A LIFE IN THE DAY OF A CRA
The Story of a Cold War Soldier

A Life in the Day of a CRA

The Story of a Cold War Soldier

by

Brigadier R. S. Mountford OBE

The Memoir Club

© R. S. Mountford 2009

First published in 2009 by
The Memoir Club
Arya House
Langley Park
Durham
DH7 9XE
0191 373 5660

British Library Cataloguing in
Publication Data.
A catalogue record for this book
is available from the
British Library

ISBN: 978-1-84104-201-5

Typeset by TW Typesetting, Plymouth, Devon
Printed by Good News Press, Ongar, Essex CM5 9RX

Contents

List of Illustrations

Between pages 82–83

Colour photographs

1. May 1964 in the Radfan after the capture of the Coca-Cola hill feature
2. June 1964 as RAF Hunter aircraft attack the enemy strongpoint on the flat topped 5,500 feet Jebel Widena feature
3. Following the capture of the Jebel Widena by 3 PARA the author relaxes in the remains of a house
4. The author was fortunate to survive a mine explosion while on reconnaissance patrol in the Radfan, May 1964
5. The artist Terence Cuneo spent a week with E Battery RHA in Detmold in 1974
6. Training in Canada with E Battery RHA in July 1975
7. 40th Field Regiment RA Farewell Parade inspection in Gütersloh, December 1980
8. The author climbs into the rear seat of a Harrier trainer fighter aircraft at Sennelager prior to take off from a public road
9. The new FH 70 guns of 38 (Seringapatam) Field Battery at conversion firing on Salisbury Plain in May 1981
10. Major Mike Smythe shows the author and the author's son Alexander his battery of 105-mm Abbot howitzers fully dug in below ground and camouflaged
11. Rear access door opened to alert a surprised Alexander
12. Alexander examines the gun pit that includes crew and ammunition shelters
13. Her Majesty The Queen reviewed the fifteen regiments stationed in West Germany as part of the 1st British Corps in May 1984
14. Early morning routine at The White House in Bad Oeynhausen, 1983–4
15. Main Headquarters 4th Armoured Division in the field in 1984

Foreword

Since 1945 the British Armed Forces have been involved in dozens of minor operations mostly linked to the withdrawal from Empire. There have also been a number of significant campaigns. Recent examples of the latter like Afghanistan, Iraq and Kosovo have received full attention from the media and are thus well known at home whereas earlier operations of major significance are now almost forgotten. In this latter category must go Greece, Palestine, Malaya, The Canal Zone, Radfan, Aden, Suez, Korea, Kenya, Cyprus and Borneo. In between there are some campaigns notable for their length like Northern Ireland, or for their dramatic nature like the Falklands.

Throughout the same period and hardly noticed, but hanging like a dark cloud for almost fifty years was the Cold War during which the Armed Forces managed to preserve peace. They managed to do this through dogged alertness in the face of boredom and by the maintenance of the highest standards of military effectiveness until the Iron Curtain crumbled in 1991.

All these operations, including the Cold War, cost lives; they imposed major logistic problems and they required flexibility in training. They also imposed turbulence and often separation from families. All this needed leadership of a high order in both the periods of excitement and of boredom.

In this book Brigadier Mountford lifts the veil on the whole gamut of military life since World War 2. He has experienced the rough and tumble of campaigns and this comes out clearly in his accounts of service in Kenya and Radfan. Equally he gives a graphic account of life in NW Europe facing the Warsaw Pact. His service has spanned the ranks from subunit command to service in a major allied headquarters and finally in a higher command appointment itself.

I believe his story is an important one for it reveals the unpredictability of service life and the dangers of becoming too wedded to one type of operations.

General Sir Edward Burgess, KBE, OBE

(General Burgess served as Deputy Supreme Allied Commander Europe from 1984 to 1987.)

Preface

Warfare has been the thread running through my life. Having spent the Second World War near enough to central London to see the horrors of air warfare, I then enjoyed thirty-seven years as a regular soldier, during which, thankfully, my short periods of active service were not of the full war-fighting variety. Having retired from the military I was then 're-engaged' for a further six years as Honorary Regimental Colonel of 40th Regiment Royal Artillery, The Lowland Gunners, a Regiment that I had commanded some fifteen years earlier. Since leaving the Armed Forces I have spent fourteen years as an advisor to Industry on personal protection for the military and police.

But the reader needs to understand the title of this book. Within the Gunners, there is always – somewhere – for every gunner a Commander Royal Artillery, or CRA. He may be a commander of a brigade of artillery within a division, rating equally with the other brigade commanders: or he may be at a higher headquarters with training, technical and certain other responsibilities for a number of artillery regiments without exercising full command. Either way, as far as the young officers and men of an artillery regiment are concerned, their CRA is their 'god' as only he understands every aspect and nuance of the science of artillery. My first CRA was the tall, elegant, moustachioed Old Etonian, Brigadier Anthony Stanton. His first visit to my first regiment in 1960 was an occasion of fear and foreboding, such was his reputation, and I admit to making a big effort to stay well clear. Little did I know that twenty-three years later I would walk those same barracks as the CRA. However, the relaxed atmosphere of a confident professional regiment led to an altogether less stressful occasion for all concerned.

The writer, almost uniquely, served two wonderful tours of duty as a CRA. The first was in an Armoured Division in Germany during the height of the Cold War; and this was followed by a tour that included duties with the United Kingdom quick reaction force for Out of Area Operations (OOA) established after the Falklands conflict.

But the meat of the soldiering part of this book covers military life in the years 1957 to 1993, a period dominated by the Cold War with 55,000

British soldiers in the British Army of the Rhine (BAOR) standing guard in West Germany as part of NATO against the huge Warsaw Pact forces that threatened. This was not glamorous soldiering – in fact it was a long slog. But in the end it was a battle won and deserves to be recorded by an officer who spent twenty-four years in every rank from 2nd Lieutenant to Brigadier preparing for the Third World War, with just a few interludes in more exciting places: hence *A Life in the Day of a CRA*.

An explanation of Royal Artillery terms

The Royal Artillery has the formal title of The Royal Regiment of Artillery but is known colloquially as 'The Gunners'.

As a Royal Artillery officer, when asked by a stranger which regiment I belonged to, I and most brother officers would reply 'I'm a Gunner'. Most senior non-commissioned officers and junior ranks would quite correctly give the same reply.

In the Royal Artillery the most junior rank similar to a private soldier is 'Gunner', which causes a measure of confusion to some. A lance-corporal is a Lance Bombardier while a corporal is a Bombardier. Otherwise ranks follow the normal names and pattern except that the second-in-command of a battery is called the Battery Captain.

Within the Royal Artillery the battery (equivalent to a squadron or company and commanded by a major) is the unit level around which history is recorded and honour titles awarded. Battery honour titles are mostly based upon daring deeds at a major battle or on the name of a battery commander at some significant point in history such as the Battle of Waterloo. I have chosen in this book to use 'batterys' as the plural of 'battery', as opposed to 'batteries' which are the objects one uses to power a torch or a radio.

There are normally between four and six batterys in a regiment, which is commanded by a lieutenant colonel. In this context a regiment usually has around 500–700 soldiers. However, the same term – Regiment – is also used to refer to the whole of the Royal Artillery i.e. The Royal Regiment of Artillery.

CHAPTER 1

The Early Years

MY VERY FIRST MEMORY DATES back to the autumn of 1940 when my parents took me outside our home in West Wimbledon near the junction of Coombe Lane with Copse Hill to watch the Battle of Britain. I remember searchlights combing the sky, sometimes catching a German aircraft. I also remember the noise of fighter aircraft on full power wheeling around the sky, with flashes as guns fired or aircraft were hit. When the attack became too close for comfort, I was taken inside and as I reached my bedroom door, a four-inch piece of shrapnel from a nearby bomb blast hit the landing window, to be stopped by the heavy protective curtain, just where I had passed seconds before.

I had been born two years earlier in a nursing home at the top of Wimbledon Hill, the first child of Stanley and Evelyn Mountford. My father had been working for several years for the Witherby publishing company in London, an internationally recognised publisher of ornithological textbooks. My mother had worked as a secretary. Soon after the start of the Second World War my father found himself drawn into the organization responsible for the civil defence of London, and was at the very heart of the 'Blitz' in 1940. He remained in that role until 1945. Meanwhile I started school at The Rowans in Drax Avenue in 1942 where I had three happy years until the start of the V1 and V2 rocket attacks on London in 1944. I remember very clearly looking up to see my first V1 rocket flying 300–400 feet above me while I was playing at the far end of the garden. As I watched, the engine cut out and in a flash I was whisked inside the house and into the Anderson Shelter by my mother. Less than an hour later she walked me just two hundred yards down the road to see the remains of the houses that it hit.

Within a few days I was evacuated with my cousins Jeffrey and Robert Holmes to Southport. After a short period we were split and I found myself very lonely in a large house with a fierce lady owner close to Arnold School, south of Blackpool. But, quite remarkably, I was soon reunited with my mother who, expecting my first brother, had herself been evacuated to a temporary maternity hospital in a hotel at Cleverleys, just north of Blackpool where Rod was born.

The war over, we were all reunited in the house in Coombe Lane with my two cousins and their parents just four houses away. Jeffrey and Robert Holmes and I became inseparable. Our homes backed onto some school playing fields on which we played football throughout the winter and cricket during the summer. We biked all over the nearby Wimbledon Common and knew every track like the backs of our hands. We were actively engaged outside from dawn to dusk. But this hyperactivity masked what were in reality very hard times for the family. I had to leave my small private school and join Bushey Junior School in the state system where I found myself in a class of forty-eight. Holidays became very simple, if at all, and we moved to a smaller house a few hundred yards away. Yet for a time we were also looking after relatives who had lost everything during the bombings in London.

My father decided that he needed to set up his own business and with two friends started a small printing company in an empty shop in Camberwell. In the depressed days of the late 1940s it was very slow and hard, but the family survived. One of my duties on Saturdays was to fold the local church weekly newsletters. But slowly the business grew, moving to Richmond and later to Twickenham and, by the 1960s, it was an extremely profitable concern.

Starting in 1947 at the age of 9 I became a regular spectator at the Oval where I watched the Surrey 'greats', the Bedser twins, Laurie Fishlock and others, play under the leadership of E. R. T. Holmes. I would take myself off for the day by train from Raynes Park to Vauxhall with a jam sandwich and a bottle of water. I always sat under the scoreboard close to the gasometer. Sixty years later I enjoy the comforts of the pavilion.

In 1948, my second brother, Roger, was born to complete the family. We were a united and very happy family, although the five years' age gap between each of us boys led to three separate groups of friends. In 1949 I failed the examination to attend a grammar school and was sent instead to the local secondary modern school for boys. After several months spending Saturdays at a crammer I passed the entrance examination to attend Kingston-upon-Thames Grammar School, starting in September 1950. This ancient school, whose Charter was granted by the first Queen Elizabeth in 1561, originated from the building of a Chapel in 1309 (which was still used as a classroom in my day) by Edward Lovekyn. Kingston-upon-Thames Grammar School was at that time a direct grant grammar school with a Board of Governors subordinate to Kingston Council. In 1957 the school was elected to the Headmasters' Conference, and in 1975 became a fully independent fee-paying day public school. Some seventy-five boys joined in my year of whom half were fee paying and half attended without the payment of fees; the term's fees for me were £12. We were streamed into three classes of twenty-five boys each and I managed to spend the next five very happy years in the C stream where I worked little but played a huge amount of sport. My cousin Jeffrey Holmes was in the year ahead of me, and subsequently both my brothers followed me to Kingston Grammar School.

The school was unique in that it played hockey in both winter terms, in the autumn term against the main London club sides, and in the spring against school teams. Unsurprisingly, in my time we were never beaten by another school. Several of my teammates became internationals. I played both hockey and cricket for the First Eleven in every year group as I moved up the school, with two years in the First Eleven in both sports. In the hockey First Eleven I played at left half while my cousin played at left wing. I also played frequently for one of the Old Boys' lower elevens on Sundays. After one such occasion followed by some beers I was interviewed by the local police as my bicycle wobbled across Kingston bridge. I also took a lead role in the CCF, attending as many courses as I could and becoming the Company Sergeant-Major which was the senior cadet post.

It became increasingly obvious that a career in the Armed Forces would be an enjoyable and stimulating way to spend my life, and this coincidentally acted as a rather late wake-up call for my academic efforts at school. Having clawed my way past the minimum five O levels to allow me to sit the Civil Service Entrance Examination for the three Service Academies, I then made a gigantic effort to pass that exam, surprising everyone by being rated in the top thirty of nearly 900 candidates. Early in 1957, I attended the aircrew selection tests at RAF Hornchurch and the Regular Commissions Board at Westbury. The three days at Hornchurch started with various physical and mental coordination tests and then moved into a demanding medical. After two days, the barrack room that had at first housed all fifty candidates had more than forty empty bed spaces, and on the third day the survivors faced a day of officer leadership tests. I returned home exhausted. Four days later I received a buff envelope informing me that I had been granted a place at RAF Cranwell to train to be a fighter pilot.

In April I reported to Westbury to attend the Regular Commissions Board for consideration for a place at the Royal Military Academy Sandhurst. The Regular Commissions Board consisted of interviews, discussions on current affairs, obstacle courses and a variety of command tasks involving imaginary rivers full of man-eating crocodiles that had to be crossed despite all available timber being too short. Some of these command tasks had an appointed leader while others were a free for all. I shared a room with a young man whose uncle, until a few months before a member of the staff there, had told him exactly what he had to do (and not do). He relayed everything to me during the first evening and as it seemed sensible advice I followed it for the next three days. I passed but he failed. I met there Robert Hall. We went to Sandhurst together, into the Royal Artillery and served together or very close for the next thirty-five years, both reaching brigadier, and remain close friends.

So by 24 May 1957 I held entry letters from both Cranwell and Sandhurst to commence training in September. The difficult decision was made for me by the then Defence Minister Duncan Sandys who in a major defence review announced that the days of the manned fighter aircraft were ending, to be replaced by guided rockets. I did not fancy spending my life guiding a rocket so the decision for Sandhurst was made. Interestingly, the eighty squadrons of Hawker Hunter fighter aircraft in 1957 had been reduced to four squadrons of Harrier by the time I completed my military service.

The final summer term at Kingston Grammar School was a lazy affair with lots of cricket and only the duties of a prefect to keep me busy. As I departed to the military my two cousins and my two brothers all in due course went to London University. Jeffrey Holmes studied law at King's College and made a fine career as a lawyer in Vancouver. Robert Holmes attended the College of Estate Management and developed the highly reputable estate agency bearing his name in Wimbledon. My brother Rod went to the London College of Printing prior to taking over the family business from my father; and my younger brother Roger studied economics and politics at the London School of Economics prior to becoming an extremely successful merchant banker in London and Hong Kong, and in later life returning to his Alma Mater as a Governor.

CHAPTER 2

Entering the Armed Forces

I REPORTED TO THE Royal Military Academy Sandhurst in August 1957 along with around 220 others in Intake 23 of whom forty were from a wide variety of overseas nations including the colonies. Allocated to Waterloo Company in Old College, my platoon was formed from four different types of entrant. From school came the Hon. Patrick Anson (later the Earl of Lichfield), Peter Dwerryhouse, John Lofting, Hamish MacNab, Christopher Peacocke, John Wilsey and myself. The Army Entrants, that is, serving soldiers who had passed the Regular Commissions Board, were Fred Walker and Simon Lowman. Jack Carter, Keith Ryding, Paul Bloxham and Michael Riggs came from Welbeck, the Army's new Sixth Form College, and we had three overseas cadets: Mohammed Al Khalifa from Bahrain, Mohammed Al Ali from Kuwait and Musa Bin Mohammed from Malaysia. There were twelve such platoons of new entrants.

The Army of the late 1950s was a conscript organization numbering around 450,000 all ranks. At Sandhurst the majors and company sergeant-majors and above were all veterans of the Second World War, while the captains and sergeants were mostly recent veterans of the Korean war, many with impressive decorations. The equipment that we were issued with was the best available but was all of Second World War vintage including battle dress and Number 1 Dress (Blues). For my first term Major (later Colonel) Nigel Birbeck was my platoon commander; seven years later he was to be my commanding officer. Officer training for the National Service officers took place at Mons, just down the road in Aldershot, or for infantry officers at Eaton Hall in Cheshire. I arrived at Sandhurst wearing a suit and with a very small suitcase containing some sports gear, a change of clothing, and little else.

The first six weeks were similar to any other initial training in the Army with two exceptions: the training sergeants were from the Guards (we had Sergeant Creveul from the Scots Guards) who had both viciousness and sarcasm honed into a fine art; and I was addressed by them as 'Mr Mountford – Sir' although both sides knew that the compliment was not intended. It was a tough period with long hours, frequent changes of uniform, much shining of boots and leather belts and a demanding fitness training regime. Most days were filled with some combination of drill, physical training, weapon training and perhaps a lecture. The wearing of civilian clothes was not allowed. There were three principal aims in this hectic period. The first was to 'pass off the square' at the six-week period which allowed a weekend off, the wearing of civilian clothes, the College servants to clean the bedrooms and authority to leave the Sandhurst grounds. The next was the Junior Intake Drill Competition that consisted of a rigorous inspection for which we wore our newly tailored best battle dress, followed by a complex set piece drill display. There followed in November the Junior Intake Steeplechase Competition that was an obstacle course through rivers and mud that had to be completed as a team event with the slowest man's time as the team time. There was a very great deal of practice on the course, not least to conquer some of the aerial challenges. We were not the only platoon to arrange for our very heavily built slowest member to report sick on the day of the competition. By this time my roommate Michael Riggs had been declared unsuitable to continue training and had left us very quietly – I returned from a lecture to find his half of our room empty.

Our platoon had now developed a character which changed little during the next two years – we were laid back, full of innovation and ideas, never first in any competition but always in the top half and very happy with each other's company. During our first field exercise on West End Common near Bagshot some of us crept out of our bivouac and climbed up the drainpipes of the nearby Paddock Wood finishing school. Although their Principal surprised us at 4 a.m. in the girls' dormitory, our instructors never did find out. On another occasion we were very late on parade to cycle as a platoon the twelve miles to Chobham Common for a map exercise. No problem. We surprised the commuters at Camberley station by boarding their train with our military bicycles to Sunningdale, before the short ride to the exercise location on Ship Hill. Unfortunately, our arrival well before the other platoons, while at first admired, was later treated with suspicion. Our over bold decision to return to Sandhurst by train was covertly observed, and on this occasion we were in big trouble.

There were now just four weeks until the Sovereign's Parade at which the senior intake would pass out. My platoon would be an integral part of Waterloo Company on parade, the first time we had been allowed to join the rest of the Company in any activity. Like everything at Sandhurst a lot of practice was deemed necessary – and so we spent even more time on the drill square.

The first Sovereign's Parade was a memorable occasion with a large crowd watching a complex and lengthy parade with everyone in 'Blues'. But in the background I learned of the harsher side of Army life when a senior cadet in my Company, charged with helping my platoon for the first term, and who the previous evening had shown us his newly tailored and very expensive regimental uniforms including an immaculate mess jacket, was told he was not suitable to be commissioned, and invited to leave. A stark warning.

After Christmas leave, I returned to Sandhurst in early January for my second term. As there was now a new intake of juniors the pressure was eased. We had a new platoon commander, Captain Geoffrey Duckworth, from the 2nd Royal Tank Regiment, an officer of great ability although serious by nature. The college servants, a wonderful group of retired soldiers, cleaned all our kit. The curriculum from now on was based on a 60/40 military studies/academic studies split, effectively two days a week in the classroom. We all studied international relations and military history plus a language, and two optional subjects. I took French, geography and a special mathematics course that included much trigonometry in order to get me through the QRA (Qualified Royal Artillery) exam. The academic work was far from arduous and so the first term pressure was off. Military studies became very interesting, mostly conducted at Corps level, while our field exercises were frequent and varied, always against a rather cynical company from the Irish Guards. I was selected for the Academy hockey First Eleven allowing me to get to know many others at Sandhurst including the senior intakes, and to meet our opposite numbers at Dartmouth and Cranwell.

I was invited to go on the Easter 1958 Sandhurst hockey tour of Germany, a wonderful trip. Travel was in uniform starting with the military train from Liverpool Street to Harwich, then the overnight crossing on the troop ship *Vienna* to the Hook, and finally the military train to Munster where we stayed with 2nd Royal Tank Regiment. At that time, Germany was still finding its feet after the war, there were few cars and many uncleared bombed buildings. The economic miracle was only just beginning. The military had its own currency, BAFVs or British Armed Forces Vouchers, with special notes but UK coins. At that time the exchange rate was twenty Deutschmarks to the pound. The hockey matches were played on the tarmac regimental square or, in some barracks, on red shale. In both cases it was an extremely fast game. Having completed our matches in Munster, we moved on to Osnabrück where we stayed with the Royal Engineers, and then to Berlin as guests of a cavalry squadron.

This was Berlin before the Wall. West Berlin was a well lit, prosperous and thriving city: in contrast East Berlin (other than the Unter den Linden showpiece development by the Brandenburg Gate) was almost the same as the day the war ended, drab, dirty, dark and very poor. The exceptions were the enormous Russian war memorials at the Brandenburg Gate and Treptow Park, the latter containing 30,000 Russian soldiers' bodies from the Battle of Berlin. We were encouraged to walk across and explore the eastern sector wearing our uniforms, which we did. It was a graphic display of communism at work, but also a reminder of the ferocity of the battle to take Berlin. It was hardly surprising that increasing numbers of Germans living in the Russian zone fled to West Germany.

The Summer Term passed quickly with several field exercises, an elaborate Company Waterloo Day celebration and first year examinations. My platoon lost its second man when Hamish MacNab departed.

The long summer break represented a challenge and so I took off on my motor scooter to tour northern Europe, a 3,000-mile journey across the channel and then through Belgium, The Netherlands (where I toured the Arnhem battlefield) and Germany to Denmark. I departed Copenhagen by ferry to Malmö and then explored north-east via Lake Vättern to Stockholm where I spent a week lodged on the *Alf Chapman* sailing ship in the harbour. Sweden and Norway were a serious challenge to the biker as, apart from the cities and towns, all roads were gravel with large wheel track marks, hollowed out by lorries, and the edges of which were of soft unpacked stones. I left Stockholm westwards along minor roads to Oslo. After a couple of days I took off northwards across the Hardangervidda mountains via Geilo towards Bergen. The descent from the mountains to the sea-level Eidfjord – twenty-three miles of hairpin bends with a sheer drop on a gravel surface with no crash barriers – was terrifying. I moved on to the seaport of Bergen, spending a few days based on Mount Fløyen above the harbour, and then returned to Oslo through the Telemark region of mountains, forests and small farms. The final leg was the ferry to Newcastle and then south to London.

By now I was an Inter-Senior at Sandhurst and well established. I continued to play hockey for the First Eleven, with life in my platoon in Waterloo Company continuing much as before. The Inter Platoon Obstacle Course competition in October sharpened up our fitness, while the November Initiative Exercise over my twentieth birthday weekend caused us to speed march from a start point in mid Wales north to the summits of Tryfan and then Carnedd Llewelyn before turning east to swim the River Conwy to reach our coach for the journey back to Sandhurst. As the term ended I had hoped that I would become a junior under officer in my final two terms, but it was not to be, for I was, I think, the victim of one of the many undercurrents at Sandhurst. Instead I became a cadet sergeant and, as a compensation, the Sandhurst captain of hockey.

As 1959 and the final straight started, life was busier than ever with the additional responsibilities of one of the junior platoons to administer. The hockey team beat both Dartmouth and Cranwell as the climax of an excellent season. In July the whole platoon supported John Wilsey, now the Company Senior Under Officer, in his attempt to win the London to Paris air race. By now my place in the Royal Artillery was confirmed subject to the final examinations. In the event I passed out in twentieth place collecting two prizes. On 24 July 1959 I took part in my fourth and final Sovereign's Parade with the salute taken by Queen Elizabeth the Queen Mother, and with that famous departure from the parade ground in front of Old College up the steps to the tune of 'Auld Lang Syne'. It is interesting to note that only four members of the original platoon completed the whole military career. John Wilsey retired as General Sir John Wilsey, having finished his career as the Commander-in-Chief of United Kingdom Land Forces. Christopher Peacocke and Keith Ryding both reached colonel and had highly successful careers in the development of technical weapons.

The next stop on my military journey was the School of Artillery at Larkhill. All of the Sandhurst graduates entering the Royal Artillery were required to complete a Young Officers' course before joining our first regiments. We lived in our own very lively mess – 'A' Mess as it was known – which was so old that we were quite unable to cause more damage however hard we tried. The prize trick was to extract a horse called Colonel Freddie from the adjacent stables and then hold a jumping competition in the ante-room using sofas as jumps. When this became too tame, the 'jumps' were moved to be exactly under the roof cross beams to give added interest.

The aim of the course was to teach us everything about field gunnery so that we could carry out any and every task that any member of a field battery might face. By November it had become clear that two of our number would be joining Corporal guided missile regiments so they had separate instruction. For the rest it was the tried and tested 25-pounder from the Second World War. In those days the Larkhill artillery ranges were frantically busy from dawn until dusk with probably between six and eight batterys firing all day long – there was no shortage of ammunition as wartime stocks were being run down.

A real highlight of these months was playing in the Royal Artillery Hockey Club team against the very best club sides in London, now in effect the main London League. The strength of the team owed much to the National Service officers who, if they wished to play at international level, were strongly encouraged to join the Gunners or Sappers. Major (later Lieutenant Colonel) Desmond Leach proved to be a most effective recruiter of these outstanding players. There were three current internationals in the team: John Neill at right back (England), Chris Key at right wing (England) and Tony Pratt at left wing – a regular officer (Wales); a former international, Trevor Selley, was at inside left (England). Another National Service officer Tom Booth played at centre half (North of England). Bill Cornock (Combined Services) played at left half while I played at right half (with internationals both in front of me and behind me). There were more regular officers – Tony Spackman played at centre forward, Guy Smith at left back, Ron Coleman at inside right and Bob Stephens in goal. During the season in which I played, this talented team beat almost every London club, Oxford and Cambridge Universities and the Sappers. Furthermore, with the Royal Artillery Mess at Woolwich, we had the best clubhouse in London hockey.

In November we received our postings. Despite having asked for Hong Kong, where there were three Gunner regiments, I was posted to Lippstadt in West Germany to join the 41st Field Regiment. But first we had to attend a short driving and maintenance course at Bordon and have some leave. One of my colleagues, Barry Grace, suggested we go on holiday together. But where in February? The penny dropped. We could both just afford two weeks at the Norwegian ski resort of Geilo, so for under £40 we purchased a return boat-and-train fare from Newcastle to Geilo via Bergen and twelve days in a small hotel on the slopes. That was the start of my skiing.

CHAPTER 3

The Magical First Regimental Tour

EVERY NEWLY COMMISSIONED YOUNG officer looks forward to joining his first regiment with a mixture of satisfaction after a long and demanding training period and of apprehension. In my case this concern was heightened because I did not know a single person in 41st Field Regiment or anything about the Regiment except that it was stationed in Lippstadt, a small town in a farming area of Westphalia and fifty miles east of Dortmund and the Ruhr industrial area. My parents took me to Liverpool Street Station for the 24-hour train–sea–train journey: as these were military trains and a troopship I was dressed in uniform and had to hand carry all my uniforms, clothes and personal possessions in five large cases, an impossible task going up and down a ship's gangplank, but that was how life was for a 2nd Lieutenant when there were more than a hundred (mostly National Service) young officers making the same journey, not to mention a sprinkling of wives and families, and hundreds of young soldiers.

I was very well aware that on arrival at Lippstadt station an initiation ceremony of some kind was likely, but it was more than half an hour before a breathless Sergeant Taylor, who I later learned was the Mess Sergeant, arrived in a suspiciously old car to take me to a barracks that was completely deserted. I wondered what was to hit me; had I been brought to an unused barracks? But he explained that the Regiment was away on a big winter exercise and would return at the coming weekend. This explanation reminded him to pull a letter from his pocket for me. It was from Major (later Brigadier) Lionel Barker to tell me that I would be joining his 135 Field Battery, but more importantly I would be playing in the regimental hockey team in the British Army of the Rhine (BAOR) cup final the following week and so I should practise daily. At that precise moment Sergeant Major (WO 2) Woods, the Battery Sergeant Major of 135 Field Battery, appeared informing me that he was also a member of the team and had been sent back from the exercise to train me for the final, which he did unrelentingly, enthusiastically and tirelessly!

This account of life in BAOR needs to explain some background to the story that unfolds. It was some twelve years since Winston Churchill described the east–west tensions as the Cold War, with the coming down of the Iron Curtain, and this period became more and more tense as relations deteriorated. The Soviet Union with its Warsaw Pact allies saw the domination of western Europe as the only way to solve its chronic economic under-performance. The Warsaw Pact forces hugely outnumbered NATO forces, being able to field up to two hundred well-equipped divisions against the thirty or so available to NATO. Up until the late 1950s the NATO strategy in Germany had been to hold a defensive line based on the River Rhine: but an increasingly forceful West German government had successfully argued for a forward defence strategy that did not yield any German territory without a fight. This coincided with the increasing operational efficiency of the new Bundeswehr, raised from 1955 onwards, and by 1960 at a strength of three army corps. Both the Warsaw Pact and NATO had large numbers of strategic and tactical battlefield nuclear weapons. It was felt that NATO was unlikely to make first use unless the battle was being lost, but that the Soviets would use nuclear weapons in considerable numbers along their chosen lines of advance. It was also anticipated that the Soviets would use chemical weapons.

Within this doom laden scenario it was planned that the sixty million strong German civil population would remain in their homes in the event of war, with most being overrun by Warsaw Pact forces who probably had revenge in mind for the the Second World War activities of Nazi Germany. Most observers anticipated that .the majority of the civil population would drive to the English Channel in a time of tension using the same roads necessary for NATO forces to move up to the new forward defensive line, as many of them were still in barracks behind the Rhine.

The Northern Army Group (NORTHAG), of which the 1st British Corps was part, was tasked to hold the territory between Hamburg and the Harz Mountains near Kassel with four army corps: from north to south the 1st Netherlands Corps, the 1st German Corps, the 1st British Corps and the 1st Belgian Corps. The Central Army Group (CENTAG) to the south consisted of two US Corps (5th and 7th) and two German Corps (2nd and 3rd), with the 1st French Corps outside the NATO command structure located around Baden-Baden on the Franco-German border. The large 4th Canadian Independent Brigade Group was attached to the British forces. The 1st British Corps sector of approximately seventy kilometres was split, with thirty-five kilometres to each of the two forward divisions, with the third division in reserve. A division had only two brigades. As a brigade had a sector 15–20 kilometres wide, an infantry company probably had up to five kilometres of frontage – an impossible task on the line of a major

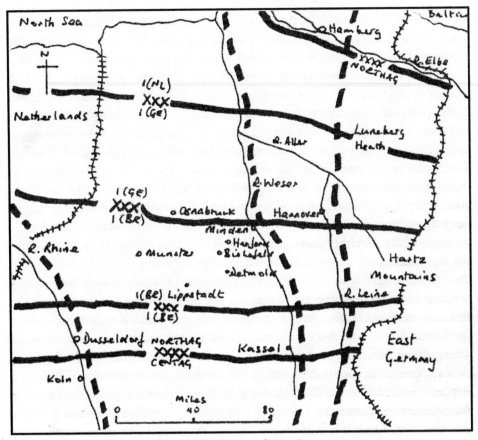

The NORTHAG area of West Germany

enemy thrust, or at night, or in reduced visibility. As most of the 1st Belgian Corps and all of the 1st Netherlands Corps were stationed in their home countries, an attack on the west without warning represented the nightmare scenario. The 41st Field Regiment was the artillery component of the 4th Guards Brigade, part of the 4th Division, with three foot-borne infantry battalions whose vehicle movement was dependent on the arrival of three-ton lorries from the Royal Army Service Corps. The other major unit was the 5th Royal Inniskilling Dragoon Guards with Centurion tanks.

This was a National Service conscript army – a very far cry from the professional army of the late twentieth century. Most, but by no means all, National Service conscripts, wanted to do their very best during their two-year period of military service; however, they all had to be trained in the very simplest of military tasks and almost as soon as they had become reasonably efficient, their service period ended and they were away to resume their civilian lives. Almost all conscripts were single-skill trained. A driver only drove; a signaller only operated a radio set; and a gunner only loaded or fired a gun. In contrast the advent from 1961 onwards of a professional army introduced multi-skilled soldiers who typically had qualifications in three or more military skills as well as drive and initiative. Most National Service conscripts were aged 18 and directly from school, but a number had deferred their service to complete five- or seven-year apprenticeships during which time they had married and started families. Conscripts were paid 28 shillings each week, £1.40 in today's currency. This embarrassingly small amount prohibited these young men from almost all activity other than lying on their beds, normally in barrack rooms of twenty or thirty men, each bed space adorned with every conceivable 'demob' chart. For the married conscripts, life was extremely difficult from the financial point of view. The British Army no longer used BAFVs and the Deutschmark was now twelve to one pound, enough to give a young officer considerable spending power. Other ranks were all still paid over the table at the weekly pay parade, a public affair where everyone could hear the amount every soldier (including senior ranks) had elected to receive. It was almost impossible to telephone the UK with any privacy.

My arrival in Germany coincided with a reorganization of Royal Artillery Field Batterys. The war-proven organisation of two troops each of four guns and a forward observer party plus a headquarters troop had a strength of around 160 personnel. To save personnel and money following the 1957 decision to replace conscription with more expensive professional soldiers, the manpower was reduced to 105 men (with an additional forty reservists arriving for war) and the guns reduced from eight to six. The new organization consisted of four sections: there were two similar gun sections each of three guns with associated ammunition vehicles; a command post section that contained all the men responsible for the technical aspects (computation, survey, etc) of firing the guns; and an observation post section containing the two forward observer parties, the battery commander's team and the line laying parties. My first command was the 135 Field Battery Observation Post Section. My section sergeant was Sergeant Grantham, an excellent signals sergeant but with little understanding of the control of artillery fire. His deputy was Bombardier Phillips with a very similar background. In addition I had thirty-nine soldiers in the rank of gunner, all but two of whom were conscripts. Some were highly intelligent while others had just succeeded in learning to read and write at school and had drifted since. My two regular soldiers were educationally in the latter category. Gunner Harry Poole had been a Yorkshire miner and drove my radio vehicle, and was a notable digger of trenches whenever asked to do so. Gunner Paddy Hill from the Irish Republic was also a driver, but very much a loner and quite without friends, probably owing in part to a negligent attitude towards basic hygiene allied to a fearsome temper.

The British Army in Germany ran on an annual cycle, but with conscripts coming and leaving on an entirely haphazard basis. The New Year until Easter was spent in barracks with most soldiers in the classrooms in the barracks on courses which covered a wide range of military skills and, for some, basic education. Low level field training (how to camouflage a vehicle or dig a trench, how to carry out a patrol or a reconnaissance, leading up to how to deploy the battery and then fire the guns) followed after Easter, initially on a small designated training area near the barracks, and later on a '443 training area'. These areas were unique to the occupation forces' agreements and allowed the freedom to train over all private land and to demand the use of barns and other farm buildings for the shelter of soldiers or camouflage of vehicles during the training. My Regiment arranged to have four '443 training areas', each sixty kilometres from east to west and forty kilometres from north to south, in the four quadrants surrounding the town of Lippstadt. They provided a magnificent training area and we were very careful to avoid damage. The farmers welcomed us, not least because they could claim for damage and be handsomely rewarded. However, they were conditioned to armies training over their lands as it had been a feature of life in northern Germany since time immemorial.

The northern part of West Germany had two huge live firing areas for tanks and artillery – Munsterlager and Hohne Ranges. Adjacent to them was a British-use only permanent '443 training area' known as the Soltau Luneburg Training Area (SLTA), in reality most of Luneburg Heath. Combined, these huge areas allowed 120 kilometres (with a varying width of fifteen to thirty kilometres) of training area of which sixty kilometres were used daily for live artillery firing. By 1960 the Munsterlager North area had been handed over to the Bundeswehr, but Munsterlager South and Hohne ranges remained under British control. The advantage was that the training months of first choice (May, June and July) were permanently allocated to the three British divisions on a rotational basis. At other times the ranges were used by German, Dutch, Belgian and US forces. The British also had a three-week period every winter for winter firing.

Therefore, after a period of work-up training near Lippstadt, the Regiment would move the two hundred kilometres to the Soltau Luneburg

Training Area for three weeks of more advanced training followed by four weeks of live firing on the Munsterlager and Hohne Ranges. The live firing period usually consisted of two weeks' battery level firing followed by one week of regimental level firing, and finally the four day Commander Royal Artillery's (CRA) test exercise with three or more regiments taking part. All this live firing was under the very close eye of the Gunnery Staff, a team of resolute and hawk-eyed gunnery instructors who worked directly for the CRA and had the ability to hasten the termination of the careers of the under prepared! Thus the technical gunnery training was completed by early summer, leaving time for leave and sport. Lieutenant (later Lieutenant Colonel) Peter Salisbury, an outstanding cricketer, ran our regimental team in which I played but never mastered bowling on the matting wickets.

The annual training cycle resumed in early September once the harvest had been gathered with six to eight weeks of combined arms training on a special '443 training area', usually in the area where we expected to fight the Third World War, at that time defending the line of the River Weser. Typically the first three weeks would be brigade training, starting at the company level, moving up to battalion level exercises and finishing with a full brigade exercise. This was usually the first time in the year when infantry, tanks, artillery and engineers trained together. Divisional training would follow for a further two weeks, to be followed by a corps level exercise with around 60,000 soldiers taking part. Sometimes these exercises were combined with other national corps to allow each side to have a period of four or five days in attack followed by a similar period in defence.

In addition to the training described, there was an overlay of command post and signals training exercises throughout the year when brigade, division, corps and then army group headquarters staffs were trained. At regimental level this gave rise to a requirement for lower controls to provide the necessary inputs.

By late October most of the army had completed training and returned to barracks for a period of repair and maintenance of equipment. This was known as the 'Admin' or administrative inspection and occupied every moment of the day from 7 a.m. often until 10 p.m. at night. Every single piece of equipment had to be cleaned and scraped back to bare metal, inspected, serviced, repaired and repainted in green high gloss complete with elaborate formation and tactical signs. The barracks had to be returned to pristine condition. More painting. Soldiers' records had to be updated and checked. Teams of experts then descended on the regiment from higher headquarters to check everything. And finally, being in a Guards Brigade, the last day of the inspection period included a formal parade and inspection by the brigade commander. I confess that this was a period of the year I detested. As a young officer, one either became a member of a paint spraying team or one stood back a little and attempted to help the organization. I chose the latter as the detail of the work was really the sergeants' matter, and they wanted to ensure that their equipment was right and ready for the next training year. So this was the lifestyle of the British Army in Germany in the 1950s and early 1960s.

Back to my story. Some four days after my arrival in Lippstadt, the 41st Field Regiment returned to barracks. They welcomed me most warmly but I soon learned that the last exercise during the command tour of Lieutenant Colonel Pat Saunders had not been a success; indeed by the final day hardly a single one of the old Second World War radios still worked. The battery captain (or second in command) of 135 Field Battery was Captain Geoff Plunkett while the senior subaltern and Gun Position Officer was Lieutenant Spencer Holtom. The living-in officers totalled around twenty, of whom twelve were national service 2nd Lieutenants. Although we were all happy in each other's company, we usually socialised in two separate groups. I tended to spend time with Captains Tom Soffe and Conn Gage, both skiers. I also got to know well Captain (later Brigadier) Tony Stagg with whom I was to serve on several more occasions.

The following week, after much more practice, we met the 1st Battalion the Somerset and Cornwall Light Infantry in the BAOR hockey final, only to lose 1–0 after a hard fought match. Fortunately I played well enough to catch the eye of the BAOR selectors, joined the BAOR Team and was awarded colours. I continued to play regularly for BAOR for the next four years.

I assumed command of the 135 Field Battery Observation Post Section and started training with them, a rewarding task as they were never happier than when out in the field. A dynamic new commanding officer with a fearsome reputation as a demanding trainer had arrived, and Lieutenant Colonel (later Brigadier) Harry Salmon was quick to impose his standards. One feature that dominated was Officer Training, with a monthly Officers' Training Day and nightly sessions on the Observation of Fire miniature range. We worked hard but it paid off. Within a month the Regiment was at the Munsterlager and Hohne ranges for winter live firing. I was a very young and inexperienced Forward Observation Officer (FOO) – visibility was very poor at the Hengst 'B' observation post (OP) – when I was summoned forward to be given my first shoot. Behind me were at least forty people arrayed like vultures awaiting my fall, including my Battery Commander, the Commanding Officer, the Commander Royal Artillery Brigadier Anthony Stanton, the BAOR Senior Instructor in Gunnery and two Instructors in Gunnery – Captains Tony Haywood and David Lloyd. My target was set by the latter only to disappear in the shifting mist and then return. I gave my orders and the first shell appeared to fall a little to the left and slightly short. After ordering, 'Go right fifty, add two hundred,' the second shell exploded with a thud but could not be seen. I was sure it had landed in the mist just behind the target, so my third order was 'Drop one hundred, one round gunfire' which drew an audible communal sucking of teeth from the vultures who felt closer to me by this stage. However, the fire was exactly on target, setting up my reputation as an accomplished FOO.

Public holiday periods such as Easter were a period of potential boredom, and therefore trouble, for the impoverished national service soldiers. The solution was for a young officer to take his section away on a cheap holiday. So my first Easter was spent with thirty members of my section at Laubach, a traditional farming village near Frankfurt where we camped in an orchard and enjoyed the local life. These 'section holiday weekends' became a very popular and inexpensive way of amusing the soldiers and showing them the different areas of Germany and I continued them throughout my time in Germany. The most successful was Gut Burau in Schleswig-Holstein north of Lübeck where the farmer owner set aside unoccupied cottages for our use, and for whom on one wonderful occasion we floodlit his fine house and put on a short military tattoo.

I settled very quickly into military life in Germany. I soon ordered my first new car, a Renault Dauphine ex-works in Paris for the special NATO price of £352. There followed my yellow Labrador bitch, who for the next few years accompanied me almost everywhere, and whom my soldiers adored.

But the training year continued at a pace. I met my infantry battalion – the 1st Battalion The King's Own Yorkshire Light Infantry – and trained with them as one of their two FOOs, interspersing this with the sequence of gunnery training during the early summer. After leave we returned to the field for the combined arms training period which culminated in our role as the enemy (simulating the Warsaw Pact forces) attacking across the Elbe-Lübeck canal north-west into Schleswig-Holstein against the 6th German Division. The initial attack was marred when the Scots Guards fixed bayonets to assault the initial German position on the grounds that 'we always fix bayonets when we fight the Germans!' The exercise was halted, apologies given and received, and then continued. After four days, we pushed through an armoured break-out force that raced northwards through Bad Bramstedt to the final objective on the Kiel Canal. I spent this break-out phase as the FOO with Major (later Major General) Norman Arthur of the Royal Scots Greys clutching the turret of his tank as we raced forward. This marked the end of my period as an FOO as on return to barracks I was moved to a Gun Section where we had exchanged our small 25-pounder guns for the heavier 5.5 inch howitzers.

I spent part of my winter leave in the Alps, skiing with Tom Soffe. In addition we drove the forty miles from Lippstadt to Winterberg most Sundays to ski there. The Regiment had a very fine cross-country ski team but lacked an alpine team. On returning from the army ski meeting the commanding officer decided that his Regiment would in future field both a cross-country ski team and an alpine team. Lieutenant Colonel Harry Salmon unusually came to the mess for mid-morning coffee and asked for a show of hands of those who had skied that winter. Four hands were raised including mine. We were instantly selected for the 1962 Ski Team and ordered to start training, which we did.

It had been decided that, as part of the reductions in the size of the army, the 41st Field Regiment would amalgamate with the 49th Field Regiment in March 1961, the latter returning from Hong Kong with just fifty officers and men destined to join us. They arrived early in 1961 and it was immediately clear that they had sent fifty very high quality people. On the day of the amalgamation – 15 March 1961 – we held a farewell parade for the 41st Field Regiment and adopted the titles, traditions and property of the 49th Field Regiment. I was now in 143 (Tombs' Troop) Field Battery, owing its name to Major (later Major General Sir) Henry Tombs, one of two Victoria Cross winners in the Battery at the Indian Mutiny. Joining my Battery was Captain (later Brigadier) Mike Perkins who was to be my commanding officer in 1st Regiment Royal Horse Artillery twelve years later, and Lieutenant (later Brigadier) Giles Arnold who went on to command 7th Regiment Royal Horse Artillery. Amongst the junior ranks we gained Lance Bombardier (later Warrant Officer Class 2) Mick Boyland, a delightful West Countryman and outstanding cricketer in the Botham mould.

At this stage the new regular soldier recruits were starting to arrive in increasing numbers as National Service began to be phased out. They were superb young men, highly motivated, and many were highly intelligent. They wanted to learn about soldiering, to improve their skills, play as many sports as possible, and of course they were much more highly paid than the conscripts whom they replaced. I would not wish to detract from the service given to their country over fourteen years by National Servicemen, but it must be said that from the military point of view the arrival of professional soldiers led to a huge improvement in the British Army. Similarly, almost all National Service officers had now been replaced by a mixture of regular and the increasingly popular three-year short service commission officers. I now commanded a Section of three 5.5 inch howitzers with three sergeants and eighteen junior ranks. The 1961 training year followed the pattern of the previous year with low-level training near Lippstadt followed by three weeks of more advanced training on the Soltau Luneburg Training Area and then the annual Practice Camp for four weeks on the Munsterlager and Hohne Ranges. During this summer I learned every aspect of the command, control and technical functioning of the Battery.

August 1961 saw the building of the Berlin Wall as a measure by the Soviets to try to halt the massive population exodus from East to West Germany. With it came the threat that the Soviets might also close the three autobahn routes from West Germany to Berlin. Some units in BAOR deployed on the inner German border with full ammunition scales ready to fight their way to Berlin if necessary. This, together with the 1962 Cuban missile crisis, was probably the closest that NATO and the Warsaw Pact came to starting a catastrophic Third World War. Exercise 'Quick Train' was the code name for the biannual emergency call-out exercise in NATO. Normally started in the middle of the night, the regiment had to be deployed to a nearby survival area within two hours, ready in all respects to go to war. Unfortunately we were never allowed to upload our war ammunition scales, a terrible weakness. We were aware that all Soviet units were 'bombed-up', that is, every vehicle loaded with the full war ammunition scales at all times and therefore with the ability to drive straight over the inner German border against NATO forces.

There was an interesting innovation in 1961 – the birth of the Allied Mobile Force (Land) [AMF(L)], a multi-national brigade-sized organization to deploy rapidly to any part of the NATO area, but probably the flanks, to deter Soviet opportunistic aggression. The UK component was the 1st Battalion Welsh Guards from our brigade and as an extra third FOO party was required I was selected to fill this role.

Come the autumn the Regiment returned to the field with the 4th Guards Brigade and the rest of the 4th Division for all arms training and the big multinational manoeuvres. The enemy this year was a superbly equipped large US Corps acting as Warsaw Pact forces. They attacked with mass and great speed, but ignored every minefield and umpire, driving west until they ran out of fuel. It took two days to refuel, return and re-assemble them, explain the rules, and then restart the exercise. But it was a salutary lesson to us and demonstrated our inability to cope with massed armoured forces. By this time Major (later Brigadier) David Wilson was my battery commander.

After the autumn manoeuvres were completed, the Regiment returned to barracks for the administrative inspection preparations, and I found myself transferred to 127 (Dragon) Field Battery. My new Battery Commander was Major (later Brigadier) Alan Woolford who had very bravely, and it was said foolishly, earned himself a Military Cross fighting the Japanese. The new four-section battery organization had been terminated. Each battery once again consisted of two almost identical Troops, each with a Troop Commander and a Troop Subaltern.

However, for me this unpleasant period of the year was alleviated by starting a strict training period prior to the ski season. The new Regimental Alpine Team of which I was a member was four strong, all new to downhill racing. Without extra team members we knew we had to avoid injuries to be able to field a team throughout the winter race season. In mid-December we set off for Ehrwald in Austria, a tiny hamlet on the north slopes of the Zugspitz where the Alpine and Langlauf teams shared the most basic accommodation imaginable. We were allowed to have light blue painted army Land-Rovers and a truck with civil number plates and documentation. Every day was spent on the slopes above Lermoos skiing both the downhill and slalom disciplines just as fast as we could. Ski teams from other regiments began to appear. We were not the worst, but certainly some other teams were better equipped and faster skiers. The Commanding Officer came down to the Alps to inspect progress. He did this often from the churchyard, and we watched nervously for the brown trilby hat that gave away his presence! We trained very, very hard and made progress. The 4th Division meeting took place in mid-January and our experienced Langlauf team won the cross-country races while the Alpine team came eighth from nineteenth teams. This well deserved result allowed us to move on to the BAOR and Army Alpine meeting at St Moritz. Our limited budget only allowed us to stay in an inexpensive hotel in St Moritz

Bad, a mile or so from the centre, but the savings made did allow us to share a racing coach with another regimental team. In January 1962 the very first snow piste machine reached Europe and arrived in St Moritz. The piste, such as it was, was made and maintained by hundreds of piste workers, local men who spent their winter months on skis on the slopes with a shovel to maintain the piste areas. Our skis were made from wood and did not have safety bindings, and we wore lace-up leather boots. Paul Schmidt, a member of the Swiss national 'B' team in 1961, was our race instructor. His philosophy was very simple – 'Follow me as close behind as you can and do what I do.' Every morning was spent on downhill training. We would ascend on the Corviglia mountain railway to a suitable start point. Paul would set off and we would follow as fast as we could. As the days progressed he found that an increasing number of us had survived the descent. Lunch was a cheese roll sitting on our skis. The afternoons were spent slalom training. There were no lifts on the slalom slopes. We would ski down a steep hundred-yard slalom course and then climb back. It was hard work but we all survived to make the race days and achieved a creditable result. I returned to Lippstadt very fit, happy but penniless.

A number of new officers had arrived in the regiment. I was the Gun Position Officer (GPO) of 127 (Dragon) Field Battery, a key position giving me almost total control of the Battery in the field, except for the Battery Commander's and two FOOs' parties. Captain (later Major) Ted Scott was the Battery Captain. My new Troop Commander was Captain (later Field Marshal Lord) Dick Vincent while the other Troop Commander was Captain (later Major) Peter Bagwell Purefoy. The junior officer in the battery was Lieutenant (later Lieutenant Colonel) Richard Kidner who was my highly trusted and very competent deputy on the Battery Gun Position. The Battery had an extremely talented group of officers and it showed in everything we took on. But this success would never have occurred without an extraordinarily skilled and devoted group of soldiers, including an influx of outstanding young professional soldiers from both the Junior Leaders Regiment RA and from 17th Training Regiment RA.

A key figure was Warrant Officer (Troop Sergeant-Major) Peter Smith, an outstandingly smart and intelligent young man who joined on accelerated promotion from 1st Regiment RHA and set the very finest example to all the soldiers in the battery. He and Richard Kidner were the two very reliable Command Post Officers (CPOs), key figures within the Battery. Sergeant Hall, always in or near the command posts, ran the radio nets meticulously, while Sergeant Heal, the TARA (Technical Assistant Royal Artillery) sergeant was an utterly reliable supervisor of all the artillery computational matters. The two Saracen six-wheeled artillery command posts were driven by Lance Bombardiers Patterson and Hemsley. These two wonderful soldiers maintained and drove those complex vehicles for the next two years with enormous skill, covering thousands of miles. There were other key figures in this outstanding battery. The two best TARAs, soldiers who turned the target information into data for the guns' sights were Gunners Mick Hanny and David Holmes, while Gunner Dennis Calvert was a hugely efficient Director Assistant responsible for maintaining the parallelism of the six guns. The six 25–pounder gun detachments were no less determined to play their role and while Sergeants Ryan, Burgess and Gooding ran particularly fine detachments, it was to Sergeant Armstrong that I inevitably turned when speed was paramount. Throughout, Gunner (later WO 2) Jim Marsh and later Gunner John Margerison (known to all as 'JJ') were the drivers of my Champ vehicle as well as the perennial friends of my labrador that travelled the length and breadth of Germany in our vehicle.

I spent most of 1962 and 1963 as the Gun Position Officer of 127 (Dragon) Field Battery. We were well trained, confident and ready for anything – the living proof of the value of a professional army. I was determined that, while the fire of our guns was always totally accurate, it was speed that became the aim of all our training. When the battery deployed to a new location, we developed the 'Master Gun' technique and could therefore report 'Battery Ready' within two minutes of the guns reaching their new position. To meet a request for fire, we expected the ranging gun to be ready to fire within twenty-five to thirty seconds of the command post receiving the target grid reference. All the gun-firing drills had demanding target times attached to them, and every member of the Battery shared the will to meet them. Within 49th Field Regiment there was enormous competition between the three Batterys to be the first to be ready on a regimental target and this team achieved it more often than not.

The extramural side of regimental and army life flourished as the constant turnover of conscripts was replaced by professionals who on average went on to serve for nine years, with many completing the full twenty-two year engagement. Only a small number chose to terminate their service after three years. I was tasked to convert the largest barrack room into a Battery Club, and this was an immediate success, as the unmarried soldiers preferred its proximity and more intimate atmosphere to the large and impersonal NAAFI club. Drinks were sold there and bar games provided. Within a few weeks Gunner Dodds, a carpenter before joining the army, had constructed a very smart bar. The other Batterys followed suit and within a few years Battery and Company Clubs were widespread: indeed they further developed into the social hubs of batterys and companies with events for wives, children and friends.

Sport flourished both in quality and variety with most soldiers being deeply involved in at least one sport, ranging from football to cricket and parachuting to cycling. At nearby Bad Lippspringe, the BAOR sporting facilities were developed with a sport parachute centre, a golf course and the annual Rhine Army Summer Show that included a full range of equine events. In both Norway and the Harz Mountains, BAOR adventurous training centres were established for climbing/sailing and winter warfare/winter sports respectively. At Kiel the sailing centre was updated and enlarged. I attended all of them at various times, enjoying the challenges of sailing and skiing.

In the Officers' Mess a more relaxed and cohesive lifestyle developed. The living-in officers met before dinner for a drink and then dined together, often in black tie. Officers' wives, formerly unwelcome in the mess unless invited formally, were much more warmly welcomed, and a so-called 'nightclub' in the cellar opened on a regular basis. By this time Number 1 Dress had been replaced by Mess Dress for the formal monthly Guest Night dinner and one such event each year was designated a Ladies' Guest Night. The Warrant Officers' and Sergeants' Mess was similarly improved and the first Junior NCOs' Mess was established. The effect of these lifestyle developments was to create a much improved harmony between all ranks, improved mutual respect and above all the creation of a strong regimental family.

There were two external duties which came round almost annually. A two-week period conducting border patrols along the Inner German Border under the watchful eye of the British Frontier Service allowed our soldiers to see the wire fences, minefields, floodlights, watchtowers, attack dogs and forbidden areas on the communist side, a mournful experience. Far less popular was the Nuclear Site guard duty when soldiers spent a similar period in watchtowers guarding the bunkers containing the nuclear weapons we hoped would never be put to use.

The Commanding Officer decreed that following the summer 1962 training on the Soltau Luneburg Training Area and annual Practice Camp on the Munsterlager and Hohne Ranges every young officer should take a party of soldiers away on an expedition of some sort. As the Regiment had played a leading role in the Salerno landings in 1943 I elected to undertake a battlefield tour. Together with five of my soldiers, each of us with a bicycle, we cadged a lift on a United States Navy aircraft from Frankfurt to Naples. We took the coast road to Salerno enjoying the delights of Sorrento, Positano and Amalfi en route and, it must be said, these exotic resorts were of greater interest to the soldiers than the Salerno battlefield. Returning to Naples military airfield, we called in on the way to see Pompeii where the wall pictures of opportunities offered in the former brothel proved of the greatest fascination to my colleagues. After an anxious wait, the Royal Canadian Air Force kindly flew us back to Germany.

Earlier that year I had applied to do a flying tour in the new Army Air Corps. I was called to the Commanding Officer's office, always a frightening prospect, where he greeted me with two letters, one in each hand. 'This letter sends you to Middle Wallop for flying training and this letter posts you to my old Regiment, 3rd Regiment Royal Horse Artillery who are in Kenya. Which letter should I throw into the waste-paper basket?' he asked with a smile. In a mini second I elected to go to 3rd Regiment Royal Horse Artillery in Kenya.

The autumn manoeuvres followed in familiar style with my Battery now working very closely with the 1st Battalion Irish Guards, an experience best described as amusing and interesting. Typically, orders for the attack were 'Up Micks and at 'em'.

Major (later Colonel) Guy Hatch had become the Battery Commander bringing a new set of characteristics to the Battery founded on a paternally based friendship with every member. The new Commanding Officer appeared in October 1962. Lieutenant Colonel (later Major General) John Douglas-Withers was preceded by a frightening reputation based largely upon his high standards in almost all aspects of military life. While this formidable reputation was in every way deserved, my view was that he found the Regiment in very good order and was content to maintain the standards, albeit with added polish and style. Within a few weeks his inspection regime as we prepared for the annual administrative staff visits reinforced this opinion.

Meanwhile training for the ski meetings was in full swing and we departed for the Alps in early December to train for the first race in late January 1963. We trained very hard, not least because the Commanding Officer planned to join us for a time. He had last skied in the Alps in the 1930s and had not maintained the skills. His first appearance on the training slopes was in his rather dusty 1930s ski kit, including skins for his skis. It was a difficult few moments. In St Moritz we stayed in the very upmarket Caspar Badrutt Hotel that proved rather more fun than the previous year. We had a good season and I was delighted to achieve 22nd place in the Army Alpine combined.

On return from the Alps in February I quickly settled into my fourth and final training season with gunnery in the spring and early summer, followed by the big autumn manoeuvres later in the year. I was by now a very experienced Gun Position Officer and totally confident in that role. Major (later General Sir) Ted Burgess had joined the Regiment to take the adjutant's role prior to assuming command of my Battery. Second Lieutenant (later Brigadier) David Creswell joined at the same time. Later in life we worked very closely together. Following the initial gunnery training in the local areas the Regiment once again travelled up to the Soltau Luneburg Training Area for more advanced training. However, the July 1963 annual live-firing Practice Camp took place on the United States Army firing ranges at Grafenwehr in Bavaria.

This was an entirely new experience for the Regiment who were themselves a novelty to their American hosts. There seemed to be very few safety rules which made life easier, but the Americans did not practise fire and movement and so found our normal routine of firing from three or four different gun positions every day rather strange. Off the range our hosts were very hospitable while the Post Exchange (PX) shop (which none of us had previously experienced) seemed like an Aladdin's cave. After three weeks, we faced the two days' return drive to Lippstadt followed by leave. My brother Rod joined me for a grand tour of Europe centred on Italy and the Alps that proved great fun.

After the leave period (owing to the need always to have 80 per cent of the strength available for war, this was necessarily a long period as we took turns to be away) we embarked on the autumn manoeuvres. It was decided that I should become a Forward Observation Officer once more which made a welcome change. This six-week period in October and November was demanding but fun. The final big exercise saw us deployed in our wartime area and attacked by the other two British divisions plus the Canadians, replicating Soviet tactics.

On 15 December 1963, I drove away from Lippstadt after four happy years in 41st and then 49th Field Regiments during which I had learned much about soldiering, and made many friends. On reflection, these four years set the tone of the new all-professional army that was to operate so successfully for the remainder of the twentieth century. But the equipment of the time, very largely necessitating positional defence against a highly mobile armoured enemy, led to an intellectually stagnant doctrine in need of urgent reconsideration.

CHAPTER 4

Adventures in Kenya and Aden

Kenya

Arriving in Nairobi on a Friday in early January 1964, I was met by my old Sandhurst friend Lieutenant (later Lieutenant Colonel) Nick Bird, the Assistant Adjutant of 3rd Regiment Royal Horse Artillery who very kindly took me to his home overlooking Lake Nakuru for the weekend. It was a stunning view from the side of the Rift Valley down to the flamingos on the lake. Every house had a small sign outside with the name of the owner and I noticed that my host's neighbour was Daniel Arap Moi (later President), the first African to gain a place in this road.

At that time, the much coveted elevation to Royal Horse Artillery was known as 'being awarded the Jacket' and allowed the wearing of 'ball buttons' and the cipher badge in the hat. Entry was conditional on an above average performance during the first tour after Sandhurst and a personal recommendation. I learned as we drove into Alanbrooke Camp at Gilgil on the Monday morning that the three previous lieutenants had proved unacceptable to the Commanding Officer, Lieutenant Colonel Paddy Victory, and had departed rather swiftly. By lunchtime, I had been to the camp tailor and shoemaker for measuring, and received my new tropical uniforms, even including a mess jacket and No. 1 dress jacket. At 2 p.m. I met the Adjutant, Captain Andrew Fowler, who warned me to be careful as he showed me in to meet the Colonel. Lieutenant Colonel Paddy Victory, a stern figure with a slightly florid face, looked me up and down before asking if I 'had twigs in my beak?' I was nonplussed and it showed. 'Are you thinking of getting married?' he explained, 'because if so you can go directly back to the airport!' I was then welcomed to the Regiment with a minimum of warmth and told not to unpack or wear ball buttons or the cipher badge for three months or until I was told by him. It was exactly as I had been warned.

I was sent to Headquarters Battery under Major (later Brigadier) John Parham to be the Intelligence Officer but also to command the Staff Troop consisting of various drivers, clerks, cooks and even Gunner Marshall, who drove the tractor of the Regimental Sergeant Major WO1 (later Major)

Ernie Lambert. It was not a very inspiring role, but was to liven up considerably within a few days. However, life in the 24th Infantry Brigade was just about perfect. Brigade Headquarters in Nairobi was three hours' drive to the south, and collocated with the Scots Guards and the Staffords. We were in Gilgil with the Gordons and a RASC company. Gilgil is a small agricultural town at 5,500 feet above sea level and exactly on the equator. Our barracks on the airfield was a mile outside town on the Thompson's Falls road, otherwise notoriously known as Happy Valley.

The barracks contained the finest hockey pitch in Kenya and, this being an Olympics year, the Kenyan national team wanted to play the army side there as often as possible. I found myself in the Combined Services Kenya team playing against the best players in Kenya twice each week, once in Nairobi and once in Gilgil.

3rd Regiment Royal Horse Artillery had two gun batterys only in Kenya, the third battery being detached to Aden. Life in Gilgil was extremely comfortable. Onyango, a member of the Luo tribe, was appointed my full time batman. I would sometimes wake as his arm stretched round my door to remove my dirty clothes basket from my room in the early hours, but everything was washed, dried, starched and returned to me before I got up! Life in the mess was fun for we had a lively group of livers-in. The stables contained four racehorses under the care of Bombardier Thompson who was also our senior jockey. We had several days at the Nairobi races after which our winnings were drunk in champagne at the Muthaiga Club. But there were undoubtedly tensions within the regiment that would not be finally eradicated for nearly three years.

Life changed on 24 January 1964 when battalions of all the East African armies mutinied simultaneously in response to skulduggery organised, it was said, by the Chinese, the aim being to take over the five nations. 3rd Regiment Royal Horse Artillery was ordered to disarm and arrest the mutineers in Kenya north of Nairobi while the Scots Guards looked after Nairobi and the south of Kenya. The Staffords took on the army in Uganda while the Gordons were dispatched to Zanzibar. 45 Commando from Aden was sent to Tanzania. Four days later it was all over, but these were four tumultuous days.

On the morning of 24 January we were called to an urgent 'Orders Group'. Information had been received that the 11th Battalion the Kenya Rifles was likely to mutiny within twenty-four hours with the aim of breaking out of their barracks at nearby Lanet with weapons and ammunition to meet up with dissidents in the town of Nakuru as a part of a nationwide insurrection. The 11th Battalion the Kenya Rifles was an 800-strong lorried infantry battalion with African soldiers (askaris) and mostly British white officers, commanded by Lieutenant Colonel Bill Stead. Our primary task was to prevent unauthorised drawing of weapons from the armoury or ammunition from the adjacent ammunition compound: the secondary task, should weapons be seized, was to prevent any mutineers from moving the eight miles to Nakuru.

The Regiment quickly reorganised into two infantry style companies based on 'C' and 'D' Batterys Royal Horse Artillery, while I was ordered to form an independent platoon from my Troop. Luckily I discovered that the three pay corporals had all fought as infantry non-commissioned officers in Korea, so they became my section commanders and we started a crash course in infantry training immediately.

The Regiment already had a covert presence in the Lanet barracks. Lieutenant (later Brigadier) Geoffrey Ransby of D Battery RHA went with Sergeants Robertson and Thompson in mid afternoon to meet the adjutant of the 11th Battalion the Kenya Rifles to find a tense atmosphere, with the askaris refusing to take orders pending a promised radio broadcast by President Kenyatta to address alleged grievances. Meanwhile the Regiment's preparations for operations continued with D Battery RHA moving forward to a hidden location near the Lanet barracks. The two sergeants were deployed in a covert position to watch the armoury while Lieutenant Geoffrey Ransby found an access gap in the perimeter wire near the armoury to allow entry without trying to pass the main gate that was under control of the askaris. As night fell there was a loud explosion and Sergeant Robertson reported that the askaris were breaking into the armoury and ammunition compounds.

Within minutes Lieutenants Geoffrey Ransby and Charles Wainwright led D Battery RHA, commanded by Major (later Brigadier) Ian Lambie, through the perimeter wire to attack the mutineers who were attempting to drag away weapons and ammunition. In complete darkness and a very confused situation the mutineers failed to seize the ammunition compound but were able to hold the armoury long enough to grab a substantial number of weapons, along with rifle and machine-gun ammunition stored there ready for range firing, before D Battery RHA seized control. For the rest of the night D Battery RHA, who were quickly reinforced by C Battery RHA but outnumbered three to one, faced the mutineers while trying to keep them contained. By this time I had taken my platoon to a position just outside the Lanet barracks on the main road to Nanyuki to prevent any breakout in that direction.

Later I intercepted Lieutenant Colonel Stead as he tried to return to his Battalion after a meeting at his brigade headquarters. My Commanding Officer, Lieutenant Colonel Victory, joined him and after discussion the two men very bravely negotiated to approach the mutiny leaders unarmed in the glare of vehicle headlights. At the same time a stream of increasingly firm orders arrived from Headquarters East Africa Command ordering 3rd Regiment RHA to attack immediately. Lieutenant Colonel Victory declined, in my view quite rightly, because he felt a night attack with inferior numbers would lead to very heavy casualties and because we now had the mutineers contained, thereby allowing chance for further negotiation.

As first light came, it was clear that around 600 armed askaris held the main part of the barracks although not the ammunition compound or the Officers' Mess, but that we had them contained within the barracks. Ominously, within Nakuru troubles had already started. Sergeant Roberts in a Ferret armoured car was raked by machine-gun fire, avoiding death by the thickness of the bracket holding the hatch. The stand-off continued throughout the morning with negotiations leading nowhere and increasingly irate messages from Command Headquarters for the Regiment to attack. By now my platoon had redeployed to the Officers' Mess where we were surrounded by the press. The attack was set for 1200 hours to coincide with a time when it was anticipated that the majority of the askaris would be in the dining hall having their main meal of the day. But they had left a small group of askaris with machine guns holding positions on the elevated roundabout in the centre of the barracks and nearby, guarding stockpiled weapons of those in the dining hall. I gave orders to my platoon for the attack only to hear them repeated on Kenya radio just before the attack after a radio reporter had covertly held a microphone by my side.

The attack was the simplest of frontal assaults, with speed given priority over tactics, and it worked. Lieutenant Geoffrey Ransby played a brave and prominent role in this action, kicking away a jammed light machine gun just as the askari cleared the stoppage, having charged from fully a hundred yards away. Despite some miraculous escapes, within ten minutes the firefight was over and we had no casualties. Sadly there were a number of askaris killed. Then came the task of rounding up and imprisoning the mutineers, identifying the leaders and securing the weapons. I was tasked with conducting a search and clear operation of the askaris' married quarters. I crashed my way into the two hundred or so single room quarters occupied by terrified wives and children to extract the last few soldiers.

There were two outcomes from this event that directly affected me: the first was the sad process of the departure of our Commanding Officer and the second was an extension of my role as Regimental Intelligence Officer responsible for northern Kenya. In the meantime the askaris were divided into three groups: a small number of leaders to go on trial, a larger number of those implicated to be discharged and returned securely to their tribal reserves, and a majority who would in due course form the new replacement 1st Battalion the Kenya Rifles.

I was tasked with making visits to District Commissioners (DC) and similar leaders all over northern Kenya, plus any installation with potential weapons for an insurrection, such as quarries with stocks of dynamite. A typical visit was to the DC of Kisimu, Gordon Skipper, where over four days we mixed intelligence gathering with confidence building measures to assist local African civic and tribal leaders. During this period I saw much of the country, including areas where the land resettlement programme could have led to instability. I also watched the 'implicated mutineers' being transferred in barbed wire caged trucks to be returned in disgrace to their tribal chiefs.

Meanwhile, unbeknown to me and most other officers, it had been decided that our Commanding Officer would depart. I was summoned to his study in his house where he handed me his letter of resignation and instructed me to use his staff car to hand-deliver it personally to the GOC which I did later that day in Nairobi. It was a very sad occasion – a brave and dedicated career had ended early.

In early April 1964 we learned that Lieutenant (later Brigadier) Mike Bremridge had been wounded in Aden and casevaced to England. Next morning I went to the adjutant's office early. By the time he arrived almost every subaltern in the regiment was there to lobby to be selected to be sent to Aden to join 'J' (Sidi Rezegh) Battery in Mike's place. I was selected and on 10 April flew to Aden.

Aden

'J' (Sidi Rezegh) Battery, commanded by Major Tony Stagg whom I knew well from Lippstadt, provided the artillery support for the Federal Regular Army (FRA). The battery rear base was in Seedaseer Lines near

Khormaksar Airfield just outside the port city of Aden, which housed the headquarter elements of the FRA. I was shown to my room there, issued with some additional kit, and warned to be ready to fly up country next morning. In the next six months I was to spend only three nights in that room although I did not know it as I departed next morning.

Until a few weeks earlier the Battery had been split into three sections, each of two 105 mm pack howitzers, located at Dhala, Beihan and Wadi Ayn, and each supporting an FRA battalion guarding the border with Yemen. The FRA battalions were well equipped and trained, but a period of rapid Arabisation had seen the early departure of all the British officers except the Medical Officers.

For many years the FRA, formerly the Aden Protectorate Levies, had exercised a degree of control over the mainly mountainous tribal regions of the Western Aden Protectorate and the Eastern Aden Protectorate (the Hadramaut) northwards to the border with Yemen (known as North Yemen at some times). The port city of Aden was a Crown Colony. The Governor, appointed by the UK Colonial Office, was the power in Aden but exercised his limited authority in the Protectorates through the Tribal Chiefs. Aden was important militarily as a staging post for ships and aircraft en route between the UK and Far East. The UK Middle East Command (a four star headquarters) was located in Aden city.

Following the 1956 Anglo-French Suez invasion, President Nasser of Egypt had tried hard to gain revenge by troubling British interests in the region. With strong influence in Yemen and Soviet money to assist, Nasser set about influencing the wilder Aden Protectorate tribes in an attempt to overthrow British rule. This included Yemeni and possibly Egyptian volunteers and instructors as well as weapons and ammunition. The Quteibi tribe in the impenetrable and very wild mountainous Radfan area, a few miles south of the border town of Dhala, and some sixty miles north of Aden city, became the focus of efforts to destabilise the whole country. The Quteibis had always been lawless, often stopping the vehicles of other tribes to extract so-called local taxes. This activity increased throughout 1963 and so the Governor asked for British military help early in 1964. As a result the section of guns at Dhala had been moved south to Thurmier (since renamed Habilayn) where the main Aden city to Dhala road ran along the periphery of the Quteibi area. It was during military activity in the nearby Danaba Basin that Lieutenant Mike Bremridge had been wounded. My arrival in April was quickly followed by a massive reinforcement from the UK.

I arrived in Thurmier in a six-seater Twin Pioneer aircraft and walked from the airstrip to the Battery gun position – six guns, a command post and storage areas all protected by sangars as we were closely overlooked by Saddleback Hill, a large hill feature. With us were a troop of Ferret armoured cars from the 4th Royal Tank Regiment (4 RTR) and a platoon of 45 Commando. It was very hot, with scorpions, the giant camel spiders and flies in profusion. During the day the rebel tribesmen were quiet, but at dusk they crept up to our position to fire at any movement or light. We had dinner in total darkness with the odd round zinging over our heads. My tent had several bullet holes where the enemy marksmen had tried to get a bullet just above the sangar wall.

Captain (later Brigadier) Tim Thompson was tasked to help me learn about the local situation and so two days later we flew up to Dhala. Once darkness had fallen we marched fourteen miles with a platoon of FRA soldiers back over the mountains almost to Thurmier to lay a first light ambush on a defile where the Quteibis had increasingly often held up local traffic. Within two hours we saw a group of tribesmen creep into position just below us, and then attack the first truck to appear. We attacked and drove them off. We learned later that our increased activity was not appreciated.

The training tempo of the Battery was stepped up: we took advantage of increased helicopter availability and even used camels to move guns and ammunition. Additional battalions moved into the area from Aden – 1st Battalion The Royal Anglian Regiment and 45 Commando – plus elements of the 3rd Battalion The Parachute Regiment (3 PARA) from Bahrain. This force was commanded initially by Brigadier Louis Hargroves as 'RADFORCE', based upon an upgunned Headquarters Aden Garrison, but it was not really suitable for such a complex task.

The Radfan area was dominated by four huge rugged mountains with sheer 1,000-feet cliffs in some parts: the fertile and well-farmed extensively terraced Bakri Ridge, the flat top Jebel Widena, the Jebel Radfan and the smaller but tactically vital feature named Coca-Cola. The Wadi Taym was a large flat area surrounded by mountains with fertile fields and sophisticated traditional irrigation systems. The Wadi Rabwa, Misrah and Dhubsan were primarily communication routes through the mountains with very steep sides, often 1,000 feet almost vertical. Thurmier, the site of the main airstrip, was simply a place on the Aden to Dhala road.

It was decided in early April 1964 to push a brigade sized force forward from the airstrip at Thurmier into the Wadi Taym to bring the dissident

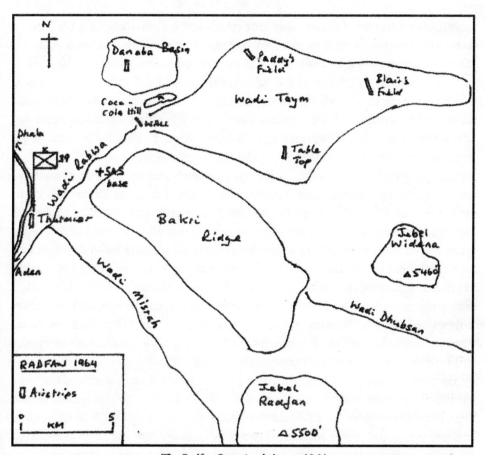

The Radfan Operational Area – 1964

tribes back under government control. The political plan was harsh. The population was ordered to vacate the entire area, although a few elderly people plus the enemy remained. The military plan was simple – a massive left hook by 45 Commando through the mountains and the Danaba Basin during two nights to link up with B Company from 3 PARA at Coca-Cola, the massive hill feature deep in enemy territory. At the same time a troop of B Squadron 22 Special Air Service Regiment (22 SAS) was to infiltrate through the mountains to the right of the main axis up the Wadi Rabwa (which was the only possible route to the heartland of the dissident tribes).

The first task of J (Sidi Rezegh) Battery was simple – to push down the Wadi Rabwa track on 30 April as a diversion to draw the bulk of the enemy force away from the area of the vital Coca-Cola feature and the proposed 3 PARA drop zone (DZ). As the Gun Position Officer I commanded the Gun Group and our guard force consisting of a platoon of 1 Royal Anglian, a section of Royal Engineers for mine clearance, and a troop of armoured cars from 4 RTR. It proved to be a memorable task.

On the night of 29 April the SAS troop moved off into the mountains to the right of the Wadi Rabwa, significantly with one of our A42 radios so that they could call for artillery fire. Soon after first light the next day we set off from the Thurmier gun position to the entrance to the Wadi Rabwa, very much enemy territory at this stage. All went well as we snaked up the progressively narrower wadi with infantry and mine clearers leading. Suddenly all hell broke loose. Rounding a tight bend the guard force ran into a 4-foot high rock road block which was well covered by small arms fire from three sides. The forward part of the guard force, the GPO's recce party, command post and first two guns were all pinned down by accurate fire. The platoon commander Paul Long ran back to me to report, and as he did so was shot through the side of the lower chest. The fire fight lasted thirty minutes or so but as ever it was extremely difficult to spot the enemy tribesmen. As the Saladin armoured cars with their 90 mm guns came forward into the action, the enemy melted away, the Saladins clearing the ambush wall by firing at twenty-metres range.

By midday the guns were in action some 3,000 metres short of the wall (a 400-foot sheer cliff) at the end of the Wadi Rabwa which stood below the 1,200-foot-high Coca-Cola hill feature. Ammunition was unloaded, sangars built and defensive fire targets adjusted. Our infantry completed their defensive positions and the armoured car troop withdrew. By mid-afternoon we were under attack again, this time an emboldened enemy some 200–300 strong skirmishing forwards over broken ground to within 200 yards to attack the gun position with a frontal assault. I ordered three guns into their low anti-tank position to engage the enemy with direct fire, the other three guns firing in the indirect role. Bombardier (later Regimental Sergeant Major) Baker was particularly effective with his light machine gun taking out the nearer targets. Back in the command post sangar, enemy fire was showering the plotters with earth as bullets hit the bank behind.

At the same time the SAS troop some 1,500 metres to our right was in trouble. They had been discovered by a young shepherd boy earlier in the day and were now also under heavy attack. Their troop commander had been killed and their radio operator shot through the chest, the bullet also damaging their primary radio. Now their only means of communication was our A42 radio relaying all messages through my command post. For the next two or three hours until last light, one troop of three guns fired almost continuously in high angle to protect the SAS patrol, alternating with rocket firing RAF Hunters, and all controlled though the J Battery command post. Fortunately, the direct attack on the gun position withered away and so the other three guns returned to the indirect fire role, mainly on harassing fire tasks to disguise the move forward of the main force far to the left.

We prepared somewhat nervously for the night. In the event we were not attacked again but continued to fire to help the SAS extricate themselves back to the gun position, which they did with considerable valour. The two dead had to be left behind and all of the remainder had gunshot wounds.

By 1 May we had completed our task as the diversion and the brigade left hook was going well, surprise having been achieved. Our next task was to withdraw back into Thurmier to join the main brigade axis with a series of helicopter moves forward until a week later we were deployed in the village under Coca-Cola, from which the enemy had attacked us on the first day. This village, situated at the western end of the seventeen-kilometre long Wadi Taym area of irrigated fields with fortified villages, was the launch pad for a move forward to control the whole area and the surrounding mountains. At a later stage the Sappers built a quite remarkable road from the Wadi Rabwa up the wall and into the Wadi Taym. After a few days it was decided that I should leave the gun position to become once more a Forward Observation Officer, which I did for the rest of my time in Aden. By this time, the 39th Infantry Brigade commanded by Brigadier (later General Sir) 'Monkey' Blacker with the 1st Battalions of the Royal Scots and the King's Own Scottish Borderers had arrived in theatre.

I joined the 1st Battalion of the Federal Regular Army with Gunner Howard, London born but of West Indian extraction, as my signaller. The racist attitude of the local Arab soldiers was immediately apparent. They would nonchalantly feel Gunner Howard's skin and later round on me for sharing my equipment with a black man. President Nasser visited Sana'a in the Yemen where he made a three-hour highly emotional and very anti-British speech calling on all Arabs to expel the British from Arab lands. Every soldier in the company to which I was attached on a high and exposed ridge listened on his transistor radio. The tension rose and I started to feel most uncomfortable: as last light approached, my Battery Commander called me to the radio to warn me of a possible attack by mutinous Arab soldiers, saying that he hoped to get a helicopter to remove us. At last light Gunner Howard and I erected a two-man tent we had found, securing the entrance. Once inside we lay with weapons cocked and safety catches off aimed at the most likely directions of attack. We could still hear Nasser's tirade from a multitude of radios. After a very long night we emerged at first light, soon to be rescued by a helicopter. After a debrief at Brigade Headquarters I was quietly told that they had not expected to see us again.

With some relief I moved a few kilometres forward to join, near Paddy's Field, the 1st Battalion The King's Own Scottish Borderers who had just arrived in the area of operations following acclimatization. A pattern now emerged whereby the infantry battalions served for four weeks up-country in the zone of operations followed by four weeks in Aden for rest and recuperation: in contrast the Gunners and a few others remained on operations throughout. As there were only enough officers in the Battery for each battalion to have one Forward Observation Officer party, I was normally located at battalion headquarters deploying to rifle companies in turn as they undertook operations. So for the next five months I switched between battalions as they came and went, and as operational priorities demanded. Captain (later Lieutenant Colonel) Rodney Cotton, a Forward Observation Officer formerly based in Beihan, arrived in the area of operations, as did Captain (later Major General) David Quayle from the Regiment in Kenya a few weeks later. By now the Battery was stretched to the limits – the Battery Commander was tied to Brigade Headquarters while the four Forward Observation Officers were allocated, one to each battalion in the operational area.

Each Forward Observation Officer had one radio operator. In my case for much of the time this was Gunner Ramsay who carried the radio as well as his own kit without ever complaining. Battle fatigue was such that some radio operators had to be rotated through the gun position command post for rest. During this period I had with me only my waist-mounted load carriage kit: two ammunition pouches, two water bottles, two utility pouches (one with food and the other with one pair of socks, one pair of underpants, washing kit and my camera), plus a bum role containing a piece of green hessian, six feet by two feet for camouflage, shade and warmth at night, and of course a map. Sometimes we carried extra water in the local *chughals*, goatskin bags that kept water cool but allowed a steady drip from the outside as it evaporated. It was a tough and spartan existence. Daytime temperatures exceeded 50° Celsius, water was very limited and there were no showers and no loos.

The 'J' Battery gun group was by this time run by the three warrant officers (Warrant Officer 2s McGillivery, Wakeford and Smith) although the battery captain, Captain (later Lieutenant Colonel) Peter Cronk, spent more time at the gun position as the guns moved forward into increasingly dangerous locations. Second Lieutenant (later Brigadier) Neill O'Connor came from Kenya to become the Gun Position Officer.

'I' (Bull's Troop) Battery Royal Horse Artillery arrived from Bahrain to give us a second battery and an additional Forward Observation Officer party. From the Far East arrived a two-gun section of 5.5 inch howitzers from 45th Field Regiment to provide a heavier shell and a much greater range. We soon heard that the enemy hated being attacked with these eighty-pound shells.

The first month of the operation had witnessed some tough pitched battles against groups of up to four hundred enemy. Once we entered the Wadi Taym, enemy tactics changed to carefully recced surprise attacks by up to twenty men at short ranges. The enemy knew the ground like the back of his hand, travelled fast and light living off the land, and had remarkably good eyesight and shot with considerable accuracy. Our task now was to expand our area of control, driving the enemy out. The plan was to control the central axis of the Wadi Rabwa and Wadi Taym while driving south-westwards into the highest mountains where the many remote villages provided bases for the enemy.

During my short time with 1st Battalion The King's Own Scottish Borderers, we cleared the ground forward in the Wadi Taym as far as the Table Top airstrip. (During the First World War the Turkish army had cleared a number of short airstrips that were visible from air photographs and quickly brought back into use.) I then transferred to the 1st Battalion The Royal Anglian Regiment who were tasked to clear down the Wadi Misrah as a prelude to the daunting task of capturing the huge plateaus of the Jebel Radfan and Jebel Widena.

On 25 May I conducted a four-vehicle armoured patrol towards the south of this great Wadi. My Ferret armoured reconnaissance car was second in the patrol, one hundred yards behind the first vehicle, and was blown up by an anti-tank mine. I was lucky to escape. The enemy had laid two old Mark 5 anti-tank mines in the wadi bed, one on top of the other, but they had dug them in slightly too deep. The first Ferret armoured car triggered only the first of the double pressure fuses. My Ferret's front left wheel triggered the second fuse, and a huge explosion. I was blown out of the turret, regaining consciousness as the lead vehicle crew came back to help. Apparently my vehicle headlamp had almost decapitated the lead vehicle commander. My driver, unhurt apart from a headache, had fortuitously closed his hatch just seconds before the explosion. We owed our lives to the good fortune of the mines exploding under the front wheel. Had the rear wheel detonated the mines, the petrol tank would have exploded in a massive fireball.

The 3rd Battalion The Parachute Regiment under the command of the legendary Lieutenant Colonel (later General Sir) Tony Farrar-Hockley was now tasked to advance south-westwards down the strongly held Bakri Ridge clearing the enemy as they advanced. The Paras stormed along the top of the ridge. When their supply helicopters had to be reallocated for other tasks, the commanding officer turned two companies into porters to allow the other two companies to fight on. I joined their D Company at this stage for the final assault onto the Jebel Widena.

Next I moved to 1st Battalion The Royal Scots who replaced the Paras on the Bakri Ridge with the task of clearing the many villages in the area. We found steep terraced fields from the wadi bottom almost to the tops of the highest mountains. All movement was always by night – two yards forward, climb a five-foot high terrace; two yards forward, climb another terrace – all as quiet as possible knowing that it would be suicide not to have secured and prepared the defence of the highest point in the area by first light. We used artillery fire a lot, mostly to attack enemy we saw but also as a defensive measure in case we were attacked, as we often were. We also used the RAF Hunter fighters in the ground attack role. Their brave pilots would fly down the valleys way below us, dive into the attack to use rockets or cannon, and then at the very last moment pull out of the dive to prepare for their next target. On occasions their pull-up was so late that their jets raised dust in the wadi bed.

I returned to the 1st Battalion The Royal Anglian Regiment who had arrived back in the area and tasked to exploit forward in the Wadi Taym. Two incidents concerning the technical firing of artillery occurred. In preparation for an ambush on a suspected enemy route through a ruined farm I had pre-recorded a target on a ridge two hundred yards to the east, fearing that they could creep up to the crest unseen to attack us in the ambush hide. Sure enough two days later soon after first light we were attacked as I had feared and so I called down the emergency defensive fire. The whine of the incoming shells lasted much longer than usual. I yelled 'Take Cover' and pressed my body into the earth by a low wall. The nearest shell exploded so close, maybe five metres away, that my lungs filled with high explosive dust. But we were still under attack and so I ordered 'Add 200 Repeat,' and then caught the eyes of some very frightened infantrymen. The shells arrived very quickly, striking the enemy who bothered us no more. The cause of this mistake was an incorrect measurement of the charge temperature. The temperature being applied was from last light the previous day but the cold night-time air had reduced the charge temperature substantially by first light.

As we advanced further east past the 00 easting on our maps, we soon noticed that our calls for artillery fire using grid references always seemed to result in the shells landing uncomfortably close. A few advanced gunnery calculations led us to the conclusion that the army map makers had omitted a one kilometre grid square at the map join, and so from then on we always added one kilometre to the easting and the problem was solved. Thirty years later I was the guest of the Chief Royal Engineer, General Sir John Stibbon, at dinner at Chatham, and found myself seated next to the Royal Engineer's head of survey, a serving major general. He told me he had served in Aden during the 1960s and so I asked him if he knew about the mistake in the Radfan maps. He replied after a long pause that he and a very small number of colleagues were aware of the mistake but were quite sure that nobody else did. He was aghast when I explained how we had discovered the error and then applied our own corrections.

It was almost impossible to have fresh food while operating in the mountains as I did continuously. At one stage my signaller and I had nothing other than tinned steak and kidney pudding for two weeks, three times each day, every day. I developed huge boils that the medical officer unkindly burst between his thumb and forefinger before cleaning the wounds with cotton wool wrapped around the end of his pencil. Major (later Major General) Barry Lane, who was the senior logistics staff officer at Brigade Headquarters, promised me fresh food. Next morning at first light I heard a Scout helicopter approaching my Observation Post position on a 5,000-foot peak. It hovered twenty feet above me, the door opened and a wooden box and two sandbags crashed to the ground beside me. The wooden box shattered to deliver twenty kippers, while a wriggling sandbag revealed a young goat and a second sandbag a quantity of rice, plus two well-read copies of the *Daily Mirror* and a bank statement!

August brought the violent monsoon season. In early afternoon the sky would darken, the wind would increase to eighty or ninety miles per hour blowing tiny particles of earth and sand into every part of one's body, kit and equipment, and then a gigantic thunderstorm would roll around the mountains getting ever closer. As the wind died, torrential rain fell for an hour or more soaking everything and producing a dangerous wall of water down every wadi. Exactly at last light the storm would end. But everybody and everything was caked in a layer of mud, a condition that could hardly be rectified until first light when a quick clean-up provided perhaps six hours before the violent cycle started once more. On one such occasion, the Battery stores marquee, secured by six-feet long iron staves into the ground and with a concrete base on which stood racks of equipment, was blown totally away. The only remains, apart from the concrete base, were the iron staves plus a few feet of shredded rope. A four-ton Ferret armoured car caught in the Wadi Misrah in such a storm was washed sixty miles downstream into the sea and never seen again.

Towards the middle of August I joined 45 Commando Royal Marines on their return from their base in Little Aden. Their first task was to eliminate a gang of forty enemy who had established themselves on very high ground at the eastern tip of the Bakri Ridge. Expecting an attack from the north-east, they had a strong position in a fortified village. A few days earlier I had registered this village as a pre-recorded target for future use. The Commanding Officer decided the best way to attack was from the south-west using the Wadi Dhubsan, a steep-sided valley some 2,000 feet below the ridge feature. Surprise would be achieved as it provided a covered approach and allowed us to use our detachment of cliff leaders to scale the 400-feet almost sheer cliffs from the top of the wadi to the Bakri Ridge. Fortuitously, the company commander was Major Mike Banks, an experienced Everest climber. We entered the Wadi Dhubsan after last light, moving up to the cliff. Once there the cliff leaders climbed the face and secured ropes, signalling the lead platoon to commence the climb. The platoon started the climb with the company commander and me, with our radio operators immediately behind, the remaining two platoons following. As the first marines reached the top the enemy attacked from about two hundred yards and the platoon commander called for artillery fire. I quietly said to Gunner Ramsay,

'DF/SOS Fire.'

Over the radio he ordered, 'DF/SOS Fire!'

The instant reply from the Guns was 'DF/SOS Fire – Shot over.'

Gunner Ramsay reported up to me on the rope six feet above 'Shot sir,' and the company commander just to my right on the adjacent rope said, 'Well done – thanks.'

We heard the near simultaneous sound of the guns eight kilometres away on Table Top, and immediately the whistle of the shells followed by six huge explosions just above us. There was panic and mayhem above. The first radio report said the shells were landing too close, quickly followed by a second report saying that they were in exactly the right place and the screaming of wounded enemy could be heard in the darkness. As we neared the top of the cliff, I ordered Gunner Ramsay, 'Four rounds gunfire,' and then as the marines asked for more, we fired another twenty rounds gunfire to enable the rest of the company to complete the climb and then attack the enemy position. At first light we exploited forward following the blood trails, but the remaining enemy had gone.

By now the main emphasis of our operations had switched back to the farthest east part of the Wadi Taym where I joined another company of 45 Commando commanded by Major 'Jungle' Basely, augmented by the reinforced Recce Troop run by Captain Ted Goddard with Lieutenant Ian Martin as his number two. This company pushed east to the hamlet of Mutber where they established a very strong defensive position both sides of the wadi, overlooking the Blair's Field airstrip. Two Vickers water-cooled heavy machine guns mounted on the top of the wadi bank could reach almost to the eastern end of the Wadi Taym and cover much of the rising ground to north and south. This position was used as a patrol base with the Recce Troop conducting deep patrolling while the company patrolled closer to the base. Some were fighting patrols but most were ambush patrols.

Captain David Quayle was also there so we had the luxury of two Forward Observation Parties located together. This enabled David and me to patrol alternately, one staying alongside the company commander at the very exposed base location and the other out on patrol. We shared the tasks but David took on most of the deep patrols while I had a majority of the closer company patrols. David's radio operator Gunner Kerr played a leading role in the rescue and retrieval of the bodies of two marines gunned down when trying to move into a better ambush position at first light. I completed so many patrols in this area that towards the end the company commander combined the tasks of patrol commander and Forward Observation Officer, and I did both. I appreciated the privilege of being allowed to command Royal Marines on operations as a patrol commander.

During the first six months of this campaign we had lost around forty soldiers killed and many more wounded or injured. More than half were caused by accidents ranging from aircraft crashes to the accidental firing of a rifle. Some, such as the Hunter aircraft cannon shells that hit two soldiers on the head, were extremely unlucky. There were the so-called 'blue on blue' incidents but none of these was caused by artillery fire. Of the soldiers killed by the enemy, most were from rifle fire while a few were from mine or booby trap explosions. By this time 3rd Regiment Royal Horse Artillery had served four years in Kenya, always with one battery detached to Aden, and it was time for the Regiment to return home. We were flattered to learn that 'J' (Sidi Rezegh) Battery was to be replaced by a full eighteen-gun field regiment, possibly an unintended tribute to the pace at which we had worked to fulfil the required tasks.

On 20 September 1964 I left the Radfan for an overnight stay in my little used room in Seedaseer Lines, and flew out next day. As we flew into Malta at 4 a.m. it was the first morning of Malta's independence. The harbour, full of ships dressed overall, was a blaze of light. The aircraft door was opened and I took my first lungful of cool fresh clean air for a long time.

Some thirty-three years later I had the chance to return to Thurmier and, armed with the photographs I took at the time, returned to the old gun position, looked up at the Coca-Cola hill (actually rather more like the rock of Gibraltar) and looked again at the dominating cliff at the top of the Wadi Rabwa. The airstrip at Thurmier is no more, replaced by a thriving market town with a satellite dish on almost every roof. This time the locals were very friendly. It appears that the British were a better bet than the Russians and later Chinese who followed.

CHAPTER 5

Return to Germany

3RD REGIMENT ROYAL HORSE ARTILLERY, now with Lieutenant Colonel Nigel Birbeck (earlier my Platoon Commander at Sandhurst) in command assembled at Airfield Camp at Netheravon on Salisbury Plain. The reunification of the Regiment in England should have been a joyous occasion; however, it was anything but. We had been informed that on return from well-deserved disembarkation leave we would be equipped with the new Abbot 105 mm self-propelled howitzer together with a range of modern tracked armoured vehicles. Now with expectations of an exciting new challenge to be faced, we were suddenly told that the arrival of the new equipment would be delayed for a year.

I spent my leave in the United States. I flew to New York via Iceland and Newfoundland and then spent a week exploring this great city. The famous greyhound bus took me to Washington where David and Eileen Wilson, from Lippstadt days and now working in the British Embassy, very kindly gave me their spare room for two weeks. I explored every corner of (the safer parts of) Washington and followed the routes of Stonewall Jackson in the campaigns of the Civil War in Virginia. I found the United States fascinating.

On return to Netheravon in November I discovered nothing but gloom. We were in an old hutted camp with almost no facilities of any kind. The promised new guns and armoured vehicles were not available. Each Battery had one Land-Rover and one three-ton truck – nothing else, not even a rifle, a radio or an artillery range table. It was the most terrible anticlimax. The most difficult problem was keeping our fine soldiers happy. As one said to me, 'It's all very well doing PT from 0900 to 1030, playing soccer from 1100 to 1245, and then having a cross-country run in the afternoon, but my body cannot take any more exercise!' The Commanding Officer tried everything to get the Regiment some equipment. Eventually we suffered the indignity of taking equipment from the Territorial Army as nothing else was available. Each battery received two Second World War 5.5 inch guns, and then a few weeks later four more to make up the six.

In January 1965 I reported to the Royal Armoured Corps Centre at Bovington to do two three-week courses: first an Armoured Fighting

Vehicle (AFV) 432 Driving and Maintenance Course, followed by a Centurion tank-driving test officers course. These were great fun. I returned to Netheravon to learn that the Regiment would move as planned to Detmold in May taking with us the ancient towed 5.5 inch guns to join the 20th Armoured Brigade. We were to replace the 1st Regiment Royal Horse Artillery, who on moving out of Hildesheim would send all their M44 155 mm self-propelled howitzers for scrap. It was a very bitter blow to join the crack 20th Armoured Brigade with such old and immobile equipment.

But a surprise awaited me. Brigadier (later General Sir) John Sharp, Commandant of the Royal School of Artillery at Larkhill and a former Commanding Officer of 1st Regiment Royal Horse Artillery, had just been selected to be the General Officer Commanding (GOC) 2nd Division in Lübbecke in Germany, and he needed an ADC. The Commanding Officer was asked to forward the names of three suitable subalterns for interview. In turn we each had lunch with the Sharps, and a few weeks later I was told that I had been selected, starting a year ahead in March 1966.

Hobart Barracks in Detmold was huge, including an airfield, and contained Headquarters 20th Armoured Brigade, The Royal Dragoons with Centurion tanks, an Army Air Corps Regiment, an Aircraft Workshop, an Armoured Workshop and several other small units. All these had to give up space so that 3rd Regiment Royal Horse Artillery could squeeze in. It was not the warmest of welcomes. The Brigade had two more tank regiments (including the 3rd Carabiniers, also in Detmold) and an armoured infantry battalion (1st Battalion The Royal Northumberland Fusiliers in Lemgo). As we were a part of the 4th Division, our operational area was very similar to my previous tour in Germany. The operational situation remained very similar, except that our Main Defensive Position (MDP) had been pushed forward from the hundred-metre wide River Weser to the much narrower River Leine to meet deepening German misgivings about giving up any territory without a fight.

I became once again the Gun Position Officer (GPO) of 'J' (Sidi Rezegh) Battery Royal Horse Artillery. We had lost many of the stalwarts of the tour in Aden and so had to work very hard from our arrival in Germany in May to reach the highest standards for the Practice Camp at the familiar Munsterlager South and Hohne ranges in July. The Regiment very soon regained its cohesion and, despite the rush to be ready in time, our first firing camp in Germany with the old towed 5.5 inch guns was most successful. On return from firing camp, I was promoted to captain, having completed six years' service since commissioning, and became once again a Forward Observation Officer (FOO).

As an FOO in an Armoured Brigade, my primary vehicle was a Centurion Mark 5 tank. In October and November we faced the annual autumn field training period in the operational area near the inner German border, and so I had to get to know a new crew with different skills. My tank driver was Lance Bombardier Talbot, one of the very best young soldiers in the battery (he later moved to 22 SAS where he had a notable career). He knew the tank backwards and his simple instruction to me was 'You talk to the tank squadron and fire the guns – but leave the tank driving and maintenance to me.' It worked well.

The five-week autumn field-training period started at the lowest level with squadron/company training followed by regiment/battalion training, and then moved up several gears with brigade training followed by the divisional exercise, and finally full-scale manoeuvres with the German army as our opponents. As ever, all this took place over German farmland in the area where we planned to fight the Third World War should it ever occur. Lance Bombardier Talbot kept my tank going throughout, and we had a great deal of valuable training. The German Army had matured into a well-equipped and organised fully mechanised army. However, their conscripts were no match for the increasingly experienced professional British Army, and it showed. It was said that they always took their boots off at night. We did not and so our mock attacks at or near first light came with a near guarantee of success!

By mid-November we were all back in barracks for the winter and, in my case, full-blown training for the ski season. The Regiment fielded both an alpine team and a cross-country team, both moving to Biberweir near Lermoos in Austria early in December. With me in the Alpine team were Lieutenants Oliver Skeen, Charles Wainwright and David Bonnor-Morris. We trained hard and started the race season with the 4th Division meeting in Lermoos. For the first month we stayed in a very cheap and quite awful Austrian 'pension'. I maintain the memory of a huge cooking range rather like a gigantic Aga populated by a dozen or so cats perched on those parts that did not get too hot and eating whatever they fancied as it was cooked. Every meal came with cat hairs! Fortuitously our next stop was the Caspar Badrutt Hotel in St Moritz which could not have been more different. As ever the Army meeting had fearsomely challenging courses and we did moderately well without winning. Finally, we moved to Oberjoch in

Germany for the BAOR races, but this location was far too low for downhill racing and was not a success.

On return to Detmold in February 1966, there was just enough time to hand over my Troop before moving to the 2nd Division headquarters at Lübbecke, an attractive market town in a gap in the steep Eggebirge hills. The task of the Divisional Commander's Aide de Camp, or ADC, is to be at his elbow throughout the working day and at every social occasion. In the headquarters, access to the General was through my office to a time schedule I ran. I planned and accompanied the General on every visit he made. In the field I was always at his side. The ADC is both a personal staff officer and a social organiser. While it is a demanding appointment with many potential pitfalls, it provides a young officer with a priceless experience of the army at a higher level. The 2nd Division took over the 1st British Corps right forward division from the 4th Division at the time I moved from the 4th to the 2nd Division, and so I already knew the tasks and ground very well.

The 2nd Division had two brigades under full command: the 6th Infantry Brigade in Munster commanded by Brigadier John Douglas-Withers (my commanding officer until two years earlier); and the 12th Infantry Brigade in Osnabrück commanded by Brigadier Sandy Thomas, a New Zealander who had joined the Hampshire Regiment. These were two very fine soldiers both with formidable records in the Second World War. In addition the 4th Canadian Infantry Brigade Group in Soest was attached to the 2nd Division for operations and training. Its two very fine commanders were first Brigadier Jim Telfer, followed by Brigadier Ned Amey. They too were extensively decorated in the Second World War. The fourth brigadier in the Division was the Commander Royal Artillery, Brigadier Phillip Rooke. Our next superior headquarters was 1st (British) Corps at Bielefeld commanded by Lieutenant General (later General) Sir John Mogg, and, above that, Headquarters BAOR/NORTHAG commanded by General Sir John (but known as Shan) Hackett who after parachuting as a brigade commander into Arnhem in 1944 had famously hidden in a cupboard for many weeks in a Dutch house to avoid capture. Both these generals and the other divisional commanders had ADCs who worked together as a close-knit team to ensure that their generals' lives did not clash, but meshed together as and when required.

The Sharp family, the General, wife Wendy, and Anne, Susan, Rosanne and Michael, plus a dog and three horses, arrived in Lübbecke a week after me. Major General John Sharp was a tough, highly-decorated soldier who had won two Military Crosses in the desert in the Second World War. His exploits in that campaign were legendary and he was severely wounded several times. Field Marshal Montgomery had selected him to be one of his liaison officers, and this led to the famous incident in May 1945 when, having been plied with drink by the Russians, he responded to the Russian 21-gun salute on departure by firing his pistol six times through the roof of the Field Marshal's plane. I had been warned never to mention this incident, and nor did I. In my year with him I only heard him mention it once, and not to me.

I lived in the Divisional Headquarters Officers' Mess, notorious for its wartime role as a pure Aryan breeding centre with the bravest blond Nazi officers being mated with selected blond women. The building was set in the trees near the top of the ridge in the most beautiful setting. The General and his family lived in the fine Crossed Keys House just fifty metres away. I was treated almost as an additional son, arriving at the house as breakfast ended and, following a day in the office, leaving after tea. In the event of a dinner party (usually once per week) then I left after the last guest and usually a discussion on how the evening went. I always sat in the middle of the table at dinner parties in order to engage those sometimes stranded between the two table-end conversations.

When the General travelled by car or helicopter, I sat next to him to assist with papers needing discussion, points of clarification on the programme, and a discussion on whom he would meet and when. I kept a little grey book with a few pages for every unit in the division, including outline details of every officer. The aim was not just that the General should never be surprised by a face, but that he would know every face, the name to go with it, when they last met and some important fact special to that officer. We developed a system that usually allowed me to receive a panic signal and provide the information in a split second.

We were of course there because of the Cold War and the possibility that we could face a Warsaw Pact onslaught at any time, and this was very serious business. The divisional headquarters staff worked long and hard on war planning and training, maintaining very close watch on the intelligence picture so that we knew as much as possible about our enemy. I worked closely with the Chief of Staff, Colonel David Pontifex, and with Major Bob (later General Sir Robert) Pascoe as the senior General Staff Officer Grade 2 Operations. The CRA Brigadier Phillip Rooke commanded two field regiments both with the very new Abbot 105 mm self-propelled howitzer and a nuclear-capable missile regiment with Honest John rocket launchers and 203 mm guns. I learned a very great deal from these fine soldiers and their colleagues.

For the first six months from March to September we were in the field frequently, both watching the divisional units training and taking part in high-level command post/signals exercises. While some were set at a low level for the division and its brigades, others such as Exercise Summer Sales and Exercise Wintex were corps and NATO exercises respectively with huge importance attached to them. Indeed, 10 Downing Street and the White House were both involved in the process of nuclear weapons release, and it was often a very long process. With the Cold War now long over, nobody should be unaware of the detail of the training that was practised or the seriousness with which such questions were tackled.

In the autumn the Divisional manoeuvres took place to the south of Hanover directed by my general. At this stage the Division had just completed the issue of the new tracked Armoured Fighting Vehicle 432 in its main variants, of which the most important was the infantry section vehicle. For the first time the infantry could now travel at the same speed as the tanks and over the same ground. Moreover, they could swim major rivers such as the River Weser, although this was not recommended for the faint-hearted as the margin between a successful river crossing and either sinking or being swept downstream was proved to be a slender one.

At Bünde, close to Lübbecke, was the headquarters of SOXMIS commanded by General Belskii. This Soviet Mission was the equivalent of BRIXMIS at Potsdam, and like BRIXMIS had become a legal spy organization. Having been asked to arrange a social occasion for Belskii, we received as a gift a huge amount of caviar that I much enjoyed. The SOXMIS officers were deeply involved in various acts not to be described here, but suffice to say they were watched with the greatest care.

The 2nd Division included six superb infantry battalions and two of the oldest and finest cavalry regiments, and I got to know them all very well. It is sad to relate that at the time of writing all eight have disappeared from the order of battle.

The role of the ADC was not all pleasure. While I developed a remarkable ability to spot pitfalls and take avoiding action, whenever anything went wrong in the General's life it was always declared to be my fault and so I received the most almighty rockets. When she was around, Wendy Sharp would pick me up and dust me down. Otherwise, I had to live with the anger and gauge when it had subsided.

Early in 1967 it was decided that I would leave the Sharps as planned in March to return to England to join the 16th Light Air Defence Regiment Royal Artillery in Barton Stacey near Andover in Hampshire. I knew that I was approaching the time to take the demanding Staff College and Promotion to Major examination. In his most generous letter thanking me for my support as I departed Lübbecke, General Sharp wrote, 'I hope your experiences of the past year will be of some help in passing the Staff College exam, which must now be *Priority 1* in your life!'

CHAPTER 6

Life as an Adjutant

THE 16TH LIGHT AIR DEFENCE REGIMENT consisted of two gun Batterys and a very large and complex workshop. Its role was to provide the low and medium level air defence of the 3rd Division with its sixteen L40/70 towed guns, each with a Fire Control Equipment (FCE) 7 radar that included an inbuilt analog predictor computer and a massive generator. In addition each Battery had an Observation Troop with one Number 4 Mark 7 radar roughly the size of a London bus to provide early warning, plus eight Observation Post parties to give quick verbal warning orders to the guns, allowing the FCE 7 radars to face the right way to pick up fast approaching aircraft. On arrival I was sent to 30th (Roger's Company) Battery, commanded by Major Peter Morris to command the Observation Troop.

16th Light Air Defence Regiment, commanded by Lieutenant Colonel (later Colonel) Peter Garnett, had returned to England from Singapore the previous summer. The old Second World War US Army camp at Barton Stacey had lain derelict for many years. It consisted of wooden huts so old that daylight showed between the wood planks. Our soldiers lived thirty to a hut with their lavatories and wash facilities in other huts up to fifty metres distant. Each hut was warmed by two huge coal stoves made in the US. If it became too hot, the soldiers opened the door; when it was too cold they added more coal. When they were away or asleep it became very cold. All of the equipment stood on a windswept car park, hardly conducive to radars and early 1960s vintage computers. It was an unimaginable way in which to house a professional army. Unsurprisingly, the *Daily Mirror* and other tabloids ran the story on a regular basis. I shared an officers' hut with Captain (later Colonel) Tim Hoggarth. We were lucky enough to have both a lavatory and a bath under the same roof, but keeping our coal fires alight was a major chore.

At this time the 3rd Division had three infantry brigades plus a 'string' to 16th Parachute Brigade. The Division had been reformed to provide the United Kingdom's strategic reserve for worldwide operations, deploying either a brigade group or a larger force. The result of this was that the 16th Light Air Defence Regiment tended to be on the fringe of mainstream divisional training, and usually deployed for training as a single Battery with a brigade, rather than the complete regiment. The CRA was Brigadier (later Major General) Drew Bethell who, having never served in air defence artillery, maintained his distance from us.

Soon after I arrived, it was hinted that I was a strong candidate to become the adjutant when Captain (later Lieutenant Colonel) John Biles departed to the Staff College in the summer. But my overwhelming priority had to be the dreaded Staff College exam, in those days eight very demanding three-hour written papers in four days (including three tactics papers and others on military administration, law, international affairs and similar). I enrolled for the Metropolitan College correspondence course and completed the sixty written papers by the December 1967 exam date. I also attended as many short courses at the universities, mostly at Bristol, as I could.

I had a very fine bunch of soldiers in my Troop (in those days air defence regiments received a higher percentage of soldiers of above average intelligence than field regiments) and I enjoyed the challenge of a new type of artillery needing different skills. In late May I was taken ill while on exercise on Salisbury Plain and whisked in to the Tidworth Military Hospital where I suddenly found myself with a nurse permanently assigned to my bedside. Twenty-fours later I was subjected to a hair-raising, police-escorted, blue-light dash to London to the Queen Alexandra Royal Military Hospital (now subsumed into Tate Britain) on Millbank. I was put into the King George VI officers' ward overlooking the river, and having watched two officers die that first night I began to realise that my predicament could be serious. This hospital was the show piece of military medicine and Matron was the undoubted boss. Her daily inspection was an experience I had never before, or since, witnessed in a very long military career. The inspection was preceded by Ward Sister's inspection for which all the patients had to lie to attention, not moving at all for the next thirty minutes until Matron had finished.

After two weeks of tests I was prepared for theatre, being told to expect to be minus one kidney on waking up. An eminent and knighted professor from Westminster Hospital had attended me and decided that the kidney could remain and so I awoke intact, if a little sore. Apparently I had picked up a virus of some unidentified kind in Aden and it had worked its way through my system. I remained in the hospital for another week. I recall being taken to the Trooping the Colour parade in a wheelchair wearing a dressing gown over my pyjamas and being placed in the front row. I was relieved that nobody recognised me.

On return to my Regiment I was invited to take over as the adjutant in August 1967. An adjutant is in effect the chief executive of an organization in which the Commanding Officer is the Chairman and the Battery Commanders are the Board. It is a demanding appointment for a young officer (I was then 28) and a pre-requisite for a serious career. I also set about getting myself seriously fit, having put on weight while an ADC, in order to play hockey again at the top level in London. This proved to be an extremely busy time, juggling my full-time duties as adjutant with examination studies and courses, and with hockey matches every Wednesday, Saturday and Sunday. The solution proved to be a personal 4 a.m. reveille to allow four hours' study before work, and then another three hours' study either side of dinner. For these months I became a very anti-social animal. I sat the examination in December and in March 1968 received the very good news that I had both passed the examination and been awarded a place at the Staff College with my Division 3 course starting in September 1969.

In the meantime I grew into the task of being the adjutant. Lieutenant Colonel Peter Garnett allowed me a very free rein and supported even my wildest ideas. Light Air Defence was at this time not considered the most exciting subject on earth, and some regarded us as the poor relation. So I set about raising the profile in as many ways as I could. We had the advantage of being on the main road from London and therefore a natural place for VIP visitors to stop on their way to the Army Headquarters at Wilton. I decided that a very impressive Quarter Guard should be formed. I selected twenty soldiers over 6 feet 4 inches in height, all of whom could form the basis of a very smart and well-drilled Guard at a moment's notice. To this we added four trumpeters. Having greatly smartened up the entrance to our dilapidated camp, the Regiment began to catch the eye of the senior people.

We set in train a plan to improve the standards in the Officers' Mess and our Regimental Dinners earned a fine reputation. Having been assigned Glasgow as our main recruiting area, we had more than our fair share of problem soldiers so I invoked a three-months' warning and discharge system that rigorously removed bad soldiers from circulation. The Regiment had four outstanding ex-Regimental Sergeant Majors, now all captains. Three of them had spent most of their careers in parachute artillery: Jock Stewart and Ernie Lambert (whom I knew from Kenya) had served in Royal Horse Artillery, while Lance Prewitt was a war-time parachute gunner with a fine record. John McGowan had an air defence background and was also a tower of strength, not least because as a Scot he understood the complex Glaswegian dimension, as that was from where many of our soldiers came. They gave me much quiet encouragement and help as I strove for improvement.

I was always in the office early to clear the paperwork before the Commanding Officer arrived. It allowed me time to be out and around the camp talking and listening. I spent an hour every morning and afternoon on my tours, learning first-hand where the problems were and what the soldiers were thinking.

I had noticed that there was no Regimental Directive of any kind, and so I wrote one and had it typed for the Commanding Officer's signature. Having put it with a brief explanatory note on his desk I expected there to be a discussion and amendments but, not at all, as the Colonel signed it as it was. Not only was I hoist, but I now had to admit to the Second-in-Command that I had written a major policy document without any consultation. I had covered most normal priorities but added a few novel ideas of my own. These included an annual regimental Skill-at-Arms camp at Shorncliffe that proved a great success, and a plan for every Troop Commander to take his soldiers away on an overseas adventurous training exercise.

Three young officers worked for me as assistant adjutant during my two years in that role, and all of them worked extremely hard. I soon discovered that the ploy of putting my in-tray into theirs before reading through it altered the work balance in my favour. After prosecuting at two Courts-Martial, I passed that task on to my assistants as well. Lieutenant (later Colonel) Johnnie Eliot was the assistant adjutant for most of the time, becoming a lifelong friend.

With regard to the Troop Commanders' adventurous training exercises, I regarded the Regimental Sergeant Major and all the regimental policemen plus the chief clerk and all the regimental clerks as my Troop, with the assistant adjutant as the Troop second-in-command – probably a total of around fifteen soldiers. The neighbouring camp at Barton Stacey housed Headquarters 12 Engineer Brigade whose chief of logistics, Major Peter Chitty, was not only a highly qualified diver but was currently leading the recovery of the *Mary Rose* in the Solent. I persuaded him to help run a sub-aqua course based on the Royal Engineer Class 3 divers course. This took place partly in the classroom at Barton Stacey and partly at the Army Diving School at Marchwood on Southampton Water. Every member of the 'Adjutant's Troop' passed this course. For me the claustrophobia test which involved one hour sitting in the silt by the army quay at Marchwood was close to terrifying. The incoming tide had washed me upstream under five large barges moored from the dock wall outwards and I simply could not find a way back to the surface, every attempt keeping me trapped under the large flat bottoms or in the narrowing space between the barges. The outcome was that once the Commanding Officer rightly decided that the chief clerk and I should remain behind, the remainder of the Troop spent two weeks diving in Gibraltar in 1968, followed by a similar expedition to Malta in 1969.

Another innovation was an Air Cooperation Camp in May 1968 on Dartmoor near Oakhampton. The Regiment deployed in a straight line formation almost wheel to wheel so that fighter aircraft could attack for several hours each day, thus providing the gun crews with very valuable training. For me the bonus was flying in the attacking aircraft – usually a Vampire two-seater jet in which pilot and co-pilot sit side by side – and always finishing with ten minutes of aerobatics.

During the mid 1960s the British Army had a battle school in eastern Libya in the area of the major battles of the Second World War, well south of Tobruk. The MOD decided that the 16th Light Air Defence Regiment complete should move to Libya from September until November 1968 for an advanced training period in close cooperation with Royal Air Force units in El Adam and Cyprus. My task was very largely to get the Regiment there and then back, including massive amounts of documentation. Once the Gun Batterys' training had started I had a certain amount of freedom. In the meantime extremely valuable training took place. An Air Defended Area or Vulnerable Point defence would be established in the desert each day and Royal Air Force fighters and bombers given targets to attack. As both the guns and the aircraft filmed every attack, the periodic after-action meetings between the aircrews and the gun detachments allowed both sides to improve their performances to a remarkable degree.

It was time to take the clerks and the regimental police on a trip to escape the base camp. Using five Land-Rovers we set off southwards navigating by sun compass to reach the sand sea. After two days' driving across large flat areas of sand and gravel it became clearer by the minute that a substantial storm was brewing up, and so we made for a small hillock in an otherwise entirely flat area of gravel. As darkness fell the rain started becoming heavier and heavier with increasing thunder and lightning. Regimental Sergeant Major Wareham called me at first light. 'You had better come and see this,' he said. I got up to a remarkable sight. Our hillock was now an island in a sea of water as far as the eye could see with only a distant ridge showing above water level. We remained on the island all day as the water drained away. An attempt to drive one vehicle off the island was thwarted as it immediately sank up to its axles. We remained there another day and night while the sun dried the mud and then resumed our journey the next day. Taking a clockwise route through the desert we reached the coast east of Benghazi in order to explore the very interesting Greek ruins at Cyrene and Apollonia before returning to base.

Back in Barton Stacey it was a great relief to discover that the long promised calor gas central heating had now been fitted to our dreadful huts – at least we would be warmer. I resumed playing serious hockey for the Royal Artillery, becoming the club secretary. Not only were we now a smaller army than eight years earlier, but crucially we had long since lost our National Service star players. The top London clubs became very difficult for us to beat, but we still managed to win against Oxford and Cambridge Universities more often than not. From the 1959–60 side only Major Trevor Selley, Captain (later Major General) Bill Cornock, Captain (later Lieutenant Colonel) Tony Pratt, Warrant Officer 2 (later Major) Ron Coleman and myself remained. The star newcomer was Lieutenant (later Lieutenant Colonel) Vyvian Smith, a current English international. During these years a remarkably talented (both as hockey players and soldiers) group of young officers played in the Gunner team. Lieutenant (later General Sir) Alex Harley became the President of both the Army Hockey Association and the Combined Services Hockey Association (as well as The Master Gunner at St James's Park). Chris Burson, Rodney Walker, Peter Wagstaffe and Roger Styles all reached the rank of brigadier while Peter Sexton and Tony Moorby became colonels. Lieutenant Nick George was a star player who left the army early as a major while, in contrast, Derek Parsley had joined the army as a young Gunner in the early 1950s and was still playing twenty years later, retiring as a lieutenant colonel in 1985.

Suddenly 1969 arrived but my adjutantal duties continued much as before, with many games of hockey every week. The Regiment continued to train as two almost independent Batterys and so I had a certain amount of time for myself. One day the Commander Royal Artillery, Brigadier Drew Bethell, called into the barracks unexpectedly. He had a simple and very attractive proposition to offer me. He owned a 23-foot Invicta sloop and needed a single crew member as part of his Royal Ocean Racing Club single-handed qualification, and wanted me to join him on six cross-channel passages to France in the coming summer. This proved both demanding and great fun, generally leaving the Solent on a Friday evening for a night crossing into Cherbourg, and then returning on the Saturday night reaching the Hamble mooring by mid afternoon. Helming across the busy channel shipping lanes at night while alone on deck is a magical experience. I also crewed in the Cowes–St Malo race that summer. The latter stages of the race were in thick fog and so nearly ended in disaster as we strayed into the infamous Minkies (Isles les Minquiers) rocks just as the day dawned, spotting the breaking waves on the rocks barely seventy yards ahead.

The Commanding Officer changed, Lieutenant Colonel (later Major General) John Stephenson assuming command in the spring. He could not have been a more different personality from his predecessor, full of ideas and new initiatives, driving everyone forward with his enormous enthusiasm, energy and vitality. These characteristics were matched by a genuine friendliness and considerable charm. I had just the last three months of my two year period as adjutant working for Colonel John, and I enjoyed the fresh challenge every bit as much as the majority of my tour working for Lieutenant Colonel Peter Garnett.

During this period I organised the Rapier Pilot Battery, a trial organization based upon one of the Regiment's gun Batterys, reinforced by Royal Air Force personnel to conduct the first Rapier missile system field trials. All of the Battery's equipment was prepared for hand-back to Ordnance, the Battery completed its internal reorganisation and the Royal Air Force personnel were about to join when, out of the blue, the Ministry of Defence announced a two-year delay in the trial. It beggars belief that nobody had an inkling of such a change in plans. My final task was to write the Regimental Standing Orders for a possible internal security tour in Northern Ireland. Little did I know in 1969 that this new task would last for thirty-six years. Captain (later Lieutenant Colonel) Paul d'Apice had been selected to take over my duties as adjutant, and he moved into the office in early August to assume the role.

It had been a very varied and enjoyable tour with, it has to be admitted, far less pressure than my service brought me before or since. It was a fascinating period militarily, for almost half of the army was being withdrawn from all parts of the world back to a role almost exclusively in Europe at a time when the Cold War was intensifying. During the late 1960s the army developed new operational roles with far more intensive training schedules, and I had been lucky enough to be a small part of this change. I learned a great deal about air defence techniques that proved of immense value later in my service.

The other change in my life resulted from a duty tour near London where I had made many friends, three of whom were to play leading roles in my life, one as my future wife. Earlier in the year I had introduced Penny Webb to my assistant adjutant, Lieutenant Johnnie Eliot. In turn I met Penny's close friend and neighbour from Crowborough, Ann Walters, a physiotherapist. The third girl in the flat was Jenny Chisholm, who was to marry Captain (later Brigadier) Austin Thorp, a hockey-playing Sapper who proved a rugged opponent on the field and a wonderful friend off it. I met Ann just as I left 16th Light Air Defence Regiment in August, the start of the most wonderful lifelong relationship.

CHAPTER 7

On to the Staff

REPORTING TO THE Royal Military College of Science at Shrivenham in September 1969 with the other Division 3 students, I commenced staff training. While Divisions 1 and 2 represented the 'scientific' part of the Army, mainly officers from the technical Corps, Division 3 students came mostly from the Royal Armoured Corps, the Gunners and the Infantry, and, it has to be said, probably had rather more operational military experience. The aim of this first three months was to give the Division 3 officers a grounding in military science and technology. In those days, unlike recent years, the Royal Military College of Science Shrivenham was a pretty awful place. The instruction was appallingly bad and the walls of the Officers' Mess dining room were adorned with unframed torn travel posters. It was unimpressive and in consequence not conducive to serious learning. Indeed my main memory of the time spent there was a day working at the face of a South Wales colliery as a miner. At the end of the day, while in the showers, these wonderful men explained how proud they were to be miners. I responded by stating that in my opinion just one day at the face was so bad that I felt no man should have to spend a lifetime in such conditions. They did not understand me and I did not understand them, but the horrific injuries and health deterioration of miners has proved me correct, I think.

It was with great relief that I departed from the Royal Military College of Science in December to start the proper Army Staff Course at the Staff College Camberley in January 1970. Major General (later Lieutenant General Sir) Alan Taylor was the Commandant – a bachelor with a penchant for late night parties and fast cars – whose example many members of the Course decided to follow with a hilariously happy year as a result.

There were 180 students of whom forty-two came from a wide variety of overseas countries. Of the remainder there were three students each from the Royal Navy, Royal Marines, Royal Air Force and the Civil Service, with the rest from every corner of the Army. The overseas students were all majors while the British officers were split equally between majors and captains. The thirty members of the Directing Staff (DS) represented the cream of the Army. With sixty students in each Division, I found myself in 'B' Division under Colonel (later Brigadier) Peter Aylwin-Foster. We soon learned that the overseas DS and students were not only of the very highest calibre, but many had unique operational experience from places such as Vietnam, the Congo and the Middle East.

The twelve-months' course consisted of six terms, with the overseas students departing at the end of the fifth term to allow free discussion of United Kingdom classified national issues. Each Division was split into six syndicates, each of ten officers working under a syndicate DS. At any one time around a third of the DS were 'swinging', that is, without a full time syndicate and usually very busy developing new exercises. The first few weeks covered the very simplest staff work but the course very soon moved up a gear, the work becoming progressively more demanding, but never really challenging or intellectually taxing. Almost everything we studied related to command and staff work in a potential conflict between NATO and Warsaw Pact forces. The average working day contained an outside lecturer addressing the whole course in the capacious Alanbrooke Hall, syndicate discussions in the many syndicate rooms and perhaps a presentation from the DS who worked in specialist teams such as European Armoured Warfare or Logistics. Some of these presentations were performed as 'playlets' most of which were highly amusing. Every evening contained enough study work for at least two hours, either in preparation for the following day or as one of the many projects.

There were also two very large three-day command post exercises during the course, the first of which featured a Soviet attack from the Chilterns towards Oxford with a British defensive position based on the River Thames. As one of the youngest on the course I was more than surprised to find that I was appointed to be the divisional commander for this first exercise, being required to wear the rank of a major general and called either 'general' or 'sir' by everyone other than the Commandant. My preparation included detailed helicopter recces, writing and preparing the divisional operation order with my staff, and then conducting both the main orders group (in which my 'brigade commanders' received their own orders) and later the confirmatory orders. The 'battle' was staged in a time frame that ensured that rest had to be taken on a regular basis and of course the key point that I had to make as the 'divisional commander' was that I was happy for my staff to run my battle plan, but nevertheless knew exactly when I had to step in and make the necessary decisions. One such was the withdrawal of the last elements of the covering force across the one remaining Thames bridge which was under threat from a breakthrough. I sensed that this was a DS 'come on' so ordered the bridge demolition guard to stand firm, and the last of the covering force just made it in time.

The Army Staff Course was by its very nature an event where one made very many good friends with whom experiences were shared for the rest of one's career. They included John Soder, from Germany, who rose to become Deputy SACEUR, Rory O'Connor, who took over as CRA 4th Armoured Division from me some years later, John Leaning, another fellow Gunner and skier, who had the room next to mine on the top floor of the Staff College, and Robin Ross, of the Royal Marines, who was always a charming host for winter warfare training in Norway in the 1980s. The DS included three officers who had served with me in Lippstadt eight years earlier, Lieutenant Colonels Ted Burgess, Mike Perkins and Charles Bromby, while the Deputy Commandant was Brigadier Drew Bethell, my CRA of the previous two years.

It was a year of great fun. With more than forty unmarried officers living in the Staff College meeting every night for a drink before dinner, plenty of wine with dinner, and often a significant amount of port afterwards, these were stimulating and amusing months. Indeed one of our student body was admitted to the Cambridge Military Hospital in Aldershot with gout and our subsequent visit armed with several bottles of port was unappreciated. I continued to play a lot of hockey both for the Royal Artillery and for the Staff College. My friendship with Ann Walters developed during this year as she was working in University College Hospital in London, which was close enough for us to meet for dinner at least once a week as well as spend weekends together.

Tension amongst the students started to increase during the summer as 'Black Bag Day' approached. During the first half of the course every officer's performance and suitability for staff appointments was assessed by the instructors and then matched to the appointments becoming available at the end of the course. Other than a few very high-powered posts in the Ministry of Defence, the plum appointments were considered to be those of brigade majors or the GSO (General Staff Officer) 2 Operations of a regular division. Those officers appointed to be GSO 2 Cadets knew that their career as a staff officer would not prosper. On 'Black Bag Day' every officer's first staff appointment was pulled out of the so-called black bag. I was posted to be the Brigade Major Royal Artillery of the 3rd Division in Bulford on Salisbury Plain from January 1971 on promotion to major at age 32.

Meanwhile the Staff Course still had (a more relaxed) four months to run. This period included two tri-service periods where we met up with our colleagues from the Royal Navy and Royal Air Force Staff Colleges for joint training and exercises. The final six weeks of the year, after the overseas students had departed, included presentations by all the senior Army commanders as well as Government Ministers. But by this time the centre of interest was the students' pantomime that mercilessly teased the Commandant and all his staff in a highly professional performance that allowed a certain amount of steam to be released as a bonus. I had my own bonus too, as I successfully persuaded Ann that we should be married in 1971.

I moved down to Bulford immediately after Christmas to take over as the Brigade Major Royal Artillery (or BMRA) of the 3rd Division from my very good friend and hockey-playing colleague Major (later Major General) Bill Cornock. As a major I was entitled to a Field Officer's quarter in the 3rd Division Officers' Mess. This proved to be a small bedroom linked to a small study, with two coal fires to be kept going rather than one. As the BMRA I was the Chief of Staff and senior operational staff officer of what amounted to an Artillery Brigade within a Division of three infantry brigades. My Commander Royal Artillery was Brigadier (later Major General) Keith McQueen, a larger than life character who had commanded 5th Field Regiment Royal Artillery in the 2nd Division when I was an ADC. In the 1950s he had served in Korea as the BMRA of the 1st Commonwealth Division and had huge experience of the control of artillery fire in a positional defence against massed enemy attack. I was assisted by a General Staff Officer Operations Grade 3 (GSO 3 Ops), initially Major (later Lieutenant Colonel) John Jago and then Captain (later Colonel) Mike Beckingsale, both of whom were outstandingly effective staff officers.

The 3rd Division Artillery had five Regiments: 3rd Regiment Royal Horse Artillery with 19th Infantry Brigade in Colchester, 5th Light Regiment Royal Artillery with 5th Infantry Brigade in Bulford, 47th Light Regiment Royal Artillery with 24th Infantry Brigade in Taunton, 20th Medium Regiment Royal Artillery in Devizes, and 12th Light Air Defence Regiment Royal Artillery in Barton Stacey. After a year the 47th Light Regiment was replaced by 25th Light Regiment Royal Artillery commanded by Lieutenant Colonel Ted Burgess returning from Hong Kong to Catterick. The three Light Regiments were equipped with the 105 mm pack howitzer while the Medium Regiment had the very old 5.5 inch howitzer. In addition, although not under full command, we had certain training and operational responsibilities for 7th Parachute Regiment Royal Horse Artillery in Aldershot and 22nd (Gibraltar) Locating Battery at Larkhill.

Life was dominated by two conflicting military priorities. The 3rd Division, following the withdrawals from east of Suez, had been offered to NATO as the new United Kingdom Mobile Force (UKMF), an un-armoured Infantry Division of three brigades to move quickly to a threatened area to take up a positional defence across a predicted main Warsaw Pact thrust. Eight different areas from Zealand in the North to Thrace in the East had been selected for evaluation and preparation. Such an operation would require coordinated artillery fire to support the defence and demanded that the regiments should train together frequently. However, there was still a strong feeling that all or parts of the 3rd Division could be deployed elsewhere in the world.

The second and more immediate priority arose from the fast deteriorating situation in Northern Ireland where the initially simple internal security task was rapidly becoming far more difficult. As an example the 5th Light Regiment was the left forward infantry battalion (with a Greenjacket battalion on their right) in what amounted to a formal brigade attack from the city centre of Londonderry up through the Bogside to secure the Creggan. This attack amounted to street fighting against a well-trained but lightly equipped enemy that had the advantage of knowing the ground. All five regiments served several very demanding tours in Northern Ireland, with tasks that required a lot of sophisticated training beforehand usually over a two-months' period, and a long period of recovery and artillery retraining afterwards. I sat through many long meetings with my fellow Brigade Majors arguing over which infantry battalions and Gunner regiments should undertake pre-planned and emergency tours. My infantry colleagues could never really understand that not only did Gunner regiments have to convert to the infantry role and then back to the artillery role seven months later when the tour had finished, but that internal conversion from a two-troop to a three-platoon organization was often far from simple.

Throughout the thirty-six years of the Northern Ireland emergency tours, the Gunners shared the infantry role security duties with the Infantry. Others performed emergency tours in their normal roles, albeit in unusual circumstances. There were undoubted benefits in these periods, training to be and operating in the infantry role, in particular in junior leadership and military skills. In the early years many Gunner regiments discovered that some officers and non-commissioned officers were 'found out' in this very demanding operational environment, and sadly several promising careers ended.

During 1971 the priority was for artillery training with occasional interruptions as regiments served in Northern Ireland: by 1972 the situation was reversed. The worsening situation leading to internment demanded huge numbers of soldiers to be in the Province, resulting in very little artillery training. 3rd Regiment Royal Horse Artillery, for example, returned to Colchester on a Friday after a ten-week emergency deployment, were deployed back to the Province the following Thursday, only to return to Colchester on the next Tuesday. Yes, this showed admirable flexibility but was in fact utter madness, as the Commanding Officer, Lieutenant Colonel Dick (later General Sir Richard) Trant told me very forcefully.

Back to 1971. Brigadier Keith McQueen was an outstanding trainer of artillery in every respect, and he taught me a very great deal. Each Regiment went through a demanding and testing four-day CRA's live firing exercise on Salisbury Plain, and this was followed by a week-long Divisional Artillery Concentration, also on Salisbury Plain. Every single aspect of artillery training was introduced to each exercise, with all the commanding officers and battery commanders put under a great deal of pressure. The firing was quick and accurate with slick movement by road and helicopter from one end of Salisbury Plain to the other, and back again. We were much helped by having a Gunnery Training Team led by Major John Allen as an integral part of the headquarters.

I spent much time on the development of plans to reinforce NATO regions, in particular Schleswig-Holstein where an option to reinforce COMLANDJUT behind the Kiel Canal was considered a high priority. This led to increased cooperation with the 6th German Division and the Jutland Division from Denmark.

On 3 April 1971 Ann and I were married in St Andrews Church of Scotland in Royal Tunbridge Wells, followed by a reception at her home in Crowborough. This wonderful day was attended by a great number of friends. We moved into an army married quarter in Bulford for a few weeks while we bought a house in Idmiston, midway between Bulford and Salisbury where Ann worked in the hospital. Our nearly new four-bedroomed house stood on the banks of the River Bourne and had a field full of cattle behind. It was idyllic. Kingfishers would fly along the river while mallards would wander up our drive and tap on the front door with their beaks to be fed. On one summer's day when I was on all fours painting the skirting board in the dining room I was suddenly conscious of something behind me. Mother mallard had marched her newly hatched family up our drive, through the front door, along the hallway, through the sitting room and into the dining room to show me. I looked through my legs to see a dozen or so ducklings between my feet with the mother just behind.

As 1971 continued, so the demands of the Northern Ireland emergency increased. Brigadier Keith McQueen's tour came to an end and he was replaced by Brigadier (later Major General) Geoffrey Wilson, a commander who could hardly have been more different in every way. While Brigadier McQueen's primary interest lay in operational matters, Brigadier Wilson's priority stemmed from his interest in the welfare and morale of soldiers in the very widest aspects, including the effects of the Northern Ireland emergency. I was left to run operational planning and artillery training with very little participation by the CRA other than matters relating to Northern Ireland. My logistics colleague, Major (later Brigadier) Robin Duchesne, gained a great deal of additional work as a result.

With the help of Major John Allen I switched most of the artillery live firing exercises to the underused Otterburn Ranges in Northumberland where sole user arrangements allowed us a great deal of freedom while live firing. We introduced as many novel challenges to regiments being exercised as possible. One such was the use of 'blow up' rubber targets such as tanks, trucks and rockets that disappeared if hit by artillery fragments.

But Northern Ireland and training for operations there was the totally dominating factor, and the five regiments performed with great skill and enormous professionalism. On one visit I found myself at the Andersonstown police station in West Belfast and opposite the Republican Milltown cemetery as a 5,000 strong IRA funeral procession approached. The police station was manned by three RUC police officers and twelve soldiers from 12th Light Air Defence Regiment commanded by Major (later Brigadier) Brian Harding. An uncompromising order from Headquarters 39th Infantry Brigade stated that the funeral should proceed but there must not be the customary volley of shots from masked IRA gunmen as the coffin was lowered into the ground. Very bravely, Major Harding marched out of the police station unarmed and accompanied only by his battery sergeant-major to halt the procession at the cemetery gates. Having given clear instructions to the IRA leaders, he returned to the police station where he and I watched the burial. There were no shots fired. For this and many other actions during a four-months' tour he was awarded the Military Cross. The 12th Light Air Defence Regiment had an outstanding tour in one of the hardest areas of Belfast with the Commanding Officer, Lieutenant Colonel Dick Vincent, being awarded the Distinguished Service Order.

Some weeks later in 1972 I was in Belfast with Brigadier Wilson and dining with the General Officer Commanding (GOC) Lieutenant General (later General) Sir Harry Tuzo and Lady Tuzo in their well-guarded residence close to Andersonstown. During dinner there was a huge explosion. The ADC quickly appeared to give the GOC a message. The first bomb of the devastating IRA bombing campaign had just exploded. The GOC told us that it had been long expected. The IRA bombing campaign continued in Northern Ireland with devastating effects, extending to the British mainland and against army bases in Germany from 1974, finally ending in 1997. I was to witness the effects of the bombing campaign on my subsequent visits to Northern Ireland, not least in Londonderry where the city centre was largely destroyed.

My work as a staff officer continued apace. With the five regiments spread between Salisbury Plain and North Yorkshire there was a lot of ground to cover. Luckily I discovered that the Army Air Corps six-seater Beaver fixed-wing aircraft fleet based near the Divisional Headquarters was underused, and so I found it relatively easy to visit all the distant regiments in a single day, as each had a grass runway adjacent to the barracks. But my time had now come to an end. Despite being reluctant to leave our first home in England, a posting order to Germany promised an interesting tour ahead, but little did we know then that we would remain on the continent for nine years.

CHAPTER 8

Battery Command

I RETURNED TO DETMOLD IN Germany to take over as the Battery Commander of 'E' Battery Royal Horse Artillery in March 1973. Part of 1st Regiment Royal Horse Artillery, 'E' Battery is one of the most senior batterys in the British Army, ranking fifth in order of precedence – it was a great privilege to be selected to take command of this fine organization. 1st Regiment Royal Horse Artillery was under the command of Lieutenant Colonel (later Brigadier) Mike Perkins with whom I had already served twice and knew very well, while the second-in-command was Major John Biles from whom I had taken over as adjutant six years earlier.

The outgoing Battery Commander of 'E' Battery Royal Horse Artillery was Major John Jago. The Battery had a very close affiliation with the City of Nottingham where we recruited and from whence most soldiers came. For training and operations we worked closely with 1st Battalion The Light Infantry (1 LI) commanded by Lieutenant Colonel Barry Lane, another friend of some years standing. They were the only infantry of the 20th Armoured Brigade that had three armoured regiments in addition. We were a part of the 4th Division, the CRA being Brigadier Ted Burgess, yet another friend from previous tours. My two fellow Battery Commanders were Major Alan Payne soon followed by Major Malcolm Hord at The Chestnut Troop RHA, and Major Robin Dent at 'B' Battery RHA.

By this time the Cold War had become increasingly tense and much more dangerous. The Soviets made and distributed freely in the NATO area an aggressive film showing their capability to launch a huge armoured attack. The 1st British Corps had completed a complex programme to turn itself from an unarmoured army to a very professional armoured force with a strong nuclear capability. My battery had the new Abbot 105 mm self-propelled howitzer, AFV 432 command posts and FOO vehicles, and Stalwart ammunition vehicles, all of which provided armoured protection for the crews, could swim across rivers and were in the new drab camouflage paint. Compared with my previous tour in Germany eight years earlier, we were in a much more dangerous situation and, as a consequence, our training standards and readiness for war were altogether far higher. In particular the threat of NBC attack in war was considered so high that we wore our respirators from 0830 to 1230 every Friday morning. It was interesting that we soon found that we could work almost normally despite the encumbrance. But the situation in Northern Ireland had reached such a serious level that regiments in the 1st British Corps in Germany had had to be drawn in to the rotational cycle of four months' tours in the Province, leaving dangerous gaps in our readiness capability for war with the Warsaw Pact forces.

I served three years as the Battery Commander of 'E' Battery Royal Horse Artillery, a quite uniquely long period as most majors were lucky even to complete two years commanding a battery. My first and third years were spent with an emphasis on gunnery training, including training periods at the new British Army Training Unit Suffield (BATUS) in Alberta, Canada, a very advanced and highly realistic battle school. In contrast most of my second year was spent training for and serving in Northern Ireland.

For most of my three years commanding 'E' Battery I had a quite remarkable stability amongst my officers, and very talented and charming they were too. My first battery captain, Captain (later Colonel) George Morris, disappeared to the Staff College after a year but then returned early in 1976 to replace me. My second battery captain was Captain (later Brigadier) Mark Douglas-Withers whose father had been my Commanding Officer many years earlier. Initially my two Forward Observation Officers were Captains Nick Hall and Charlie Crawford, to be replaced after a year by Captains Mike Smythe (later a Brigadier), Peter Smeeth (later a Major) and Johnny Howard-Vyse (later a Lieutenant Colonel). The final member of the team was Lieutenant (later Brigadier) Richard Smith, the Gun Position Officer. I was very well served. However, there was a downside as the four bachelors (Douglas-Withers, Smythe, Smeeth and Smith) led a wild social life both in the mess and beyond that was not only totally beyond my control, but also caused me the occasional interview with the commanding officer as well as a near arrest by police in Gastown, Vancouver. In fairness to Mark Douglas-Withers, it was the 'Three Ss' as they were known that caused the troubles, although I sensed that Mark was often an amused observer!

The battery also had superb non-commissioned officers and soldiers, probably the very best in the whole British Army, outstandingly well led by the Battery Sergeant Major, Mick Blackmore, later to become a major. They were intelligent, well trained, full of initiative and brave. Their loyalty was legendary. As an example, early in 1973 I promoted Gunner Parvez, a talented sportsman as well as a magnificent soldier at only 20 years old, to lance bombardier, a year later to bombardier and in 1975 to sergeant. As this book is being written, in 2008, he is still serving, now a lieutenant colonel, having spent almost all his career in 'E' Battery and/or 1st Regiment Royal Horse Artillery.

A few weeks after I arrived in Detmold, Ann joined me and we moved into a married quarter just three hundred yards from the barracks. We bought a new car and, thanks to generous local overseas allowances, we suddenly found we could afford to live well. I decided to write a battery directive two or three times a year, laying out in great detail what we would do, how we would do it, and who would take the lead, even specifying aims, tasks and outline plans for such events as the inter-battery cricket competition. All the officers and non-commissioned officers received their own copies, and so every soldier in the battery was familiar with future activities and plans. At first sight it appeared over bureaucratic, but in reality it proved to be a masterstroke as everyone could see clearly six to eight months ahead, time enough to make good sound plans.

Just before I arrived, 'E' Battery had returned from a four months' tour in Northern Ireland and, as a result, the gunnery was fairly rusty. It had been decided that the Battery would accompany 1st Battalion The Royal Irish Rangers to BATUS near Medicine Hat, Alberta, in Canada, for an eight-week training period in June and July and so the instant priority was a live-firing camp on the Munsterlager/Hohne Ranges followed by all-arms combined training. The 1st Battalion The Royal Irish Rangers Battle Group was commanded by Lieutenant Colonel Mervyn McCord, a tough no-nonsense Korean War veteran. The reason for this association was that both their battery and my battalion (1LI) were serving in Northern Ireland. The other component of the Battle Group was a tank squadron from the Queen's Royal Irish Hussars.

The Battle Group assembled in mid-May at the two large live-firing areas for tanks and artillery, Munsterlager and Hohne Ranges, where we conducted live firing. Immediately I noticed that the artillery ranges, now under German control, had introduced restrictive safety measures such as taping of gun barrels to eliminate the possibility of shells landing outside the range impact area. These measures reduced substantially the effectiveness of our training but clearly had become necessary to ensure safety with the many NATO conscript armies. Once live-firing practices were completed the Battle Group joined together for a series of tactical exercises in the adjacent Soltau Luneburg Training Area (SLTA).

In early June I flew to Calgary with the advance party of the Battle Group that included the commanding officer's 'R' Group (the commanding officer, battery commander and company and squadron commanders) as Colonel McCord wished to have the time for advanced planning of the training before the main body arrived.

BATUS is 160 miles south-east of Calgary and an area approximately the size of Surrey, of which half had been allocated to the British Army as a Battle School. The other half remained restricted to experiments related to chemical and biological warfare by the Canadian government. The area consisted of rolling grassland with just one tree and a few tracks. The mid-summer and mid-winter temperatures were extreme; in fact it was impossible to train between October and April owing to the wind, cold and deep snow. The British infrastructure consisted of two main elements: a team of thirty officers and non-commissioned officers who designed and ran the exercises and provided safety parties; and all the guns, tanks and other vehicles to equip the Battle Group to the same scale as in Germany. The Permanent Staff had designed exercises to reflect a possible Third World War in Germany and arranged suitable targets in the appropriate places.

The main body of the Battle Group arrived ten days later, took over the equipment and then drove out onto the prairie. The first five days' training were devoted to special-to-arm live firing. I met for the first time Major (later Lieutenant Colonel) John Pitt who was the permanent Instructor in Gunnery (IG) at BATUS and who proved an enormous help in polishing our gunnery skills as well as assisting me interpret the local range safety rules in such a way as to introduce the maximum realism in training. This was certainly proved when I tasked my two Forward Observation Officers (Captains Nick Hall and Charlie Crawford) to conduct 'danger close' fire missions during which the shells were brought to within seventy metres of our position.

The next fourteen days involved the complete Battle Group conducting live fire combined training against an enemy consisting of old armoured vehicles and painted canvas screens some of which moved, though none fired back. It was nevertheless exciting stuff, particularly for the infantry and their FOO parties who, once dismounted from their armoured personnel carriers, had tanks firing over their heads and artillery shells landing very close. It was certainly the most realistic training we had ever encountered, and the most exhausting. The Battle Group practised the advance to contact, the quick, deliberate and night attacks, the withdrawal, demolition bridge guards and both the quick and deliberate defence. All of these were conducted with live ammunition and plenty of it.

We were only the second Battle Group to undertake this new facility and so we had plenty of senior visitors. The Chief of the General Staff was the most senior and wanted to give both Nick Hall and Charlie Crawford a target to attack. When he did so, both very cleverly hit the target first time, with Nick somewhat luckily getting a shell to strike the turret of the target tank with a blinding orange flash. We returned to the base camp – Camp Crowfoot – very satisfied with our performance as Gunners. More importantly we had all learned a huge amount about combined arms armoured warfare, and enjoyed some demanding challenges. As soon as all our borrowed equipment had been cleaned, serviced and handed back to the BATUS staff we were allowed five days' leave prior to flying back to Germany. I decided to spend my time first at Calgary watching the spectacular Calgary Stampede, followed by two days driving through the magnificent Rocky Mountains to Vancouver, and then returning by air to Calgary. In those days Vancouver and Victoria Island were not unlike Bournemouth in very many ways.

As we returned to Germany, the Commanding Officer changed, Lieutenant Colonel Mike Perkins being replaced by Lieutenant Colonel (later General Sir) John Learmont.

Summer leave followed, prior to the familiar autumn training routine, but this year with quite a story. The predominant exercise was a huge multinational event in which the 20th Armoured Brigade provided the UK element alongside US, German, Dutch, Belgian and Danish troops, all under the command of the Commander-in-Chief Allied Forces Central Europe (CINCENT). The authorities had decided that the end of the exercise would be marked by a parade to honour the retiring CINCENT, who was General Benneke, an enormous and remarkably humorous German officer. Queen's Regulations state very clearly that Royal Horse Artillery on parade with its Guns has seniority over all other regiments and takes its place at the 'Right of the Line'. However, The Life Guards had a new commanding officer from The Royal Dragoons who, unfamiliar with this particular Queen's Regulation, stated publicly that he would eat his hat if his Regiment did not lead the parade. The matter was referred to Buckingham Palace who confirmed that 1st Regiment Royal Horse Artillery would lead the parade. The 1st Regiment Royal Horse Artillery chefs constructed from icing sugar a life-size replica of a Life Guard's ceremonial helmet that was duly presented to The Life Guards' commanding officer whose request to be allowed to take it back to his own mess to eat with his officers was readily agreed. Subsequently, as the Battery

Commander of the junior Battery in 1st Regiment Royal Horse Artillery, I had The Life Guards immediately behind me during the parade drive past General Benneke, and received a friendly 'V' sign from their commanding officer as we started the drive past.

As ever, the six weeks in the field for the autumn manoeuvres passed quickly with everyone enjoying the culmination of a busy training year. Compared with my previous autumn manoeuvres some ten years earlier in 1963, the standard of training was far higher, and the British Army was now genuinely ready for war.

Life in BAOR had developed swiftly, none more so than from the influence of the married families, as nearly half of our soldiers were married, with their wives and children in Detmold with them. The Regimental Wives' Club, in which my wife played a role, was very active looking after the interests of all the wives, but particularly the younger ones. My main concern was for the younger and newly married, who tended not to qualify for a quarter in one of the so-called British areas, but lived in a hiring in the German community. From time to time, and with twenty-four hours warning, I invited myself to tea with such families, taking the husband home in my car and spending an hour or so talking to the couple in their home.

The remaining weeks of the autumn were devoted to preparations for the administrative inspection and the annual Lord Mayor of Nottingham visit. Councillor Eric Foster was the Lord Mayor and a most charming guest who never ceased to be amazed that all his Nottingham soldiers in the Regiment knew a great deal about him and the affairs of their home city. But in truth our minds were now focusing on the 1974 tour of duty in Northern Ireland for which training had already started. Our four months' tour of duty was scheduled for April to July 1974 with 1st Regiment Royal Horse Artillery responsible for the security of the Belfast city centre and the small but violent Roman Catholic enclave immediately east of the River Lagan, known as the Short Strand. My Battery was selected to be responsible for the Short Strand while the rest of the Regiment would look after the city centre, an area subjected to a massive IRA bombing campaign at that time. By Christmas my Battery had put all the artillery equipment into care and preservation and reorganised into an infantry company with three platoons commanded by Lieutenants Mike Smythe and Richard Smith, and Warrant Officer 2 Brian Redding, with Captain Mark Douglas-Withers as second-in-command and operations officer.

The reconnaissance party spent the first week in January in Belfast while the Regiment practised the wide range of infantry skills. 'E' Battery would be taking over from a company of the Welsh Guards in the Short Strand commanded by an old friend, Major Charles Dawnay, whom I shadowed for four days to learn the area and tasks. He led a fine and effective company but I found their tactics stereotyped and unimaginative. I set about developing ways to bring a new approach and of course these had to be introduced and evaluated during the intense two months' training period just starting. Firstly I decided that we would improve our 'hard targeting' by conducting all our training and shooting with the rifle (the 7.62 mm self-loading rifle) in both the left and right shoulders on a strict 50/50 basis. Although the experts quickly described this as impossible, the final shooting results showed that most soldiers were proficient firing out of either shoulder. The second new measure was, as soon as we were fired upon, to charge the firer immediately rather than taking cover, with the aim of disrupting the well-known IRA tactic of handing the weapon on to women and children while the firer strolled away. And finally, rather than always patrol in the well-known four-man half section, we put together up to six or even eight half sections for limited and irregular periods, in order to maintain a degree of uncertainty in the IRA minds.

The training was hard, demanding and imaginative, mostly taking place at the nearby Sennelager training area, both on the ranges and in special facilities built to represent urban areas in Northern Ireland. 'Tin City' was a section of a large town made from corrugated iron with streets, shops, terraced houses and open spaces used for patrolling and riot training. The 'enemy', usually soldiers from other units, would throw stones, bricks and petrol bombs for hours on end with each episode normally concluding with attacks using blank ammunition. The 'Close Quarter Battle Range' was smaller but much more realistic and used for live firing with electronic targets. Instructors in the control tower could move people and targets inside the houses. One such speciality was a life-size model woman with baby in pram suddenly emerging from the front door of a house during a gun battle. The control tower had a number of 'gunmen' they could activate to fire at us, each shot being accompanied by a very realistic 'splat' normally set in a wall close to the target soldier. The soldiers on patrol had to identify the gunman and fire back using live ammunition. A fifteen-minute action inside this facility left the patrol exhausted, but was exactly what we were to face once we reached Belfast. Specialist training also took place for search teams and close observation. By the end of February we

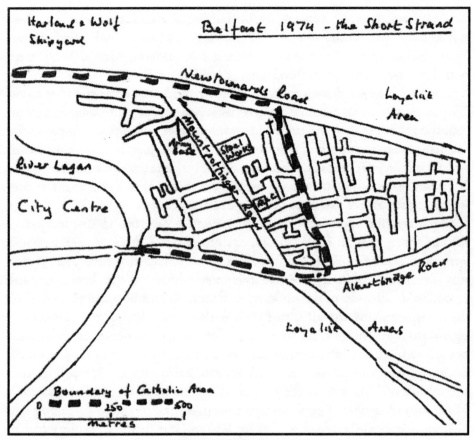

Belfast 1974 – the Short Strand

were ready for action and morale was high. The training package had been superb and we were very confident.

The sketch shows the Short Strand area, then Victorian terraced houses in poor repair with outside lavatories and many alleys and cut-throughs, split by the Mountpottinger Road with the isolated and heavily fortified RUC police station in the centre and the Protestant-only workforce Sirocco steel works further north, with our base a few yards further on. All of the buildings on both the Roman Catholic and Protestant sides of the interface streets had been burned out and bricked up – ideal for snipers and used by them, but also providing a ready supply of bricks for riots. The final twist was St Matthew's Roman Catholic Church on the Newtownards Road, three quarters surrounded by Protestants and a prime target for fire bombing for which my orders were protection above all else. The unpopular priest added a further dimension. I allocated the potentially more difficult area to the west of Mountpottinger Road to Mike Smythe's platoon, the area to the east to Richard Smith's platoon, and gave Sergeant Major Redding and his platoon a roving role allowing him to work with both his fellow platoon commanders.

The IRA knew full well that the Welsh Guards would leave on or about 1 April and as usual planned to give us a hot reception to allow them to gain the initiative. But the unusual measures I had put in place, in particular the hard targeting routine, flummoxed them completely. We soon heard via the intelligence network that they could not understand why they could rarely see us, yet they knew we were always about, and of course the reason was that they rarely saw more than a quarter of a face.

However, the remainder of 1st Regiment Royal Horse Artillery based in the Grand Central Hotel in Donegall Street in Belfast city centre had a very hot welcome. Within an hour of their arrival a massive lorry bomb was detonated by the IRA at the front door of the hotel, causing considerable damage to the building in which 300 soldiers were based. One officer showed me the effects of the shards of glass that the explosion had blown through and into his wooden wardrobe. Every piece of clothing had been shredded, yet his room was at the rear of the building on the fourth floor. Within four weeks the IRA repeated this attack with yet another massive bomb. The two Batterys operating there had a thankless task. Major Malcolm Hord with The Chestnut Troop was tasked with patrolling and keeping secure the city centre. Major Robin Dent with 'B' Battery had to man the gates in the huge steel fence that surrounded the city centre in an effort to keep the bombers out at a time when the IRA were exploding up to ten and sometimes twenty bombs each day. They were assisted by the Royal Military Police who did much of the searching. It was always interesting to watch the reaction of the female members of the Royal Military Police search teams when a transvestite tried to enter the city centre through the female search gate at Queen Street. It was brutal.

Back in the Short Strand we faced an IRA battalion with about sixty active members who lived in the area but undoubtedly had the support of all 3,000 inhabitants. The IRA in this area were on the defensive as it was felt likely that a Loyalist backlash against the carnage being caused by the IRA bombing campaign would start by the elimination of the Short Strand. However, the area was without doubt being used for the movement of weapons and explosives. The alleged IRA Belfast Brigade commander, Gerry Adams, was our number one target. The Short Strand was completely surrounded by hard-core Protestant areas with six Ulster

Defence Association (UDA) or Ulster Volunteer Force (UVF) battalions whose aim was to drive all the Roman Catholics in the Short Strand out of east Belfast. The terrorists' day started at around 2 p.m. and ended well after midnight. Therefore we maintained a hefty presence on the streets from around 4 p.m. until 3 a.m. although search operations always started before mid-morning. I was out on the streets every day from 4 p.m. until well after midnight. As a result I generally woke at around 10 a.m. in time for briefings and operational meetings followed by 'brunch'. Most of the 110 members of my battery followed a similar routine.

Our base, surrounded by a high wall, was in the old bus station and consisted of portakabins of various sizes and was not uncomfortable. It did not take long to learn why we had a small sauna in the base.

The first few weeks saw a gradual escalation of violence along the eastern and southern interfaces. The exchange of stones and rocks, with my soldiers in the middle trying to maintain distance between the two sides, would grow increasingly violent with each side bringing in reinforcements until we had to become rather more aggressive to assert control. At this stage the IRA and UDA/UVF guns would come out. The daily rioting increased both in area and intensity. I identified the main instigator, a mild-looking but very aggressive Loyalist who started most riots but never strayed into them. I arranged to meet the local UDA battalion commander in his area to the south of the Short Strand. I reached the RV with an escort of three soldiers while he arrived with ten of the most unpleasant looking thugs I have ever seen, but with no visible weapons. I told the UDA man that I was fed up with the antics of his man and that it was distracting me from my main task of chasing the IRA. He told me that he agreed and would move him immediately. Two hours later I walked past the house where the man had lived and found a delightful white haired lady leaning on the gate. I commented that she must have moved in very recently to which she replied with a smile that she had lived there for years. Such was the power of the terrorist paramilitaries.

Violence and poverty were endemic in the area. The one public house in the Short Strand, which I visited every night, was always full to bursting and with vast quantities of alcohol being consumed. Yet many houses held no food at all. The corner shops operated tick on a huge scale and I frequently saw mothers bargaining with shop owners to have a quarter of a bread loaf plus a small tin of baked beans to feed their large families. I reckoned that more than half of all unemployment and other benefits was spent on alcohol. There were several so-called 'romper rooms', normally the preserve of Loyalists to beat their enemies to death, while the IRA tended to use one variety or another of 'knee capping'.

Our operations continued although we received very little intelligence from the various agencies. We conducted endless searches often catching fleas in the process (but ten minutes in the sauna was the best way to remove them). We knew that the IRA listened in to all our radio traffic, and then used their own radio systems to inform their members where we were and what we were doing and planned to do. I learned that the IRA had three times the number of radios that my battery had, and I even heard them re-transmitting my own voice while crouching under the window of the IRA's chief radio operator. On one such occasion we were very close to seizing an IRA weapon that was being moved in the area – in fact so close that the IRA brought out their women to form a cordon around the weapon. I managed to get a dozen female members of the Royal Military Police to the scene very quickly. Their very tough sergeant saw the problem, asked me to stand back but provide cover, and then attacked the IRA women in a manner that left me and my soldiers stunned by the violence used. Feet and fists only but hugely effective and the IRA never used their women against us again. But the weapon we sought had gone.

I used covert observers, soldiers whom we inserted into empty buildings or roof spaces to lie up secretly for up to five days. Lance Bombardier Smith was one such whom I placed to spot Loyalist gunmen moving up to the Albert Bridge Road to fire into the Short Strand area. Lance Bombardier Smith received a Mention in Despatches award for an action in which he spotted a possible gunman and called for assistance, and then shot the gunman as he opened fire before rushing down from his roof space both to arrest the gunman and seize the weapon and empty cartridge case – vital evidence.

The Ulster Workers' Council strike took place from Wednesday 15 May to Tuesday 28 May 1974. The strike was called by the Protestant community in protest at the political and security situation in Northern Ireland and more particularly at the proposals in the Sunningdale Agreement which would have given the government of the Republic of Ireland a direct say in the running of the Province. The leadership of the strike was able to harness the deep sense of alienation that had grown in the Protestant community during the previous five years, not least as they saw the IRA bombing the Province to destruction. The strike lasted two weeks and succeeded in bringing down the power-sharing Northern Ireland Executive. Responsibility for the government of Northern Ireland then reverted to the British Parliament at Westminster under the arrangements for 'Direct Rule'. These were historic days in which a million British citizens, the Protestants of Northern Ireland, staged what amounted to a rebellion against the Crown and won. During those fifteen days, for the first time in over fifty years a section of the nation became totally ungovernable. A self-elected provisional government of Protestant power workers, well-armed private armies and extreme politicians organized a strike that almost broke up the fabric of civilized life in Ulster. They deprived most of the population for much of the time of food, water, electricity, gas, transport, money and any form of livelihood.

For me these were dramatic days with high tension and during which three battalions were moved from the mainland and Germany to reinforce my Battery, yet we maintained control, just. The streets of the Short Strand had nothing – no water, no food, no sewage disposal, no power; and they were surrounded by very aggressive Protestant paramilitaries who sensed they could drive the Roman Catholic population out. We were moving towards a civil war and, if such a disaster were to happen, I felt sure it would start in my area. I had every man I could find out on the interface streets keeping the two sides apart, while I kept watching, listening and talking in order to maintain a feel of the fast-changing situation. Remarkably the IRA moved in, not with weapons, but with food and water to set up street kitchens to feed the local population. Suddenly they were talking to me as they realised that only the army stood between them and the Loyalist paramilitaries.

Every morning and every evening for two weeks Lieutenant General (later General) Sir Frank King came to see me. It was always the same: 'What is going on here, what are you doing about it, and what do you think will happen then?' I would respond, he would give a nod of approval and depart. Almost immediately Major General Peter Leng, Commander Land Forces, would arrive and ask me to repeat the conversation word by word. And as soon as he departed Brigadier Bob Richardson, Commander 39 Infantry Brigade, would get me to go through the same routine. Many years later I asked General King why this had happened and if he knew that his subordinates followed his every visit. His answer with a wry smile was that only he was receiving some very sensitive information, and the indications were that the survival of the Short Strand was in the balance.

The strike ended swiftly once Direct Rule was reimposed but the area remained quiet even when the Loyalist marching season began in early July. For this we erected huge canvas screens between the marchers' route and the Roman Catholic areas to prevent any visual contact. The 12 July march contained almost a hundred bands, every one of which played at maximum volume as it passed the Short Strand during the four hours the marchers took to pass by. In previous years there had been many an exchange of stones, but after the tension of the strike the appetite for violence was diminished temporarily. Our tour of duty ended the following week and we returned to Germany and some well-earned leave.

It had been a most successful tour in a very difficult area of Belfast at the height of the IRA shooting and bombing campaign. The soldiers had advanced both their infantry and low-level leadership skills to a very high level, and their initiative, self-confidence and self-reliance had developed in a remarkable manner. These skills proved to be the foundation stones for an army far better prepared for war with the Warsaw Pact forces or any other tasks in the future. Some time later Lieutenant Richard Smith was awarded a well-deserved Queen's Gallantry Medal, and I was pleased to receive a General Officer Commanding's Commendation.

Ann and I spent our leave in Corsica, returning in August to the totally unexpected news that I had been selected for promotion to Lieutenant Colonel in 1975, but there was now a great deal to do to return the Battery's gunnery to the required skill levels, having last fired over a year before. More importantly, we had to recognise that the forty-five married members of the Battery had hardly seen their families since January, and also that we now had to cram in a year's training, sport and regimental activities into just four months. Furthermore, some fourteen new young soldiers had joined the Battery while we were away and they too needed to be trained and integrated into the Order of Battle (ORBAT).

By September we were back on the artillery ranges at Munsterlager for a shortened Practice Camp, followed almost immediately by the usual autumn manoeuvres south of Hanover where we practised defensive armoured warfare against NATO forces simulating a Warsaw Pact attack. The Main Defensive Position (MDP) had been pushed forward to the River Leine and so we were now operating in the Coppenbrügge and Springe Gaps east of Hameln.

Returning to barracks in mid-October brought more frenetic activity. I had arranged for the internationally renowned artist Terence Cuneo to produce an oil painting of the Battery deployed in the field. For a week 'E' Battery deployed on to a hillside overlooking our barracks and married quarters in Detmold while Cuneo sketched and took photographs. The painting depicts the moment when the guns have just reached their new position with the ammunition vehicles racing forward. Sergeant Major Blackmore is seen supervising the occupation of the gun position while Sergeant Major Whiteway checks that the foreground gun, commanded by Sergeant Ward, is 'on line'. Behind, Lieutenant Richard Smith and Bombardier Parvez at the Director are passing the line. Sergeant London, whose father had been the Battery Sergeant Major of 'E' Battery some years earlier, is depicted supervising the ammunition unload. This fine all-action painting now hangs in the 1st Regiment Royal Horse Artillery mess together with three more paintings by the same artist, a unique late twentieth-century collection.

The Lord Mayor of Nottingham, now Councillor Shelton, arrived in late October for the annual Nottingham week. The highlight was a ceremonial parade by 'E' Battery to mark Foundation Day on 11 November for which every man wore Number 1 Dress (Blues), followed by a traditional Battery Dinner. Regimental sports of every kind continued, from hockey (which I played), soccer and rugby, to boxing, cross-country and orienteering. Indeed the average professional soldier was now spending six to twelve years in West Germany and needed a wide variety of sports both to fill the off-duty hours and to promote fitness and team spirit. Participation in sport mushroomed, with 80 per cent of the soldiers skiing each winter and an increasing number taking up the more exotic sports such as free-fall parachuting, golf and sailing.

Preparations for the ski season began with fitness training prior to our departure for the races in the Alps. Potentially, we had a good ski team with Major Robin Dent (earlier a British Olympic cross-country skier) running the cross-country team while Lieutenant Donald Fraser ran the Alpine team, of which both Captain Johnny Howard-Vyse and I were also members. The training period followed the usual routine, although we did not move to the Alps until after Christmas. However, the teams were beset by injuries and the only trophies gained were the Veterans' Awards, Robin receiving the cross-country while I won the alpine cup. Soon after our return from the Alps our first daughter Victoria was born in the British Military Hospital at Rinteln after we had made an unexpected dash over the hills in a snowstorm. Life changed.

In order to improve the operational performance of artillery, the concept of Stay Behind Observation Posts started development at this time with the outstanding Territorial Army soldiers of the Honourable Artillery Company (HAC) filling the role. As 1st Regiment Royal Horse Artillery had enjoyed a very long affiliation with the HAC, we played a lead role in these developments that aimed to place observation posts in places where Warsaw Pact heavy (including nuclear) artillery might be deployed. My Battery was linked to 3 Squadron, an affiliation that followed me for the next ten years.

During 1975 a most curious (some would say absurd) development took place in the British Army of the Rhine under the name of the 'Wide Horizon' trials. In order to make financial savings the Ministry of Defence decided that a level of command should be removed from the 1st British Corps. Clearly this could not be the Corps level as this would unbalance NATO, so it was decided that the brigade level of command should go. Battle Group commanders (Lieutenant Colonels) would command up to six Combat Teams while Division commanders would take command of six to eight Battle Groups. The obvious weakness, proven beyond doubt after eighteen months of field trials, was that a division headquarters simply could not apply itself simultaneously to the intimate details of the current battle and the planning required for operations two to five days ahead. I found myself involved in these trials, starting in January 1975 as the Battery commander with a Battle Group headquarters. Major General (later General Sir) Nigel Bagnall was the trials leader in his capacity as the General Officer Commanding 4th Division.

In the meantime the other battery commanders had changed again with Major (later General Sir) Mike Wilkes taking over The Chestnut Troop RHA while Major (later Major General) Brian Pennicott assumed command of 'B' Battery RHA. The new CRA was Brigadier Aubrey Fielder, a renowned skier.

My third year commanding 'E' Battery, 1975, was dominated by a second deployment to the BATUS battle school in Canada, this time with the Royal Scots Dragoon Guards (RSDG), commanded by Lieutenant Colonel (later Major General) Stephen Stopford. Once again my Battery was out of synchronisation with the rest of 1st Regiment RHA as we had to complete our artillery live firing at an early Practice Camp before joining the RSDG Battle Group on the Soltau Luneburg Training Area for the work-up training period.

We arrived in Canada in May just as some warmth started to reach the wide open and windswept prairie. Since our 1973 visit BATUS had been improved and enlarged, with the Battle Group now consisting of two tank squadrons and one mechanised infantry company. The targetry was more realistic and the exercises had been developed to be more demanding. Due to some very successful recruiting, as well as a high rate of retention of our soldiers, 'E' Battery was well over strength, allowing me to take to BATUS

1. May 1964 in the Radfan after the capture of the Coca-Cola hill feature. A Battery of 105-mm pack howitzers formed from a Troop from each of J (Sidi Rezegh) and I (Bull's Troop) Batterys RHA is deployed to fire along the Wadi Taym. In the foreground the lightweight command post

. June 1964 as RAF Hunter aircraft attack the enemy strongpoint on the flat topped 5,500 feet Jebel Widena feature

3. Following the capture of the Jebel Widena by 3 PARA the author relaxes in the remains of a house

4. The author was fortunate to survive a mine explosion while on reconnaissance patrol in the Radfan, May 1964

5. The artist Terence Cuneo spent a week with E Battery RHA in Detmold in 1974 to produce an oil painting of a battery deployment. In the background ammunition is unloaded from a Stalwart vehicle

6. Training in Canada with E Battery RHA in July 1975. The author's crew for three years, from l to r: Gunner Tollput, Gunner Breward, Lance Bombardier Spencer, Bombardier Bishop and Gunner Rutty

7. *40th Field Regiment RA Farewell Parade inspection in Gütersloh, December 1980, from l to r: Major Guy Dodgson, the author, Major-General Ted Burgess (MGRA 1st British Corps) and Burgermeister Grawe of Gütersloh*

8. *The author climbs into the rear seat of a Harrier trainer fighter aircraft at Sennelager prior to take off from a public road*

9. *The new FH 70 guns of 38 (Seringapatam) Field Battery at conversion firing on Salisbury Plain in May 1981. Gun Position Officer 2nd Lieutenant (later Major-General) Gerry Berragan reports to the author*

10. *Survivability was a key aspect of training in the 1st British Corps in Germany in the 1980s.*
Here Major Mike Smythe shows the author and the author's son Alexander his battery of 105-mm Abbot howitzers
fully dug in below ground and camouflaged

11. *Rear access door opened to alert a surprised Alexander*

12. *Alexander examines the gun pit that includes crew and ammunition shelters.*
To the front of the gun is a ramp to allow low-angle firing and drive-out

13. *In May 1984 Her Majesty The Queen, the Captain-General of The Royal Regiment of Artillery, reviewed the fifteen regiments stationed in West Germany as part of the 1st British Corps*

14. *Early morning routine at The White House in Bad Oeynhausen, 1983–4. Ann, Alexander and Bombardier Wallace await the departure of the staff car driven by Bombardier Brown to Herford taking the author to Headquarters 4th Armoured Division and Victoria and Elizabeth (in car) to their school in the same barracks*

15. *Main Headquarters 4th Armoured Division in the field in 1984. The eight AFV 432 command vehicles are shown deployed in a German farmyard. Camouflage for exposed vehicles was either black hessian, hessian painted to represent red brickwork or woodland camouflage – all three are shown in this photo. To avoid radio direction finding all active radio aerials were remoted to a distant 'radio village'*

16. *At Sennybridge in May 1986 the author presented the coveted red berets to soldiers of The Parachute Regiment who, having just passed 'P' Company, were about to commence parachute training*

17. *The author (right) with the Finnish 10th Armoured Brigade near Hameenlinna in 1992, seen here with the Defence Attaché Lieutenant Colonel Freddie Clement and two Finnish soldiers. This visit included being on the objective for an attack by the brigade equipped mostly with fast-moving Soviet-made armoured vehicles such as the BMP, a chilling experience*

18. *Some of the participants at a DuPont ballistic and fire-protection clothing seminar in Geneva in 2002. The international nature of the author's post-military life is well illustrated by the participants, from l to r: Finn-Ove Gaasoy, MOD Norway military clothing development, Jaakko Barsk, Finland FY Composites, Kari Nygren, Finland FY Composites, Linda Eriksson, MOD Sweden ballistic protection research, Elzbieta Wojciechowska-Zalewska, DuPont Poland, Virpi Hermio, MOD Finland aircrew clothing development, Marina Danilova, DuPont Moscow, the author, unknown male, Sophie Birraux, DuPont France and Sonia Favaro, DuPont Geneva*

*19. Kiev 2005 – the author with Serhiy Zavadsky of DuPont Ukraine
explaining the finer points of ballistic protection to the Ukrainian Army*

*20. Colonel (Retired) Nikolai Stelmakh, late of the Soviet Rocket Forces, seen here with the author in the
Kiev Military Museum with the SS 20 missile system that he had commanded during the Cold War*

twelve more men than I would need for any exercise. Throughout the four weeks I ran a private Battery Adventurous Training Camp in the Rockies led by Bombardier Thompson, a former jockey with whom I had served in Kenya some years earlier. With borrowed horses it enabled our soldiers to take turns to have five days riding and hiking in wild country as well as complete their gunnery training. However, wild bears were a problem. Bombardier Thompson experienced a brown bear spending an hour or more sitting on his feet in his tent at night. The bear was caught the following day and taken high up into the mountains to be released. Bombardier Thompson was less than pleased when the ranger predicted that it would take about ten days before the bear returned.

Our training on the prairie started with five days of gunnery firing. As an experienced and emboldened Battery Commander, although sometimes restrained by an occasionally nervous instructor in gunnery, Major (later Lieutenant Colonel) John Adams, I pushed the safety limits to the edge and beyond. We brought artillery fire in as close as fifty metres for our soldiers in trenches. To make emergency withdrawal more realistic I took one gun to the flank and then fired it ever closer to the other guns until the shrapnel could be heard striking the armoured turrets. All these activities imbued a greater self-confidence and ability to measure risk. It also created training that was not soon forgotten.

We moved on to the main training period with the remainder of the Battle Group to conduct every phase of war firing live ammunition. The advance, quick attack, deliberate attack, main defence, quick defence, minefield breach, demolition guard and withdrawal were all practised. The only night exercise, owing to safety constraints, was the Battle Group in defence. 'E' Battery was technically near perfect and acquitted itself well. Indeed the complete Battle Group had a very successful period at what was then the most advanced training facility in the world. Nevertheless, the BATUS facility had restrictions: the application of casualties was arbitrary and inaccurate, and of course the enemy did not fire back. These were matters that I was to solve ten years later. However, the standard of training was already much higher than two years earlier and demonstrated the high state of readiness of the British Army for a Third World War should the Warsaw Pact forces attack the West, but this could not have been said of all our NATO allies.

As ever my Armoured Fighting Vehicle crew, led by my technical assistant Bombardier Bishop, consisted of Lance Bombardier Spencer, the chief signaller, later to become a Nottingham police officer, Gunner Rutty, the driver, and Gunner Tolputt, the second signaller, with Gunner Breward driving my Land-Rover. Excepting Tolputt, who joined only in 1975, these wonderful soldiers comprised my crew for the three years I commanded 'E' Battery RHA, and very good they were in every aspect of their jobs. They were also my escort patrol in Belfast the previous year and were very typical of the excellent soldiers we had.

The customary five days' leave followed and once again I drove through the Rockies to Vancouver with all the Battery officers, Captain Mark Douglas-Withers, Captain Johnny Howard-Vyse, Captain Peter Smeeth and Lieutenant Richard Smith. It was great fun to relax for a few days with this exciting and amusing group before returning to Germany and summer leave.

In 1975 the autumn manoeuvres were designed to practise the 'Wide Horizon' concept of the removal of the brigade level of command, with the Divisional Commander exercising direct command over the Battle Groups. For me as a Battery Commander working closely alongside my Battle Group commander, Lieutenant Colonel Tony Hare of 2 LI, who had replaced 1 LI, it provided an intimate view of the trials and the futility of the concept. It was proven beyond any doubt, and stated with great clarity by Major General Nigel Bagnall, that the brigade level of command needed to be reinstated. But of course there was now egg on the faces of some Whitehall Warriors. The result was that the Brigade Headquarters in the 1st British Corps were all cut slightly in size and renamed Task Force Alpha through to Task Force Foxtrot. In the United Kingdom the title Field Force was introduced. Within a few years the original well tested brigade organisation returned.

However, there was one very good consequence of these trials, the adoption of the so-called 'Square Brigade' and 'Square Battle Group'. Hitherto, the brigades in the 1st British Corps contained either three mechanised infantry battalions and one tank regiment or three tank regiments and one mechanised infantry battalion. By changing the brigade to two mechanised infantry battalions and two tank regiments, it enabled Battle Groups to be better balanced, typically consisting of one or two mechanised infantry companies and one or two tank squadrons. A subsequent additional bonus was the increase in size of all the Close Support Artillery Regiments from three gun batterys to four, thus enabling every Battle Group to have a dedicated battery. These changes substantially improved the combat power and fightability of the 1st British Corps.

I had been wondering why there had been no announcement of my next appointment for more than a year since my selection for promotion had become known. It seemed strange, as some of my peers had already started their lieutenant colonel appointments. Eventually I was told that I was to be the Military Assistant to the Commander-in-Chief Central Europe (MA to CINCENT) but not until July 1977 – twenty months ahead. On enquiring, I discovered that I was not being given many months off but that I had to become an interpreter in German, as my new boss was always a German Army officer.

My last few weeks commanding 'E' Battery RHA passed very quickly as we started to pack up the house and consider the move to a language school. These were sad days as we said goodbye to the many friends we had worked and shared life with for three years. On 31 December 1975 I became a lieutenant colonel, spending my last ten days in this rank while still commanding my battery. Major (later Colonel) George Morris returned to take over 'E' Battery RHA, and we were away.

CHAPTER 9

Back to the Staff

MY GERMAN LANGUAGE COURSE WAS at the Royal Army Education Corps Higher Education Centre at Mulheim in the Ruhr area of Germany. The only other student with me was Lieutenant Colonel David Ransley who was destined for the Senior Liaison Officer post at the German Artillery School. Ann and I were allocated a married quarter in Kettwig near Essen almost on the banks of the River Ruhr. Even the simplest of tests would have indicated my basic unsuitability for language training, a weakness worsened in recent years by hearing damage caused by many years with the guns. So I embarked on the unhappiest year of my entire military career, but balanced by a blissful domestic year. For the very first time I had no operational role and the family had my entire attention.

Every day from 9 a.m. to 12.30 p.m. and then from 2 p.m. until 4 p.m. we were taught German. In the evening there was precious little appetite to study more. As we moved towards translating technical equipment procurement papers my interest waned fast. Both the staff and I realised that very little was being gained by my presence there. I therefore moved to the *Bundessprachenampt* (German Government Language School) in Köln for the autumn 1976 term where the instruction was considerably better. By living there during the week I experienced 'total immersion' in German. Then came the news that the tour of the present MA to CINCENT was being cut short and that I was to report for duty in February 1977. On arrival at Headquarters Allied Forces Central Europe (HQ AFCENT) my new chief, General Franz-Joseph Schulze, immediately asked me what I had been doing for the last two years. When I replied 'Learning German,' he declared with some anger, 'What a total waste of time. I do not want a British Officer trying to speak German. I want a British Officer who speaks and writes perfect English!'

HQ AFCENT was a joint Army and Air Force NATO headquarters immediately subordinate to the Supreme Allied Commander Europe (SACEUR), at that time the mercurial General Alexander Haig. General Schulze arrived at HQ AFCENT a week before me from being General Haig's Deputy Chief of Staff for Operations, which was the key HQ SACEUR senior staff appointment. They maintained a very close working

86

relationship. There was a British Deputy CINCENT (D CINCENT), Air Chief Marshal Sir Peter le Cheminant. The AFCENT headquarters was located in an old but only recently disused coalmine at Brunssum in the south-eastern corner of the Netherlands. It was responsible for all land and air operations in war between Hamburg and the Swiss border. Subordinate to HQ AFCENT were two Army Groups (NORTHAG and CENTAG) with a total of twenty-one in-place Divisions, two Allied Tactical Air Forces (2 ATAF and 4 ATAF) and three Air Support Operations Centres (ASOCs). This was a huge force and I found myself at the very heart of it, dealing at the highest levels of both the military and political leadership within NATO at the height of the Cold War with the greatest arms race in history. In peacetime these forces remained under national command, but in a build-up to war would be placed under NATO command.

CINCENT had a formidable team. He operated the French Army 'cabinet' system with Colonel Lutz Moek, German Army, as *Chef de Cabinet* although he was soon replaced by Colonel Klaus Bodenstein. The team was completed by four lieutenant colonels of which I was one. My responsibilities were centred on all land operations and allied matters, plus speeches, conferences and land warfare papers. My US Air Force colleague looked after all air warfare matters and dealings with the US authorities. My Dutch Army colleague dealt with all matters concerning the host nation, and finally there was a German Air Force officer in a national appointment who covered all CINCENT's national responsibilities, mainly with MOD Germany, for General Schulze was the German Armed Forces' second most senior serving officer. In addition there was an aide de camp from the German army. The peacetime headquarters in Brunssum was complemented by a huge underground nuclear-protected war headquarters in the hills west of Frankfurt and a separate mobile headquarters.

The situation in the Cold War was very serious. The Warsaw Pact was spending huge amounts of money introducing the very latest equipment into their vast armies that stretched from Murmansk all the way to Turkish Thrace, not to mention those facing the Chinese. They were supported by a huge air force, and a navy operating in and below every ocean. All had adopted a very aggressive posture in their training, equipment, planning and preparedness. In short they were absolutely ready for war and could probably launch a Third World War within twenty-four hours of a decision in Moscow. They had built up a vast stock of chemical weapons including thousands of tons of the latest nerve agent VX. Their massive stock of nuclear weapons with launchers to reach anywhere in the world was being augmented by the introduction of the SS20 missile system based on a highly mobile truck but able to reach any part of Europe and much of the United States with each rocket containing three Multiple Independently Targetable Re-entry Vehicles (MIRVs). The United States reacted to this threat by planning to deploy the new Neutron Bomb in Europe that had a much enhanced radiation warhead that would penetrate and kill the crews of the thousands of Warsaw Pact armoured vehicles while causing much less collateral damage to West Germany. Unsurprisingly, the communists soon persuaded all their western sympathisers to mount huge protests.

We knew that the Warsaw Pact plan was based on a sudden and huge armoured attack with up to two hundred divisions, mostly fully armoured, that would be supported by tactical nuclear and chemical warfare agent weapons. Their attack into the Central Region was planned around swift armoured thrusts across the North German Plain to seize the Channel Ports before the United States could use them to bring in twenty-eight reinforcing divisions. As the United Kingdom was visualised as a large United States air base, it was estimated that an initial barrage of up to two hundred nuclear weapons on both military and civil targets would reduce most of the country to the dark ages.

Consequently, I found myself at the centre of the thrust to improve the NATO performance: a more sophisticated 'warning of war' intelligence plan, increased numbers of improved anti-tank missiles such as the new Milan weapon, reduced peacetime to operational area deployment times, increased numbers and efficiency of deployable reserve forces, improved training of governments to make the necessary early decisions in times of crisis and war, more effective targeting of NATO airpower, the building of large Forward Storage Sites to house ammunition and fuel nearer to the battle areas, and many more similar initiatives.

General Schulze was known in the German Army as 'Eierkopf' (or Egghead) partly on account of his abnormally large head and partly owing to his prodigious intellect. He was a brutally self-centred man, almost totally devoid of real friends, and quite without any charm. When in the office he would work from 9 a.m. until 2 p.m. and then disappear for lunch followed by an afternoon sleep. Sometimes he would reappear to work from 6 p.m. until 9 p.m., and sometimes not. Even his driver would not know until he reappeared at the door of his chateau. So his entire staff would wait endlessly in case we were needed.

The Chief of Staff was Belgian Army Lieutenant General Roger Dewandre, who had served with great distinction in the British Army during the Second World War, winning a Military Cross. His Military Assistant was Lieutenant Colonel (later Lieutenant General Sir) Richard Swinburn with whom I worked closely, and who put much effort into maintaining a working relationship between his boss and mine, a difficult task that almost became an inter-governmental issue. The British and Americans were the dominant staff officers at the ranks of brigadier and below, with Colonel Tony Stagg (my third tour with him) holding the key land operations post.

Against this background I arrived in the headquarters and was soon given my initial major task. General Schulze, also newly arrived, was faced with giving his first major policy speech to the UK Royal College of Defence Studies, to be followed a week later by almost the same speech to the NATO Defence College in Rome. His tasking guidance to me was minimal: 'I do not know what I want to say, but you write the speech and prepare the overheads.' So I spent a week meeting every single staff officer researching their problems and possible solutions, selecting the twenty-two issues that appeared to be the most important and, with the help of the one star (brigadier) staff level, putting together the first draft. It was returned to me a week later with a line through every paragraph of twenty-one pages of type. It said: 'I do not know want I want, but I know that is not it!' After six weeks and twenty-nine typed versions the final speech was finished, together with the overheads. Over the next two years this first speech was modified many times but always provided the base line for any occasion. I was its 'keeper' and accompanied the General all over Europe whenever it was to be presented.

I became steadily more involved in the detailed operational staff work that was done by the appropriate staff officers in the various staff branches. As the MA, my task was to arrange the various detailed subject meetings, ensuring the correct papers were produced and examined beforehand, then attend the meeting noting CINCENT's comments and wishes, and finally reporting when the actions had been completed, or very often arranging further meetings. It was fascinating and vitally important work.

In June 1977 Ann and I were thrilled and delighted when our second daughter Elizabeth was born in the Royal Air Force Hospital in Wegburg, just across the border in West Germany. As there were no married quarters in Brunssum we lived in a small Dutch house in Heerlen just a few miles from the headquarters. These were happy days despite the frustrations of my work.

I found myself increasingly used by CINCENT as his travelling companion, which proved interesting. As General Schulze was keen to keep as close to General Alexander Haig as possible, we sometimes travelled around Europe in General Haig's personal aircraft. The generals would sit at a small conference table at one side of the aircraft while the MAs sat across the aisle, following the conversation and chipping in when appropriate. We attended several large conferences as well as smaller meetings. Visits to capital cities usually included official meetings with the host nations' defence ministers and senior military staffs. All required a great deal of planning and preparation, not least to try to improve individual nations' military preparedness by raising issues at the very highest levels.

The staff both at AFCENT and at national Ministries of Defence were handpicked and expected to use their initiative. As an example the Franco-German-Italian MILAN anti-tank missile was desperately needed by the British Army in Germany but the UK was four or five years down the production queue. At the same time MOD Germany had the missile systems ordered in large quantities but a limited budget to pay for them. The UK Minister of Defence Fred Mulley was set up by the staff to visit AFCENT. During the briefing he was informed of CINCENT's concern over the lack of anti-tank missiles in the 1st British Corps. This was the cue for Mulley who told General Schulze that a deal could be done whereby he would find the money to take the unbudgeted German Army missile systems if Schulze would persuade MOD Germany to forgo an early part of the production of both aiming units and missiles. It was at the dinner that General Schulze innocently asked Mulley (who as a sergeant in the Worcestershire Regiment had spent five years as a prisoner of war in Germany) if he had had much opportunity to enjoy touring in Germany in earlier years. The dry reply was that he had tried but tourism had been actively discouraged during his time in Germany.

HM The Queen came to West Germany in June 1977 as part of her Silver Jubilee visits to the Armed Forces. General Schulze was invited to Sennelager (his home town) for both the dinner and the huge armoured parade on the following day that I attended with him. I gave him a very clear briefing for the dinner at which he was seated between the Queen and the Foreign Secretary. Next day I asked how he had enjoyed meeting them. He replied with a smile that the Queen appeared to have a much finer grasp of foreign affairs than many other officials.

The work of the AFCENT headquarters continued apace with two main thrusts: trying to improve NATO forces' preparedness and training all the headquarters' commanders, staffs and communications in the wartime roles. The latter was taken very seriously with two major command post exercises each year (Exercises Able Archer and Wintex) in which the whole of the NATO command structure took part, including national governments. For these we moved into our war and mobile headquarters knowing that the war rooms in London and other capitals were being manned and that every single NATO headquarters of division level and above was taking part. The exercise play was so realistic that it had to be graded at a very high security level. The passing of national units to NATO command was an important issue, but very minor in comparison with the procedures for the release of tactical nuclear weapons to try to halt the Warsaw Pact advance. This procedure was taken with exceptional care and seriousness. It was said that Margaret Thatcher was the first British Prime Minister to take a full part in the procedure, and found it stimulating as well as recognising its fundamental importance. We all knew that any escalation from the limited use of short-range tactical nuclear weapons to general release would devastate the world.

My work continued in this domain throughout 1977 and into 1978. Remarkably, my German had improved to the extent that General Schulze even took me once to a national meeting at the German Ministry of Defence in Bonn. I handed my report, in English, of the meeting to him next day. It was returned with a rare smile and a note that I had totally misunderstood two of the issues. I also discussed with him the most appropriate training for my successor. General Schulze wanted the candidate to attend the six months' NATO Defence College course in Rome, and was totally indifferent to any German language training. I reported this to London but my successor, Lieutenant Colonel (later Colonel) Paddy King-Fretts of the Devon & Dorset Regiment, was made to spend six months in Rome and six months language training.

By early summer I was beginning to become concerned about my next appointment due at the year end. The Royal Artillery Command List on which I hoped to feature should have been published a week earlier and I had heard nothing. I telephoned Major Richard Kidner, my colleague from Lippstadt days, who now worked for the Major General Royal Artillery (MGRA) at Headquarters 1st British Corps, to ask when the list was due out. There was a long pause, then 'Haven't you heard? The list came out ten days ago. You've got 40th Field Regiment in Gütersloh.' I was delighted. Although I had not previously served in 40th Field Regiment, they were one of the very best regiments with a role in the right forward Division of the 1st British Corps, an area and task I knew well.

The last few months of 1978 passed quickly as I turned my mind increasingly towards command of 40th Field Regiment. At the same time I was able to reflect on two very dramatic years at the heart of the higher echelons of NATO, a period in which the NATO nations all 'raised their game' thanks to the intellectual and politically aware drive of General Haig and General Schulze. This was the beginning of a process in which NATO started to gain ground and eventually overhaul the Warsaw Pact supremacy, leading to the end of the Cold War in the late 1980s. These two years taught me just how fine the balance had been between potential defeat and victory during the most tense years of the Cold War, a danger that relatively few citizens in western nations understood. But despite a lack of sympathy in governments for the military requirements of the time, it was the sheer hard work and determination of the people around me that led to improvements, and eventually to victory some ten years later.

CHAPTER 10

Regimental Command

WE MOVED INTO the commanding officer's dedicated house in Hochstrasse next to the park at Gütersloh in early March 1979. Lieutenant Colonel (later Major General) David Quayle, an old friend from Aden and Detmold days, had left a few days earlier. I had just four days there before departing with the regiment for the CRA's winter firing exercise on the Munsterlager amd Hohne artillery ranges – a tough call.

I had almost no knowledge of 40th Field Regiment. As The Lowland Gunners, most recruits came from the Lowlands of Scotland but excluding Glasgow. The Regiment was huge: four gun batterys each with eight 105 mm Abbot self-propelled howitzers, an armoured counter mortar troop with Cymbeline radars, a REME Workshop numbering over a hundred soldiers and the usual headquarters battery. In addition 'C' Battery Royal Horse Artillery with thirty armoured Swingfire long-range anti-tank guided missile systems were under administrative command. In all there were more than 800 officers and men (plus one woman), with another 400 wives and over 600 children ranging from aged twenty down to a few days. But that was not all. I was also the Station Commander for Mansergh Barracks that additionally contained 61 Ordnance Company and a German Air Force Signals Squadron, plus two British Schools with a total of 90 teachers and 2,000 children.

The main components of my new command were:

38 (Seringapatan) Battery led by Major Tony Boyce
49 (Inkerman) Battery led by Major Chris Brightman
129 (Dragon) Battery led by Major Neill O'Connor, with whom I had served in Aden
137 (Java) Battery led by Major Tony Kingaby, whose remarkable career had seen him go from gunner through every rank to sergeant-major, and then second lieutenant to major
Headquarters Battery led by Major Patrick Hazlerigg
and under administrative command C Battery RHA led by Major (later Major General) Graham Hollands with Captain (later General Sir) David Richards as his deputy. Major David Walmsley was my

wise and knowledgeable second–in–command while Captain Patrick Hunt was the very efficient adjutant who clearly did not suffer fools gladly.

40th Field Regiment was part of the 2nd Armoured Division that had the role of the right forward division of the 1st British Corps, a task I had undertaken during my three previous field artillery tours in Germany. My CRA was Brigadier (later Major General) James Templer, an outstanding sportsman with a reputation as a tough no–nonsense soldier. My Regiment supplied the artillery support for Task Force Delta (as the 12th Armoured Brigade had been temporarily re–titled following the Wide Horizon trials) which was commanded by Brigadier (later General Sir) Brian Kenny, amongst other attributes an outstanding hockey player. Living in a nearby village was Major General (later General Sir) Ted Burgess, then the Major General Royal Artillery at Headquarters 1st British Corps in Bielefeld.

The four very hectic days from arrival until departure for the CRA's winter firing just about enabled me to meet the officers and warrant officers as their soldiers loaded the Regiment's guns and vehicles on to the trains at Gütersloh station to take them to Munsterlager sidings. I also met the two headmasters, put my two daughters into their new school and kindergarten, and hung a few pictures in our quarter. Lieutenant Colonel David Quayle had handed over to me a very fine regiment: happy, efficient in their role, and good at sport. He also very kindly passed on to me his driver Lance Bombardier Joe Brown who quickly became a much appreciated additional member of the family. This wonderful soldier was to spend more than seven years as my staff car driver.

As I was about to depart to the CRA's winter firing I was warned to be in my office for a telephone call from London. When it came I learned that I was to move the Regiment back to England, to Colchester, two years later, in February 1981, after twelve years in Gütersloh. To complicate matters only a little over half the Regiment would move as C Battery RHA. 49 (Inkerman) Battery, the Cymbeline Radar Troop and the REME Workshop would all remain in Gütersloh to join 47th Field Regiment with whom we were to exchange barracks and roles. Furthermore, on arrival in Colchester we would receive the new (and very temperamental) 155 mm towed FH70 howitzer.

I arrived in the regimental bivouac area on Munsterlager Ranges with my head in a buzz. First and foremost I had to get to know the soldiers and, equally important, let them get to know me and what I stood for in life. But at the same time I faced a very important live firing exercise in extreme cold during which, after just four days, I would be commanding my Regiment on a testing CRA's exercise when it was inevitable that we would be measured against the other two regiments. The immediate task was to get the Regimental Sergeant Major, RSM Tom McSherry, who had joined the Regiment only a few days before me, to assemble everyone in a hollow square so that I could introduce myself and address the Regiment. Not least I had to tell them of the move back to England, probably an unpleasant surprise to the fifty or so soldiers who had married into German families and taken on their lifestyle.

The CRA's exercise went well over the two-week period, with my Regiment proving themselves well trained in almost every way, but I quickly determined that our gunnery skills had to be much quicker in their application with a marked improvement in the sense of urgency.

On return I learned more about the two schools located in the barracks and with whom we shared many facilities such as the gymnasium and sports grounds. King's School, under the inspired leadership of Headmaster Ken Jones, was the comprehensive school for 1,600 children coming by bus daily from all the garrison towns within fifty miles. Haig School with 350 children was a junior school with a catchment area of Gütersloh only. There were ninety teachers who all belonged to my Regimental Officers' Mess, which in the past had led to almost unmanageable tensions. The other huge problem was that more than 1,000 soldiers and 2,000 schoolchildren had to share one football pitch plus a small practice pitch, one rugby pitch, one tarmac hockey pitch and a single gymnasium. David Quayle had solved the problems of the mess and so I decided that I would tackle the sports fields problem.

Also in Gütersloh was a very large Royal Air Force base, the home for three Harrier squadrons and numerous helicopters, all dedicated to supporting the army. They were a great crowd, outstandingly led by the two station commanders in my time, Group Captains Mike Stear and Richard Johns, both of whom went on to become Air Chief Marshals.

There was a great deal to do and, as ever, time was the enemy. The greatest strength of the Regiment was the Sergeants' Mess. The CRA's winter firing period had showed that the Regiment's gunnery was good but too slow for the requirements of the potential battle, unsurprising as they had been distracted by a tour in Northern Ireland the previous year. A fast moving armoured enemy advancing in mass (the Warsaw Pact tactic) would provide many high priority targets. A regiment with 105 mm calibre guns would only really be effective when three or more batterys fired simultaneously at one target. The requirement therefore was speed – very fast engagements of targets to allow every major target to be attacked and fast movement to new positions in order that the guns were in action for the maximum time. A vital element was the provision and supply to the right place of the required natures of ammunition. The other side of this coin was survivability, the need to avoid detection and hence destruction by artillery or air attack. This led to increased use of fully dug positions for both guns and their ammunition, and command posts. Forward Observation Officer (FOO) parties also needed to be fully dug in. A gun or FOO party fully dug in is by definition totally below ground level with some eighteen inches of overhead cover, normally packed earth, for personnel survival – no mean task.

The Regiment had a massive and very well equipped training wing with nine large classrooms, some of which were specially equipped for such subjects as driving and maintenance. But when I arrived nearly every single classroom had been turned over to single soldiers' temporary living accommodation, and horrifyingly, they were in two- and three-tier bunks. This had resulted from a delayed programme to turn the single soldiers' twenty-man barrack rooms into single soldiers' flats, a new concept that gave each small group of soldiers a single or a shared room with its own ablutions, and with access normally only to the soldiers who lived in the flat.

There was also the need to get to know and act as the public face of the British Army in the town of Gütersloh. The *Burgermeister* (mayor) Herr Grawe and *Stadtdirektor* (chief executive) Dr Wixforth became both close working colleagues and friends, visiting the Regiment very regularly. After all, my British community made up 10 per cent of the local population, and including the Royal Air Force some 25 per cent. I used my German language skills a great deal, far more than when working for General Schulze. I got to know two of my neighbours, Karl Miele, who founded the washing-machine company, and Reinhard Mohn, who headed the Bertelsmann publishing empire. These two generous benefactors had set up a very large fund to help British servicemen enjoy the facilities offered by the town.

Against this background, while the soldiers had a period of intensive individual training to upgrade their military skills and therefore improve their pay grades, I considered the year ahead in detail and the year after in outline. To an extent my hands were tied as both 38 and 129 Batterys were scheduled to train at BATUS in Suffield, Canada which was in total a three months' process, and the full annual live firing camp at the Munsterlager and Hohne ranges was scheduled for July, followed by a divisional Field Training Exercise (FTX) in September. There was also the very important question of sport and adventurous training, both vital to improve the fitness and self-confidence of the soldiers. We were the army champions at judo and tug-of-war, and probably in the top three at athletics in the army. Our soccer, rugby, hockey and cricket teams were amongst the best in the 2nd Armoured Division.

The basic structure of life in BAOR had changed little since the early 1960s as described in Chapter 3. Individual training in the winter was still followed by the '443' local area work-up training prior to moving north-east to the Soltau Luneburg Training Area (SLTA), and then on to the live firing artillery ranges at Hohne and Munsterlager South. Summer leave followed, a long-drawn-out affair as 80 per cent of the strength of the Regiment had to be kept in the Gütersloh area in case of a short notice Warsaw Pact attack. As ever the major autumn manoeuvres started in late September once the harvest was in, and then followed a period of intense equipment maintenance.

But now there was one big difference, the need to balance the conflicting wishes of the young unmarried soldiers, who wanted to be out of barracks on military training or on adventurous training as much as possible, and on the other hand the entirely justifiable aims of the married soldiers to be at home with their families whenever possible. To this latter category could be added the older middle-ranking single soldiers with more sophisticated lifestyles. In addition our top ranking sports teams needed training time to win competitions at the highest levels. The achievement of the right balance needed huge amounts of sympathetic planning, almost a weekly activity bar chart for every man, ensuring that they were all available for the priority training periods such as live firing.

Our soldiers were of the very highest quality, with very few serving only the minimum three-year engagement. While a number decided to leave the army at the six-year point, the majority served for nine or twelve years or completed the full twenty-two-year pensionable term. Lance Bombardier Brown and Lance Bombardier McMullen, who drove my staff car and Land-Rover respectively, had both already served for nine years, while Gunner Pickup, who drove my AFV 432 tracked command post vehicle, had completed seven years. We ran a full-time and very active recruiting campaign in the Lowlands and had many more soldiers than the establishment allowed – up to eighty over strength that allowed enormous flexibility in our manpower planning.

The facilities in BAOR for leisure and adventurous training had grown continuously. Most soldiers would ski every winter and sail every summer as well as play all the normal team sports. Golf courses had been created, stables with regimental horses enlarged, parachute centres provided, and many other sports introduced. A surprising number of members of the Regiment had taken up these sports and reached a very high standard, even competing in the Olympic Games. One had to recognise not only the personal commitment, but also the way in which it almost always enhanced their military skills.

Within three months I was away again to SLTA with the Regiment (less one battery who were in Canada) for advanced training prior to the annual summer live firing period on Hohne and Munsterlager ranges. I decided that, rather than take over a hutted camp or erect a tented camp for the period with its inevitable overheads in personnel, we would live with our detachments for the whole six-weeks' period, which worked very well and introduced a new cohesiveness.

I obtained a stopwatch from the Quartermaster and conspicuously timed and noted many of the gunnery drills. The time for the report of 'Battery Ready' after a move soon dropped from an average of twenty-three minutes to less than two minutes from the first gun reaching the new position. We also introduced the digging-in of guns and FOO parties. They would start at last light with the aim of being below ground and camouflaged by first light, and achieved it. Interestingly, unless Royal Engineer digging machines arrived before two hours after last light it was quicker to dig by hand. The problem with the digging machines was that they disturbed an enormous area that was almost impossible to camouflage. The Quartermaster obtained a vast amount of ammunition for all our weapons other than the guns. A special range was set up where every soldier spent half a day to fire the more unusual weapons such as rocket launchers and heavy machine guns. A member of the Workshop, with a smile a mile wide, told me that he had fired six weapons he had never fired before, and fired his rifle for the first time in six years. I relearned the important lesson that training had to be fun, and I never forgot it. The live firing part of the period at Hohne and Munsterlager Ranges included anti-tank and direct firing, a best gun and best FOO party competition, battery and regimental exercises, and finally a CRA's exercise. We returned to Gütersloh a very well trained Regiment, ready for the summer leave period.

In the meantime I had also taken a close interest in 'C' Battery Royal Horse Artillery for, although I was not responsible for their operational preparedness, I nevertheless had to write their annual confidential reports. By 1979 they had been in the anti-tank guided missile role for only a few years but had achieved remarkably high standards. Tactically they had developed huge awareness and a self-confidence that was widely respected by armoured corps and infantry commanders. Technically they were superb. On one visit to the ranges a bombardier guided his missile to hit three targets in under twenty seconds. Two canvas targets were at 1,000 metres and 1,500 metres and a hard target (an old tank) was at 2,000 metres, and they were offset as opposed to being in line. The canvas targets, smaller than a tank, had a wooden frame including cross reinforcing struts in the shape of an X. The bombardier guided the missile through the top left corner of the first canvas target, swerved it right to guide it through the top right of the second canvas target (avoiding the wooden frame and cross struts both times), and then guided it left to hit the old tank hulk – remarkable skill.

During these busy months, the judo and tug-of-war teams retained their positions as army champions while the athletics team managed a very creditable second place in the army championships at Aldershot. It was time to draw breath and so Ann and I, with our daughters, headed first for Denmark to see Legoland and then holiday on the beautiful island of Funen, before returning to England to spend some time with our families.

One of the measures that David Quayle had introduced to improve relationships between the Regiment and the schoolteachers with whom we shared the mess was the formation of the 'Mansergh Dining Club'. Four times each year the fourteen members (effectively the senior managers of the Regiment and the schools) plus two guests dined together, with one guest making a speech during dinner. Every chef in the Regiment was involved under the direction of the master chef and we dined exceedingly well. All the chefs joined us after dinner for a glass of port. Ken Jones and I invited the guest speakers alternately. My first guest was Sir Oliver Wright, the British Ambassador in Bonn and also the British high representative in West Berlin. We also asked him to spend a day, visiting the Regiment and the schools, which he obviously enjoyed. As the staff at HQ British Army of the Rhine (BAOR) had made no progress with the extension of the sports fields, my next guests were General Sir Bill Scotter and Lady Scotter. He was then the Commander-in-Chief of BAOR and his wife a former schoolteacher. They too were invited to spend a day with the Regiment and the schools that proved highly successful. I knew well that, when the Commander-in-Chief visits, the host would be allowed one 'wish'. I asked for the sports fields problem to be given a higher priority. Within nine months the land was ours and only three years later it contained five soccer pitches as well as tennis courts and other facilities – such was the power of the senior officer. The Mansergh Dining Club continued as a most useful concept to enhance the relationships within this large community.

By mid-September, the Regiment was deployed in the very well known operational area east of Hameln based on the Rivers Nette and Leine with the adjacent Sibbesse, Coppenbrügge and Springe Gaps for the 2nd Armoured Divison FTX, in many ways a rehearsal for probable tasks in the huge Spearpoint FTX scheduled for the following autumn. Each Battery deployed with its affiliated battle group for work-up training while I joined Headquarters Task Force Delta with my Tactical Headquarters under Brigadier Brian Kenny. We spent much time practising the coordination of fire at divisional level in order to use artillery decisively in an armoured battle. The final phase of the FTX was the Division in all phases of war against a live enemy. While there were rules for the exercise participants to avoid inflicting unnecessary damage to the German countryside, we were nevertheless allowed a great deal of freedom of manoeuvre. We could drive our tanks and smaller armoured vehicles over any field (excepting asparagus beds) and through any forest. Our dismounted infantry could enter gardens and farm buildings but not private houses or schools. This exercise enabled the consolidation of all the training during the year, in particular the practice of the combined arms battle in the defence and counter attack. By the time it ended all my Battery Commanders and Forward Observation Officers were totally integrated not only into their respective tank and infantry tactical headquarters, but also into the tactics to be employed. Similarly, the Gun Batterys had mastered the pace of the battle and how to deal with the threats that faced them. We were ready for war should it come.

We returned to barracks briefly before returning to the field for one of the most interesting demonstrations I have ever witnessed. The aim was to show the sometimes sceptical armoured corps and infantry commanders that concentrated artillery fire was a battle winner. The CRA, Brigadier James Templer, had arranged for the 2nd Divisional Artillery, plus a typical divisional slice of the heavier Corps Artillery totalling over 110 guns, to deploy on Hohne ranges ready to fire at a carefully chosen piece of ground. The area of the target was accurately surveyed and dug with properly constructed field defences – trenches with shelter trenches according to current teaching. Just sixty metres from the target was a line of 60-ton main battle tanks, arranged track to track with the heavily armoured fronts facing the target area. For safety reasons the line of fire was parallel to the line of tanks. I was in the turret of a Chieftain tank with Brigadier Brian Kenny while every other divisional, brigade and battle group commander in the 1st British Corps similarly had his 'Gunner' with him. The first single 105 mm shell exploded just in front of our tank. I asked Brigadier Kenny if he would be happy to drive through that explosion. Answer – 'No problem!' Next came a 105 mm battery. Same question. Answer – 'I would drive round it!' Next was a 105 mm regiment of four batterys. Same question. Answer – 'No!' We them moved on to the 155 mm calibre and life became distinctly frightening. Next came the 175 mm guns followed by the 203 mm guns, even worse. Finally the target was engaged by all the guns and the effect was dramatic beyond description. The blast waves alone caused the front of our 60-ton tank to be lifted three feet off the ground. Every single piece of equipment mounted on the outside of the tank was shredded to pieces and the optics were rendered useless. The field defences in front of our tank were completely destroyed. It was a timely lesson of the firepower of artillery that nobody present would ever forget.

After returning to barracks we started the usual deep clean and maintenance of equipment with all the customary external inspections ranging from guns and vehicles through personal documentation to secret documents. It also allowed me to conduct my own inspections. Typically the guns and vehicles of a Battery would take most of a day. I wore coveralls and always carried a torch and a screwdriver. The final straw in the inspection of one below standard Battery was to find the remains of a long forgotten half-eaten meal from the September exercise. Having ordered a re-inspection of the entire Battery three weeks later, I could not resist going to the same tool bin, but this time it contained a plate of smoked salmon on fresh brown bread and an ice-cold bottle of champagne with appropriate glasses.

Our move to Colchester, still more than a year away, provided much food for thought. On returning to the UK, we would lose cheap tax-free cars, petrol, alcohol, TV, electrical goods and much more, including the important 'local overseas allowance' that enhanced salaries considerably. Most of our married soldiers had spent their entire service married life in Gütersloh cushioned by these benefits as well as free transport for children to schools and wives to the shopping centres. The Paymaster started an optional savings scheme in which officers and soldiers could make a monthly payment into a special Regimental account in order to receive around £1,000 as they arrived in Colchester to pay for the new essentials such as a car tax disc and a TV licence. The scheme worked very well.

Christmas when serving abroad is a very special time for a Regiment. A concert party was organised in which every one of the eighteen Troops or equivalent in the Regiment was required to put on an act. The cinema was packed with every standing place taken. For close to fours hours we screamed with laughter, tears rolling down our faces as act after act provided rich entertainment. The Christmas period also included all the normal traditional activities – sergeants to the officers' mess; officers and sergeants to the junior non-commissioned officers' mess; officers to the sergeants' mess followed by both messes serving the junior ranks' Christmas Dinner; and of course 'Gunfire' served to all the single soldiers in bed on Christmas morning, followed by an 'officers versus sergeants' rugby match on Boxing Day.

By this time the Regimental Ski Team had been away training for some weeks, but I had declared myself too old and too busy to take part. However, I did go to watch the races at the divisional meeting and received quite a shock. The team captain, Lance Bombardier Brunn, met me at my hotel on arrival to explain that one of our best skiers had fallen badly during the downhill fast practice earlier in the day, and that I was now the fourth team member. I was on the race course early next morning trying my best to loosen up, having not skied for a year. I watched the first twenty racers and then went to the start. Brunn arrived at my side. 'Our second racer crashed out, so your time will now count,' he announced. I did finish, but my time was slow.

I returned to face a very busy final year in Germany culminating in Exercise Spearpoint in September 1980, the largest and most comprehensive FTX for the 1st British Corps, and partly a political demonstration to the Warsaw Pact of our readiness for war. But I also had to turn my attention to sport and after that the move to Colchester. By this time Captain (later Colonel) Paddy Clarke had become my adjutant and, mindful of the extreme pressures on that role, Lieutenant (later Colonel) Chris Nicholls had been warned off that he would move into the adjutant's busy chair towards the year end, including masterminding the move.

We needed additional talent for the Athletics Team. A special day was organised in February in which every man would try a hundred metre sprint, a 800-metre race, shot, discus, javelin, high jump, long jump and finally the pole vault where we were very weak. It turned into a wonderful high-spirited Regimental Day, the highlight becoming the pole vault area surrounded by highly amused soldiers watching comrades suffering all sorts of problems and indignities in their attempts to clear a modest height. But we did find three really promising prospective pole vaulters as well as other potential athletes who joined the training squads.

The late winter and early spring was the period set aside for our soldiers to spend time in the classrooms learning new or upgrading existing skills to enable them both to earn higher rates of pay and have greater employment flexibility. It enabled me to fulfil other commitments of which an important one was to spend some time in our recruiting area. We had a small team permanently in the Lowlands with a recruiting caravan and display. Once a year we enlarged the team and included an Abbot 105 mm tracked howitzer. Captain Steve Sanderson, normally a Forward Observation Officer, had the additional task of running the recruiting effort and had begged, borrowed and stolen many more guns than normal for the 1980 tour. Accompanied by the Regimental Sergeant Major, Tom McSherry, I spent a week speaking to schools and groups of cadets as well as liaising with the Headquarters Scotland recruiting staff. The highlight of the week was a meeting with the Lord Provost of Edinburgh after which he took the salute, from the steps of the Royal Scottish Academy in Princes Street, of a Regimental drive past for which we mustered twelve guns. Our recruiting picked up well after this very successful initiative.

On 9 April 1980 the Regiment deployed once again to Hohne and Munsterlager Ranges for the spring live firing, our first live firing since the previous July. During an intense ten days we quickly regained our skills, having introduced the many new soldiers to their roles, as well as allowing several officers and non-commissioned officers to settle into new appointments within the order of battle. This was also a very necessary training period for 137 Battery who departed with their Battle Group for the BATUS battle school soon afterwards.

Major General (later General Sir) Martin Farndale had recently taken over the command of the 2nd Armoured Division, and continued to work closely with Lieutenant General (later General) Sir Nigel Bagnall, widely regarded as the greatest British strategist of the second half of the twentieth century. A new and very welcome mobility and flexibility was introduced into tactical thinking and clearly these would be a predominant aspect of the huge Exercise Spearpoint FTX in September. Regimental life quickened, as study days and command post exercises were used to explain and practise new concepts. There was still a Covering Force largely based upon armoured reconnaissance and a Main Defensive Position behind a large minefield, but the maintenance and use of large armoured reserves to destroy enemy main forces in their first echelon was to be given a far higher priority.

In the event of a period of tension possibly leading to war, the Regiment would deploy well forward to a concentration area in hides near to the planned operational areas well to the east. But simultaneously all our ammunition vehicles led by the Quartermaster Technical would drive west to the main ammunition depot at Sennelager to out-load our artillery ammunition. This worried me considerably. I did not like the idea of sending thirty ammunition vehicles away from the Regiment, and nor did I want to move so far east without any artillery ammunition. So I asked to visit the ammunition depot to see how the out-load would work, and eventually my request was agreed. It was a worrying visit. One narrow gate, poor roads in the compound, an old storehouse with narrow entrances limiting the use of Mechanical Handling Equipment and, worse still, an obvious shortfall of ammunition compared with my expectations caused me some sleepless nights. It was at this time that my Quartermaster Technical changed, Captain John 'Dodger' Green being replaced by Captain Syd Simpson. These two outstanding soldiers both reached Lieutenant Colonel a few years later, having started life in one case as a boy soldier and the other as a 17-year-old recruit.

The Regiment was planned to spend the first half of July at the major CRA's 2nd Armoured Division Artillery Firing Camp, dates that exactly matched those of the army tug-of-war finals, where we wanted to defend our title, and the army athletics finals that we hoped to win. Both were to be held in Aldershot. The combined squads totalling seventy men included some key officers, warrant officers and senior non-commissioned officers. This conflict posed an agonising dilemma. The CRA's annual firing camp was both a test and the most important event of the year; on the other hand I had seventy dedicated athletes who on average had probably completed six to eight such similar firing camps in previous years. I sat down with the Battery Commanders (whose reputations would also be on the line) to examine the roles of every man in the squads, and who could take over their roles in the order of battle. I took the decision, based on the extraordinary depth in our training, that we would go to the CRA's annual firing camp without our seventy athletes. It was a risk that not only succeeded, but provided two benefits: the officers and soldiers who moved up a level in the order of battle all performed well, thereby gaining in self-confidence; and in Aldershot the tug-of-war team retained the army title, while the athletes very nearly won the army championships.

Next we had to prepare for the CRA's annual firing camp. In order to provide variation I had applied for a '443' dry training area stretching westwards from Gütersloh to the Ruhr industrial area. This allowed us to train in the built-up area and factories, which was a previously almost untried novelty but what we expected to do in war. Some of the Forward Observation Officer parties climbed the old slag heaps to gain good observation. By early June the Regiment was back at the Soltau Luneberg Training Area (SLTA) (less 137 Field Battery who were in Canada) for advanced training in preparation for the annual summer live firing period on Hohne and Munsterlager ranges. The two-week live firing period started with exercises run by the Battery Commanders prior to my exercise for the Regiment. This included the time-honoured fire plan that I set for each Battery Commander in turn, with the aim of giving them a fair test but always retaining sufficient flexibility to allow me to tighten the screw so that each was stretched. They all passed with flying colours as I knew they would after many hours' training in the miniature range in Gütersloh. However, I did introduce a light-hearted element with a serious intent. I brought along a watering can to give each battery commander's party a rain shower just to test their ability to work through heavy rain. It worked but in one case was a close run thing. We then moved onto the CRA's exercise, with two other regiments also taking part. It was a demanding three days, with little sleep and many novel twists to ensure we stayed alert. As a Commanding Officer, one knew of the dangers of firing live artillery shells full of high explosive into a small impact area when one small mistake could cause a shell to explode in the middle of a busy market place in a local town or village. But the Regiment, and especially all those whom I had moved up to more important roles, performed very well. But sadly we all knew that it was the last time we would fire our beloved Abbot howitzers after twelve years with them.

Summer leave followed and this time we put the car onto the train to Nice and stayed for a glorious fortnight with Johnnie and Penny Eliot at his parents' villa on the coast near St Tropez. It was a memorable holiday in perfect weather that allowed our young daughters to play in the warm sea for hours on end.

The active manoeuvre part of Exercise Spearpoint was scheduled for 19–27 September 1980, a nine-day exercise within the two-week period that allowed the Territorial Army (TA) units to practise mobilisation followed by the move to Germany for the FTX, and then return to the UK. However, we all deployed into the field on 4 September to allow the full and realistic build-up of planning, logistics and intelligence, including the out-load of thousands of tons of simulated ammunition, mines and defence stores. Meanwhile our barracks in Gütersloh was taken over by a TA Field General Hospital from Bristol who would take 'casualties' from the forward areas to prepare them for the hospital trains for return to the UK. All their hospital equipment was permanently stored in the cellars of our barracks. As an integral part of Task Force Delta, I joined Brigadier Brian Kenny's headquarters in a forest east of Hameln. The weather was extremely hot and almost immediately we were ordered into NBC suits. It proved to be a demanding and tiring period while the adoption of full NBC protection was tiresome to say the least.

The Task Force (or brigade headquarters) was formed around a cruciform of six AFV 432 tracked armoured command vehicles linked together by a blackout and weatherproof tentage system. The four main components were Plans, in which Brigadier Kenny and his brigade major (Major, later Major General) Mike Scott, worked mostly on future plans; Operations, where the junior staff officers fought the battle using the secure brigade command radio net as well as the Bruin trunk telephone network; Artillery Operations, where I worked with Major Patrick Hazlerigg who was my Headquarters Battery Commander; and Intelligence, staffed by the Task Force intelligence section plus my own artillery intelligence staff. The other components, some of which were outside the cruciform, varied, but Engineer Operations, Signals Operations and Flank Formations Liaison Officers were amongst the more important. In addition the head-quarters had a very small armoured tactical headquarters consisting of only Brigadier Kenny's and my vehicles that could deploy forward when more immediate command of the battle was likely to be required, and we used these often.

During this preliminary period, which included very accurate and lifelike intelligence information, the build-up of our force continued. Gun positions were dug and prepared, with the guns well hidden nearby. Alternative gun positions were also prepared while possible future locations and routes to them were planned. The Battery Commanders and Forward Observation Officers (including the third TA party in each Gun Battery) were totally integrated with their supported battle groups and combat teams where they also prepared positions and future plans. Field defences were put in place, with the Royal Engineers preparing countless demolitions and laying huge minefields with their bar minelayers that laid sand-filled cardboard dummy bar mines that rotted in the ground after a few weeks, plus prepared demolitions on all major routes. Meanwhile the Royal Air Force flew countless missions and 20,000 TA soldiers moved into their positions. It was very busy and all in a well populated part of Germany where the informed but slightly bemused local population tried to carry on with normal lives.

By 18 September we were ready for the 'battle', expected to start the following morning. I was sitting in the Task Force Mess (a barn) having dinner with Brigadier Brian Kenny and Major Mike Scott when we heard, unusually, a helicopter landing at the close in VIP pad. Simultaneously, one of my signallers rushed in. 'Sir, Sir, your wife is in hospital and you have got to go there straight away, in that helicopter,' he excitedly explained. Brigadier Kenny's face turned white as I picked up my weapon and respirator and rushed to the helicopter. Neither my signaller nor the pilot could tell me more, except that we were going to the British Military Hospital at Rinteln. On landing just before last light, I ran to the entrance where a nurse was waiting to take me straight up to a delivery room in the maternity wing where I found Ann. Ten minutes later we had a son, Alexander, who looked remarkably well despite arriving a month early. After a few minutes the midwife indicated it was my turn to hold our son. I asked if this was wise in view of the filthy condition I was in. The reply 'As it's only a boy, I don't think it really matters' gave me the green light to take him. I looked around the maternity suite to see spread across the floor my respirator, NBC suit, weapon, map case and small rucksack as well as quite a lot of mud. It was quite a moment. I was told that I needed to disappear for an hour or so after which I could come back. A nurse took me to the Nurses' Home, found me a large towel and suggested (with her nose held slightly in the air) that I ought to take a long bath. It was very refreshing, my first proper wash for two weeks. As I emerged Lance Bombardier Brown arrived with my Land-Rover. After a while with my wife and baby son we drove back to the headquarters, arriving soon after first light. The 'battle' had not started but all the indicators showed that an attack was imminent. I took up my customary station at the door of my AFV 432 command post, with my radio head set on. Within minutes radio silence was lifted, the 'battle' had started, but I was asleep!

My tasks were many and varied. As my regimental radio net was insecure, and because I had all my Forward Observation Officers on that net, I was receiving accurate minute by minute situation reports (SIT-REPS) from the forward combat team battles: in contrast the brigade commander and his staff were reliant on periodic tactical summaries from the battle groups headquarters. Therefore I provided the best source of information. But equally, I was on the Commander Royal Artillery (CRA) secure net to Headquarters 2nd Armoured Division to whom I provided information but also requested the fire support from other artillery regiments. However, principally, my task was to ensure that the part of our Task Force accorded the highest priority by the commander received the correct allocation of artillery fire and ammunition at the correct time. At the same time I had to manage the deployment of the Gun Batterys, ensuring that they were in range but not endangered, that they had plans to move if required, and that the ammunition was at the right place at the right time.

As the battle started, the Gun Batterys were all deployed forward to help the break clean of the Covering Force, but they had to be withdrawn with great care through the Main Defensive Position (MDP) to their main, fully dug, gun positions with huge supplies of ammunition pre-dumped.

The 'battle' raged for several days. First the Covering Force withdrew in close contact behind the barrier minefields in order to reconstitute itself as the divisional reserve and counter-attack force. The enemy then faced their break-in battle to seek inroads into the Main Defensive Position (MDP) in which our Task Force Delta was the right forward brigade of the division. It proved to be a real dogfight lasting three days. For me the problem was the overwhelming number of targets that required at least a regiment's fire of four batterys while the promised fire of a Direct Support battery to an infantry battle group, including the sacred Final Protective Fire (FPF), was not one that could be lightly discarded. The 2nd Armoured Division fought the 'enemy' to a standstill before being forced to withdraw behind a reserve division to reconstitute and prepare for future operations. This, on the last day, was a counter attack against a much weakened enemy force, allowing us to regain our initial positions. The exercise gave the participants an invaluable experience of all arms and combined operations and was for that reason alone worth the costs amounting to millions of pounds. But more importantly it was a clear political demonstration to the Warsaw Pact that, should they attack, we were ready and fully prepared for war.

The exercise and the various initial debriefs over, I returned home to be reunited with Ann, our two daughters and our new baby son. After a well-earned long weekend it was time to prepare for the Regiment's move back to England. Every single piece of equipment had to be serviced and returned to pristine condition. With the advance party leaving for Colchester before Christmas, our farewells all had to be completed by mid-December. There had to be a farewell parade to mark our goodbyes both to the town of Gütersloh and to local army units and schools with whom we had worked closely, and of course an occasion for our families. Conventional wisdom dictated that the parade should be held on the hockey pitch, a rather soulless area at the back of the barracks. I wanted better so decreed that it would take place in front of Regimental Headquarters adjacent to the main gate, but close to the messes where lunch would be taken afterwards.

After much scraping and painting, the parade took place in mid-December, a light covering of snow on the ground, with the salute being taken jointly by the *Burgermeister* of Gütersloh and Major General Ted Burgess, in his capacity as the Major General Royal Artillery at HQ 1st British Corps. Every tracked armoured vehicle in the Regiment, immaculately painted, was drawn up track to track and just inches apart with their crews in best Number 2 Dress in front, and the band playing. A crowd numbering over a thousand people watched intently. After the general salute and inspection came the tricky bit. Every armoured vehicle had to reverse, track right and drive forward simultaneously, and then with extreme care exit the barracks to allow space to turn for the drive past. Having led the drive past, I jumped off my AFV 432 tracked armoured command vehicle to return to the saluting dais. This was one of the proudest moments of my life as I watched my Regiment drive past in immaculate order just weeks after playing a leading role in one of the largest military exercises the British Army had ever held.

The Regimental Christmas followed, the skiers departed and as the New Year dawned the packing cases came out. Having been abroad for nine years we had accumulated quite a lot – enough to fill eighty-three packing cases and a large white van.

But for me there was an unexpected highlight to come. Owing to the poor and often ill-informed expectations and tasking of the Harrier Force during the previous autumn FTX, the Commander-in-Chief of RAF Germany had recommended that every brigade and more senior commander in the 1st British Corps should take a two-day course on the Harrier aircraft, including flying a complete mission. Group Captain Dick Johns rang to ask if I would be the guinea pig for the course they had devised. I could not say yes quickly enough. Day one at the RAF Harrier base in Gütersloh was a medical, followed by instruction on the various safety pins in the rear seat of the two-seat trainer, ejection procedures and then mission tasking, weapon loads, operating ranges, etc. For day two, 5 February 1981, I joined Number 4 Squadron Royal Air Force deployed in the forest on the Sennelager training area, covered in six inches of overnight snow. I was shown the entire site, all deep in the forest and heavily camouflaged, and then went through the complete mission briefing for an attack on a target in the Bremen area of northern Germany. Take off from a narrow road temporarily closed to public traffic was a remarkable experience. We then flew low level to the target area before descending even lower for the 'attack' at very high speed, the target just being a blur as we roared past. Finally, after demonstrations of Harrier capabilities we returned to the Sennelager forest to descend vertically onto a tennis court-sized pad before taxiing off into a camouflaged shelter, another remarkable experience.

Nine days later we, and hundreds of our regimental colleagues, drove out of Gütersloh heading for the Channel Ports and Colchester. At the same time Lieutenant Colonel (later Brigadier) Denis Williams and the 47th Field Regiment, with whom we were exchanging locations, were driving in the opposite direction. Coming off the overnight ferry to Harwich, we soon arrived at Kirkee McMunn Barracks in Colchester where Captain Chris Nicholls was waiting in Regimental Headquarters (RHQ) with the keys to our new home – Reed Hall House. The barracks was an open camp that allowed unrestricted access to any civilians and many used it as a short cut into the town centre. Reed Hall House, the officers' mess and RHQ with the adjacent guardroom formed a triangle at the entrance to the barracks. Compared with Gütersloh the barracks was tiny, all the single soldiers living in one large unmodernised 1930s brick barrack block. We decided to explore Colchester. It took over an hour to cover 500 yards as we met a great number of other members of the Regiment with their families doing the same as us. Overwhelmingly they were delighted with their new homes and being back in England – for me this was quite a relief – but the single soldiers were hugely disappointed with their new accommodation.

We were now part of the 7th Field Force (the new post Wide Horizon name for 19th Infantry Brigade) commanded by Brigadier (later Major General) Keith Spacie, a lean and ultra fit member of the Parachute Regiment. The 7th Field Force consisted of five light infantry battalions plus the 13/18th Royal Hussars in the light reconnaissance role. Three were regular battalions: 1st Battalion the Devon and Dorset Regiment, 2nd Battalion the Queen's Regiment and 3rd Battalion the Royal Anglian Regiment, while the 5th and 7th Battalions of the Royal Anglian Regiment were fully integrated Territorial Army battalions. The operational role of the Field Force was very simple – as a part of the 3rd Armoured Division to reinforce the rear of the Main Defensive Position (MDP) of the 1st British Corps in Germany with five large infantry battalions well dug in to form a block in the form of a framework defence based upon villages between the forest-covered steep-sided hills around which armoured forces could manoeuvre for counter-attack. Until our arrival their artillery fire support from 47th Field Regiment had been of 105 mm from the Light Gun. But we were to take over the new 155 mm FH 70 towed howitzer, and inevitably these much heavier weapons would be sucked forward into the main armoured battle.

For the first time I did not have a Commander Royal Artillery (CRA) and so this role was filled by the Brigadier Royal Artillery (BRA) at Headquarters Army Strategic Command at Wilton, a role I was to take over three years later, albeit in a different place and with a different title.

My command team had changed, with Major (later Colonel) Peter Kirby taking over 38 (Seringapatam) Battery, Major (later Lieutenant Colonel) Guy Dodgson commanding 129 (Dragon) Battery while 137 (Java) Battery passed to Major John Tulloch. Inevitably, I had to impose myself to get them and many other new officers to follow the tried and trusted line from Gütersloh days, but they very soon proved to be an excellent team. I also had a new Regimental Sergeant Major as we reached Colchester. As soon as the last few members of the Regiment arrived from Germany, we all went on disembarkation leave.

On return the most immediate task was to send parties to the Ordnance Depot to draw up eighteen new 155 mm FH 70 towed howitzers and thirty-six huge Foden 18-ton trucks, half of which were built as gun tractors and the other half (with the capability to act as a temporary gun tractor) for carriage of the balance of the first line ammunition. In addition there were several fork-lift trucks for each battery to assist in handling the enormous tonnages of ammunition. But the promised new garages had not been built and so once the guns and command posts had been squeezed into the existing sheds, every other piece of equipment had to be parked on the Regimental Square, completely filling it. Not a happy situation. But life had to continue with the urgent priority of re-training the gun detachments and drivers for their new roles, and by mid-April this task was completed but as yet unproven.

The Regiment's two-week conversion firing camp on Salisbury Plain started at the end of April but I had to spend the first week on operational reconnaissances in Germany with the command group of 7th Field Force. I returned directly to Salisbury Plain to disaster. The new guns had been supplied with faulty obturator rings and there were few spares. Morale was at rock bottom with a loss of confidence in our new equipment. I had to put in a major effort then and for the next few weeks to get this problem sorted and confidence restored. Much of the problem lay with an inexperienced Light Aid Detachment commander and some poor gun fitters, and so the big stick was firmly applied.

By this time I had given the new Regimental Sergeant Major several warnings for poor performance as well as excess drinking, and as I knew he would never make the grade I sent him home on permanent leave. The Royal Artillery Records Office had anticipated my call. Within ten minutes they rang back to say that they had selected a replacement, who would come to my office at 2 p.m. that same day for me to meet. I was told that it was Warrant Officer 2 Witham, then the Battery Sergeant Major of 'J' (Sidi Rezegh) Battery RHA in Germany. At 2 p.m. I was to meet a man who became a close and valued friend. Mick Witham had been on leave in Colchester with his in-laws when the call came and he was immediately very obviously the man for the job. Within a week he had moved his home back to Colchester to take over as the Regimental Sergeant Major, instantly widely respected, and of course went on to a glittering career, finishing as the senior quartermaster of the Honourable Artillery Company in London.

There was just time to fit in all the normal sporting fixtures and enjoy the family aspects of regimental life. One such was the christening of our son Alexander in the fine and elegant Colchester Garrison Church for which the Master Chef made an enormous christening cake surmounted by an FH 70 howitzer with a baby in a shawl suspended from the muzzle brake. The cake was duly cut, with a quarter going to the officers' mess, another quarter to the sergeants' mess, while the remainder was enjoyed by the junior ranks in their dining hall.

The Regiment's major firing period for the year, the annual Practice Camp in July at Otterburn in Northumberland, was preceded by battery and regimental training in the local training areas, including Stanford in Norfolk. The Regiment conducted the move to Otterburn as a non-firing fire and movement exercise using every possible small training area between

Colchester and Otterburn, a real test for the drivers, some at age 18, driving huge lorries with a heavy gun behind. For most it was their first experience of the demanding Otterburn live-firing area situated in the Cheviot Hills just a few miles south of the Scottish border. For the drivers it was a particular test with narrow range roads and most of the area unsuitable for heavy trucks to leave the tracks at risk of being bogged in the marsh and peat.

The two-week live firing period was based on the normal pattern of battery training followed by a testing four-day Regimental Firing Exercise. A highlight was the middle weekend when the Regiment deployed close to Redesdale Camp with all the families, many from Scotland, and the Regimental Old Comrades from the Lowlands spending the day with their Regiment. Led by Colonel Tommy Weston, later to become the Regiment's first Honorary Regimental Colonel, all the visitors marched across the heather towards the three Battery gun lines, while I led the officers and soldiers of the Regiment to meet them, a piper playing in the background. It was an emotional moment, marking the return home of the Regiment after twelve years overseas.

As our last guests departed my final regimental exercise started. All the earlier problems with the obturator rings were long forgotten and the soldiers swung our great 155 mm howitzers around the training area as if they were toys, such was their self-confidence. Having put each Battery Commander through a demanding fire plan, I assembled all the Battery Commanders and their Forward Observation Officer parties at the north-west corner of the range high up by the source of the River Coquet to fire regimental targets in a close steep-sided valley just below the Observation Post. Time and again eighteen shells from our eighteen guns hit the targets below us with huge explosions echoing around the valleys. We all learned a lot about the power of medium artillery. As the last rounds fell I realised that to all intents and purposes my time as a commanding officer was over.

The Regiment returned to Colchester for a short period of maintenance followed by summer leave. For me it was a fortnight of farewells, including the move of my family to our new home in Haslemere. I returned to Colchester for a final few days culminating in farewell drinks in the sergeants' mess, after which I was taken from the mess on a 155 mm howitzer through the Regimental Lines lined by my soldiers. Later I was dined out at a Regimental Dinner Night, at the end of which I got into my staff car, and away.

After regimental command

After handing over 40th Field Regiment to my longstanding friend Lieutenant Colonel (later Brigadier) David Creswell, I had a few weeks' leave before reporting to the Royal School of Artillery at Larkhill to become the Chief Instructor of Tactics Wing and with it promotion to Colonel. In the event this tour of duty was to last only one year.

Tactics Wing had four main roles. By far the most glamorous were the quarterly All Arms Tactics Courses and Commanding Officers' Courses for lieutenant colonels, and the annual Brigade Commanders' Course. The second role was the teaching of artillery and all arms tactics, including fire planning, to all the principal Royal Artillery courses, while the third task was to run all artillery intelligence training. Finally a small specialist study team of very experienced officers provided the justification papers for the Director Royal Artillery in his submissions to the Ministry of Defence for improvements to, or the provision of, new equipments.

I had a top rate team to achieve these diverse tasks. Lieutenant Colonel (later Brigadier) Robert Hall, with whom I had attended the Regular Commissions Board twenty-four years earlier, held the key position, running all aspects of tactics relating to the Royal Artillery. He had a team of excellent majors and captains to help him. Lieutenant Colonel William Le Blanc-Smith, 4/7th Royal Dragoon Guards, ran the all arms courses. Major Charles Harcourt-Smith, The Life Guards, our neighbour in Detmold nine years earlier, and Major Tom Brooke from the Irish Guards completed the all arms team. In the event all these officers combined well, working both on all arms courses as well as Royal Artillery courses. Lieutenant Colonel (later Colonel) Tony Bennett headed the study team, while Major Dominic Campbell ran the artillery intelligence courses. In Brigadier Derek Jones I had a superior who was most supportive and with a light touch.

During my many years serving in Germany I had worried about how we as Gunners could both attack all the many targets that would present themselves, but also survive the inevitable heavy attacks by the numerically superior Soviet artillery. I was sure they had to have a weakness that we should try to exploit. I asked for permission to conduct a study entitled 'How to defeat the Soviet artillery'. First I attended a short course at GCHQ in Cheltenham that I followed up with a meeting with the previously unknown Artillery Cell there. I learned that the latter had set its own priority tasks for many years without regard to the Field Army.

Robert Hall took over the running of the Study and was able to task GCHQ with certain questions, as well as spend time with the CIA comparing information and studies. The conclusions proved most interesting, with the weak link identified as the unique regimental command post armoured vehicle with a triple aerial configuration that had to be sited well forward in a position of observation. We then developed a procedure that could identify where this command vehicle could probably be found to allow radio intercept to search small specific areas with the aim of disrupting the enemy command and control system electronically or by direct attack. It proved a most interesting and valuable study.

The highlights of the year were without doubt the all arms courses. The All Arms Tactics Courses brought the finest officers from the Royal Armoured Corps and the Infantry, as well as the gunners, sappers and signallers, to Larkhill immediately before they took over command of their regiments. The five-day course provided updates on the threat, our current organization and doctrine, and then had two days in the field on Tactical Exercises Without Troops (TEWT) covering all phases of war according to current 1st British Corps operational plans. We took all students into the Bombard Observation Post on the Larkhill artillery ranges. We entered an (hopefully) impenetrable bunker with nine-inch armoured glass windows before firing a battery of 155 mm guns at a target ten yards in front of the bunker to provide a realistic and sobering demonstration of the power of artillery. Some students would back away from the windows and so I found it necessary to push them gently forward.

For the second week the course was joined by all the Service and Logistics officers to become the Commanding Officers Designate Course. The week covered every aspect of command of a regiment from morale to administration, and legal to recruiting, with most lectures being provided by outside speakers. These courses attracted the crème of the army to give lectures and presentations. After the Falklands War of June 1982 the complete Land Forces command team came to address the All Arms Tactics Course. The presentations started at 2 p.m. and I had to halt the question period at 9 p.m. for a late dinner, such was the interest and value of the occasion.

The one-week Brigade Commanders' Course held in November concentrated on operational issues and attracted all the brigadiers about to take over command and the very best speakers. Brigadier (later General Sir) John Stibbon, then commanding 20th Armoured Brigade, spent the week with the course, giving up-to-the-minute advice and comments on the issues the students were about to face. By this time I knew I was soon to move back to Germany to become the Commander Royal Artillery of the 4th Armoured Division and so I benefited greatly from the week.

During these high profile course periods a multitude of other courses continued in Tactics Wing, providing valuable training for all ranks, from gunner to lieutenant colonel. However, in December I once again said my farewells, and also celebrated my promotion to brigadier.

CHAPTER 11

Commander Royal Artillery – the First Time

MARCH 1983 SAW MY RETURN TO Germany to become the Commander Royal Artillery (CRA) of the 4th Armoured Division and simultaneously Commander Herford Garrison. Since I departed from Germany two years earlier the 4th Armoured Division had assumed the role of the forward right division of the 1st British Corps, the identical ground east of Hameln over which I had trained for war during five previous tours totalling over twelve years. Once again I took over this appointment from Brigadier (later Major General) David Quayle, and at the same time Lance Bombardier Brown resumed as my driver.

In peace the 4th Armoured Division Artillery consisted of three regiments, each of four gun batterys. The 25th Field Regiment in Paderborn, with Abbot 105 mm self-propelled howitzers commanded by Lieutenant Colonel (later Major General) Graham Hollands, was a year or so later to amalgamate with the four Royal Horse Artillery Swingfire batterys on their conversion to field artillery to resurrect the 3rd Regiment Royal Horse Artillery. Similarly equipped was the 47th Field Regiment Royal Artillery in Gütersloh commanded at first by Lieutenant Colonel (later Colonel) Norman Arnell and later by Lieutenant Colonel (later Brigadier) Mark Douglas-Withers, both very old friends. 27th Medium Regiment in Lippstadt was equipped with nuclear capable M109A1 155 mm self-propelled howitzers and was commanded initially by Lieutenant Colonel (later Brigadier) Ian Townsend, to be followed by Lieutenant Colonel (later Lieutenant General Sir) Edmund Burton. These three fine regiments supported respectively the 33rd, 11th and 20th Armoured Brigades. In addition, the Divisional anti-tank battery role with Swingfire was filled by 'J' (Sidi Rezegh) Battery Royal Horse Artillery based in Paderborn and commanded by Major (later General Sir) Tim Granville-Chapman.

In war, and therefore also for much training, up to another three regiments came under command from both the Regular and Territorial Army (TA) including a Rapier Regiment (air defence), a Light Regiment (TA), a Blowpipe Battery (air defence), an Observation Post Battery (TA) to provide the twelve additional Forward Observation Officer parties, and

3 Squadron of the Honourable Artillery Company that provided the stay behind Observation Posts.

My own Headquarters Royal Artillery (HQRA) was an integral part of the Divisional Headquarters and split into three parts: Artillery Operations run by the Brigade Major Royal Artillery, Major (later Lieutenant Colonel) John Pitt; Artillery Logistics by Major Ronnie Young; and Artillery Intelligence run by Major David Jackson. All my operational vehicles, radios and signallers were provided by the 4th Armoured Division Headquarters and Signal Regiment. Headquarters Herford Garrison was collocated with HQRA and run by Major Ronnie Young assisted by three very able Women's Royal Army Corps (WRAC) captains, Liz Towell, Lottie Raley and Angie Howell, and a Station Staff Officer, Lieutenant Colonel Tony Taylor, with whom I had served twenty years earlier. Under my direction this team ran all the non-operational aspects of military life in the Herford area where there was a multitude of units of which the largest were the 13th/18th Royal Hussars, the 4th Armoured Division Headquarters and Signal Regiment and the 7th Signal Regiment. I had a further disconnected task as the superior authority for the widely spread 4th Ordnance Battalion. In essence I wrote their confidential reports and reviewed their courts martial.

Home for the next two years was to be The White House at Bad Oeynhausen, a spa town ten miles east of Herford. As the Second World War ended the British Army had arbitrarily selected Bad Oeynhausen for their peacetime headquarters, arriving overnight to encircle the town, including the *Kurgarten*, with barbed wire and then evacuate the population who were allowed to return only seven years later. A high priority had been the building of a substantial house for the commander-in-chief that was now to be our home. We inherited Bombardier Wallace as our house bombardier and the long-serving Waltraud as our cook but, unfortunately, no gardener. It was, however, a difficult house for my family as the nearest other British families were ten miles away.

As the CRA I had two broad tasks. The first was to command the regiments of the Divisional Artillery in much the same way as the three brigade commanders commanded their tank regiments and armoured infantry battalions, that is, to ensure that they were ready for war in every respect, and in war to command them. The second task was to be an integral part of the Divisional Headquarters, a role that combined detailed war planning with regular training to ensure that the headquarters was fully trained for war.

My time in Herford proved to be the period in which the Cold War approached its climax. US President Reagan, strongly supported by UK Prime Minister Thatcher, introduced a policy designed to bankrupt the Soviet military economy to bring communism to its knees and then collapse. At the Divisional level this translated into much increased levels of activity, in particular intelligence gathering and preparations for war. At the same time General Sir Nigel Bagnall at Headquarters Northern Army Group (NORTHAG) and Lieutenant General (later General) Sir Martin Farndale at Headquarters 1st British Corps finalised the new operational and tactical concepts based on mobility and aggressiveness, introducing hand-picked commanders to implement them. We knew that the Soviet 3rd Shock Army based around Magdeburg would be the Warsaw Pact First Echelon Force to attack us and that we needed to fight its divisions to a standstill while the air forces held off the Second and Third Echelon forces with a massive interdiction plan known as the Follow On Forces Attack plan.

But the Soviets were also active. A few months earlier Army General M. Zaytsev, Commander-in-Chief of the Group of Soviet Forces in Germany, published a tactical paper:

> TACTICS ... to a military man the very sound of the word means movement, changes in the situation and constant mental effort. And that is what tactics really are – an integral part of the military art: ever developing, reacting sensitively to changes in technology, in armaments, in means of control, in the enemy's methods of operation. Tactics and routine are poor bedfellows. This has been convincingly proved by the whole history of war and the development of the Soviet military art, particularly the experience of the Great Patriotic War. A creative approach to tactics is being graphically demonstrated nowadays, and was particularly evident during the 1981 manoeuvres and in many exercises carried out by troops of the Group.

In the meantime General Sir Nigel Bagnall was developing the concept of the Counter Stroke, a massive armoured attack against enemy troops that have achieved a penetration of the Main Defensive Position before they are able to take up a defensive position.

Against this background I had to think through my priorities for the year ahead. As the CRA's annual live firing period was scheduled for November I had time to learn the strengths and weaknesses of the Divisional Artillery before selecting the exercise aims. Knowing that the standards of gunnery were well above average, I decided that the development of artillery tactics and training would be a high, if not the highest, priority. Working closely with the three commanding officers, I started a series of Artillery Tactical

Notes that continued throughout my time as the CRA. The first explored the tactical development of gun batterys in either tight or dispersed gun positions, essential measures to improve survivability. The second tactical note provided four options to improve our ability to control artillery fire when more than one regiment was attacking the same target, while the next tactical note covered the control of fire during a divisional fire plan in support of a brigade Counter Attack or Counter Stroke operation. Subsequent tactical notes discussed the deployment of the artillery regiment Regimental Aid Post and the artillery support of HELARM (helicopters with anti-tank guided missiles) operations.

At the same time I set each regiment a project to consider. Lieutenant Colonel Mark Douglas-Withers and 47th Field Regiment were tasked to examine ways to overcome the 'stacking' of targets, a problem caused by too many demands for artillery fire to prevent the saturation of the defence when attacked by mass armour. The aim was to increase the response to calls for fire for a regimental target from one engagement every 3–4 minutes to an engagement every 1½ to 2 minutes. A procedure called 'Sequential Fire Missions' was developed and practised, and later successfully demonstrated to the whole of the 4th Armoured Division.

As I was concerned about the lack of realism for a gun battery when live firing (partly due to increasingly obtuse German range safety restrictions) I set Lieutenant Colonel Edmund Burton and 27th Medium Regiment the task of finding ways of making improvements. The importance of providing realistic training during live firing was well understood, but existing training facilities lacked the necessary capabilities to meet the needs of professional artillerymen. They developed the Field Battery Training Unit (FBTU) concept, a quite brilliant plan to construct a permanent battery gun position at the Zabelshof observation post on Munsterlager ranges allowing both direct and indirect live firing as well as the firing of all other weapons in the battery.

The FBTU gun position offered scope for indirect fire and direct fire dial sight engagements under NBC State HIGH; small arms training; using electronically controlled targets from the gun position and on a skirmishing range; anti-tank firing using Carl Gustav and 66 mm LAW (with both sub-calibre and practice rounds); All Arms Air Defence Weapons from the Abbot and M109 self-propelled guns and FV432 vehicles against remotely controlled targets; battle simulation of small arms, counter-battery fire and chemical weapons, together with a variety of other activities, such as casualty simulation, ammunition re-supply, and the employment of reservists and battle casualty replacements. This enabled battery commanders to exercise and train their detachments, technically and tactically under real pressure.

The range was built and in use within three months of the statement of requirement and has since been extensively improved. The rapid and effective response was made possible by the personal support of Colonel Rottlander, the Commandant of the Munsterlager Training Area, Lieutenant Colonel Steber, his senior staff officer, and the combined efforts of the 27th Medium Regiment planning team and the British range liaison staff, who developed the essential range safety procedures in parallel with the construction work.

The FBTU developed into a unique and important training facility designed to form the culminating component of every field battery's annual live fire training programme. The training options available were comprehensive, addressing the needs of command posts, logistic teams and gun detachments. The real strengths of the facility were based on its realism and flexibility. The exercise controller could increase the pressure by introducing additional activities, such as battle casualties, refugees, in-coming fire and incursions onto the gun position, during the execution of live-fire plans and fire missions. This build-up of concurrent activities placed significant pressure on junior commanders to establish priorities, providing experience and self-confidence in their ability to make sound decisions under stress. A visiting German army officer observed that the realism of this demanding training would be beyond the capability of his army.

The development of this tactical thinking progressed throughout the year, but this story must now return to the spring of 1983 and the customary series of command post exercises. In all command post exercises, it was normal for at least two levels of command to be exercised, and this almost always included the corresponding Royal Signals units. Thus the Divisional spring command post exercise, Exercise Main Brace, would normally have the three brigade headquarters with their Signals Squadrons plus the divisional headquarters and its Signals Regiment as players, all deployed fully tactically, moving every twenty-four hours. In this case the lower controls (LOWCONs) provided by battle group headquarters and the higher control (HICON) from corps headquarters would normally be static and work from a carefully planned battle events list. As CRA and part of Headquarters 4th Armoured Division, I would expect to be a 'player' on divisional and corps command post exercises, a LOWCON on NATO and army group command post exercises such as Exercises Able Archer and

Wintex, and a HICON on brigade command post exercises. This totalled around six weeks in the field during the spring and early summer. At this stage Major (later Lieutenant Colonel) Tim Stokes arrived to take over as my chief of artillery logistics and garrison matters.

The command post exercises were always extremely realistic and, as they were usually a rehearsal of the real war plans, including nuclear release and firing procedures, all exercise papers and radio messages were classified SECRET. Locations were close to planned wartime headquarters positions, providing very realistic training for headquarters staffs and the signals units. For us the most important and demanding command post exercise was the annual 1st British Corps Exercise Summer Sales, held in July. It was both testing and demanding, with careers able to fail after a poor performance. It was the only time I ever saw senior Royal Signals officers panic en masse!

The November 1983 NATO Exercise Able Archer included the practice of nuclear weapon release procedures (as it had done for several years) but the politico/military tensions at the time were such that the Soviets interpreted their monitoring of the exercise as NATO going to war. They ordered the Warsaw Pact forces to war readiness and to deploy to emergency dispersal locations fully armed. Fortunately a Third World War was averted, as US and UK signals intelligence identified the Soviet deployments, halted Exercise Able Archer and used diplomatic channels to reduce the tension.

The Divisional Headquarters had two identical field headquarters, known as 'Main' from which command was being exercised, and 'Step-Up' which, having been the previous 'Main', was on the move to, and setting up in, a new location. Both headquarters consisted of eight AFV 432 tracked armoured command vehicles parked back-to-back, with a light-proof rain-resistant canvas shelter joining them together with a corridor. When under attack they could continue to operate, although with difficulty, with their rear doors closed. The functions (in approximate order of importance) of these vehicles were: Operations, Plans, Artillery Operations, Intelligence, Engineer Operations, Artillery Intelligence, Army Air Corps Operations and Signals Operations. Logistics and Flank Liaison Officers were normally just outside the main complex but well within the closely protected and wired area. Radio Village, the site of all the radios and their masts, was normally on high ground within two miles distance. In addition, there was a small commander's tactical headquarters based on four AFV 432 tracked armoured command vehicles arranged in a cruciform, of which I was a part.

I also ran my own Divisional Artillery Command Post Exercises held every two months in one of my regiment's barracks in such a way that the exercise could be stopped, issues discussed face to face, and then resumed. These were high tempo occasions to practise artillery decision-making processes and divisional fire missions, with the commanding officers and battery commanders under pressure needing to develop all their skills to cope with a fast-changing situation. The exercises paid off handsomely for we became always the master of every situation however complex.

My first six months as CRA were spent not only taking part in many command post exercises and developing artillery tactics, but also getting to know my regiments by visits to see them in barracks and in the field. During 1983 nearly half of the batterys deployed with their battle groups to train at BATUS in Canada, and I wanted to see as many as possible towards the end of their work-up training. At the same time I had many duties to perform in getting to know the twenty-three major and minor units that comprised Herford Garrison. With more than 2,500 soldiers and over 3,000 dependents there was much to do. I felt that the garrison should have an indoor heated swimming pool rather than only a large open-air fire fighters' water tank in which the soldiers were allowed to swim in hot weather, but my efforts came to nought. So I settled on a less ambitious project, the provision of a bookshop. It may seem incredible but at this time there were only two English bookshops in the British Army of the Rhine – one at the München Gladbach headquarters 120 miles to the west, and a very small bookshop at Hohne, 95 miles to the east. Thanks to the efforts of Major Tim Stokes, any number of difficulties were overcome and the bookshop was opened with a fine selection of books, and soon drew visitors from many miles around.

During the spring we had given much thought to the survivability of gun positions, knowing that Warsaw Pact forces with both Hind 'D' attack helicopters and large numbers of fighter ground-attack aircraft could find and destroy our gun batterys that would be mostly sited on the eastern edges of towns and villages. The key seemed to be the construction of a dummy gun position just a few hundred yards to the east (the normal direction of air attack) of the real position that would be entirely plausible and realistic to a pilot, causing him to release his weapon load before spotting the more professionally camouflaged real gun position. As the practice developed, usually under control of a sergeant, each gun's ammunition vehicle carried enough poles, pegs, camouflage nets, a tent and a length of plastic drain pipe to make a dummy gun. As soon as these vehicles, normally the six-wheeled high mobility Stalwart, had unloaded their ammunition, they would race off to lay out the dummy gun position. These proved highly effective and I soon found the soldiers displaying all sorts of initiative to improve them, even scrounging old field cookers that, once lit, provided a realistic thermal signature. While I was observing one exercise the senior Master Gunner in Germany came to tell me that the guns of 27th Medium Regiment were poorly camouflaged. I told him to take me to the battery that he had criticised. He strode menacingly to the nearest gun, stooped under the camouflage net and stopped dead. The concept was so cleverly implemented that he had been deceived from a distance of just a few yards.

By early summer my priorities for my CRA's annual firing camp in November had firmed up. Exercise Four Square would start with a non-firing exercise to include the full preparation of main gun positions and a simulated ammunition out-load, then contain best battery and best observation post competitions, and finally have a four-day live firing exercise.

But first, after summer leave, came the autumn 4th Armoured Division Field Training Exercise (FTX), Exercise Quarter Final that, as ever, was held in the operational area to the east of Hameln. The complete division took to the field in what proved to be a very wet period. Brigade level training occupied the first two weeks and included a very interesting experiment. The operational area consisted of steep-sided well-maintained forests with many foresters' tracks, wide enough for a tank to move easily, that stood over east to west valleys two to four miles wide and containing small towns such as Sibbesse, villages such as Nette and many substantial farm complexes. All of these were fronted by impenetrable minefields and covered by long range anti-tank guided missiles: for the enemy it represented a difficult task. Although all the forest tracks would also be mined, it had been considered relatively easy for Warsaw Pact tanks to simply drive through the forest, smashing the trees to the ground as they went. We were allowed to drive our tanks through various sections of the forest with both mature and young trees. In every case the tanks had no problem for the first thirty or forty yards but as the felled trees collapsed forward on to the next trees they gradually piled up against each other, and the tanks bellied on the larger trunks.

The final ten days of the FTX was a divisional exercise in which Warsaw Pact forces, played by the 1st Armoured Division reinforced by brigades from other NATO nations, attacked first our brigade-sized Covering Force and then our two-brigade Main Defensive Position (MDP), allowing the

Covering Force brigade to recover and be reconstituted for further operations. These were specifically to practise the Counter Attack and Counter Stroke operations in the development of new tactics and in preparation for the large exercise scheduled for 1984.

A most interesting demonstration took place as a direct result of the official MOD report of the Falklands War that highlighted the total lack of awareness of the effects of the firing of both Rapier and Blowpipe air defence missiles. When Rapier, in particular, was launched, such was the noise that many soldiers thought they were under artillery fire. The Commander 1st British Corps, Lieutenant General Sir Martin Farndale, arranged for two Royal Air Force transport aircraft to take around 160 senior officers from BAOR to the missile firing range in the Outer Hebrides to watch missile firings, normally always from a concrete bunker two hundred yards behind the firing point. On arrival we were told that special dispensation had been given for two senior officers at any one launch to watch the firing from the missile launcher. As we approached the missile launcher, we all noticed two chairs no more than six feet away from the launcher. General Farndale grabbed my arm saying that we would be the first (ever) to be so close to a live missile launch. The remaining officers retired to the safety bunker while I watched nervously for the target towing aircraft and then the much smaller target, knowing that all my friends in the bunker would be watching my every move on the TV screens. As the target reached the engagement area there was, just to my right, the loudest explosion I have ever heard as the missile ignited, and I felt that I had probably jumped a good foot off my chair in shock. The missile destroyed the target and so General Farndale and I returned to the bunker to receive the debrief and watch the engagement film. As the recording countdown reached zero I cringed lest the film should show my leap off the chair in fright. Happily, and to my surprise, my bottom remained motionless, stuck firmly to the chair. It was an incredible and most unusual experience.

Exercise Four Square took place on the Soltau Luneberg, Hohne and Munsterlager South training and live firing areas from 15–25 November 1983, a period of heavy rain and intense cold. Fortunately I had designed the exercise in such a way that everyone worked flat out for the whole period. Every battery deployed with eight guns and several infantry Mortar Platoons were fully integrated into the exercise. I had also included some novel training ideas to stimulate and maintain interest. The first three days were centred on the complete 4th Divisional Artillery digging in, including Regimental Headquarters and Regimental Aid Posts, with the full range of dummy gun positions deployed and with a simultaneous divisional command post exercise. 19 Squadron Royal Corps of Transport brought 1,000 pallets of SIMMO (simulated ammunition) which they delivered both to Ammunition Points (AP) and to the Chinook helicopters for direct supply to the gun batterys, allowing the gun detachments to gain experience in handling vast tonnages of ammunition. The Divisional Artillery then did a night withdrawal under radio silence to a new Main Defensive Position.

Next came the Best Battery and Best Forward Observation Officer competitions. The former was judged on a deployed gun position with teams of specialist instructors testing every possible military skill. The latter also included the Advanced Posts (AP) from the Sound Ranging Troop and Listening Posts (LP) from the Counter Mortar Troop and included digging in and a range of technical tests. I noted at the time that the bombardier-led APs and LPs were all remarkably professional.

The final four day live firing period was based upon the planned sequence of events in the case of a real Warsaw Pact forces' attack with divisional fire plans and many divisional targets. Throughout, 57 Locating Battery were deployed as enemy, tasked to find the gun battery locations using their Sound Ranging and Drone Troops. Many soldiers had the chance to fire machine guns against model aircraft. But I also wanted to enhance the usual casualty evacuation procedures.

During each morning and each afternoon, an exercise control team visited every battery gun position and every observation post to inflict carefully selected personnel and vehicle casualties. The former had to be treated and then sent to the Regimental Aid Post from which they were extracted to a reinforcement holding area. The vehicles (normally guns and observation posts, but also some command posts) were withdrawn to a simulated Armoured Reinforcement Unit also in the reinforcement holding area. Overnight both men and vehicles were returned to the battle via the Ammunition Points as battle casualty replacements would be in war. But here was the twist – no man or vehicle returned to his own battery, and in the case of personnel and vehicles from the Abbot Regiments, not even to their own regiment. After three days only the three commanding officers and the twelve gun battery commanders remained in their original positions; every one else was in a different battery or regiment. Yet the standard of training was so high that the most demanding live firing continued without any discernible difference. At the conclusion one commanding officer told me that despite not recognising a single voice on his regimental radio net, everything worked normally. All the soldiers thoroughly enjoyed the experience of joining another battery or regiment.

We returned to barracks after an active year. As ever people left and others arrived. We gained a new divisional commander Major General (later General Sir) John Waters, a cerebral infantryman who was totally in tune with the developing operational and tactical arts – he 'lifted' the headquarters within days. I received a new Brigade Major Royal Artillery, Major (later Lieutenant Colonel) Will Townend, and Captain Syd Simpson rejoined me to take over the new discipline desk in my headquarters. All eyes were now already focusing on Exercise Lionheart to be held in 1984, the largest exercise ever held by the British Army.

During these years the problems associated with terrorism in Northern Ireland remained, with regiments continuing to serve emergency four-month tours in the province. But there were also several attacks, some fatal, against the army in West Germany. For a very short time in 1983 I found myself as the target and, much to the amusement of our small son, we were told to have a machine-gun team in our kitchen covering the now firmly locked main gates of our house.

Christmas allowed us to invite our entire family to come to stay, making rare use of every corner of our vast house. As chairman of the 4th Armoured Division Ski Club, I was expected to spend ten days at the Divisional Ski Meeting held in Austria at Ischgl and Galtür. I raced in the Downhill, down a horrifyingly steep course and in the fifteen-kilometre individual cross-country races.

In April 1984 21 (Gibraltar) Air Defence Battery armed with twelve Blowpipe short range air defence missile systems mounted on Spartan light tracked armoured vehicles arrived in Germany and joined 47th Field Regiment. Another tactical note was issued to say that these weapons systems would mostly deploy to protect armoured counter-attack forces when on the move. In another reorganization the four Royal Horse Artillery Swingfire anti-tank batterys handed over their equipment and role to the Royal Armoured Corps and then moved to Paderborn to amalgamate with the 25th Field Regiment. The latter was placed into suspended animation as 3rd Regiment Royal Horse Artillery rejoined the order of battle.

There was unprecedented activity in all the major headquarters in the 1st British Corps. We studied our potential enemy more closely than ever, both overtly and covertly. We knew that the Warsaw Pact had completed an underground communications system that allowed them to deploy and attack without a single radio switched on, that they had pre-positioned warlike stores in our areas for their Special Forces and saboteurs, that their senior commanders had driven their attack routes in the guise of East German truck drivers, and that their exercises indicated early use of parachute forces and chemical weapons against us, with tactical nuclear weapons used should their dash for the Channel be unduly delayed. To thwart the massed Soviet armoured forces, the Counter Stroke philosophy, already three years in development, was re-examined by Brigadier (later General Lord) Charles Guthrie then commanding the 4th Armoured Brigade in the 3rd Armoured Division. The essence of the Counter Stroke was to create shock action by the attack of our concentrated armoured forces into the flank of Soviet massed armour, either on the move or temporarily halted, thereby exploiting the weakness created when massed forces are disrupted with their command and control system put under extreme pressure. Major General Waters, tasked by the Corps Commander to comment on this new paper, passed it to me for an initial evaluation. My major concern was that we had yet to find a way of being sure that we could hold or delay a Soviet armoured thrust to allow our counter stroke force to attack its most vulnerable part (the middle, which would include the command and control elements). Timing was crucial and so additional artillery and HELARM needed to be allocated to this task. Subsequently, my work formed an important part at the Divisional Commander's study day just a few weeks before Exercise Lionheart.

As 1984 was to be a very busy year, my annual 4th Armoured Divisional Artillery live firing exercise was scheduled for April. Exercise Quadriga was a concentrated all-action three day exercise, quickly followed by the annual Corps artillery Exercise Sheldrake Spear. In addition to my own three regiments I had a Heavy Regiment with M107 175 mm guns. My exercise aimed to improve the use of the Divisional Artillery by using the 1983 Option Plans that allowed Battery Commanders and Forward Observation Officers to fire batterys and regiments other than their own, and also to allow each Commanding Officer to practise a divisional fire plan for a Counter Stroke operation. The exercise also included two divisional artillery night moves, the whole range of target acquisition devices, manoeuvre of guns within a large gun area, line laying and deception (or dummy) positions.

But the highlight was a live firing demonstration at Zabelshof on Munsterlager ranges of divisional fire missions using the newly developed 'Sequential Missions' procedure to 250 officers and senior ranks from the 4th Armoured Division. A tactical picture was painted of a Warsaw Pact division advancing rapidly astride a road leading to the audience position. The Divisional artillery of ninety-six guns engaged six targets in nine minutes, each with three shells from every gun. Everyone then entered the Zabelshof bunker for a final engagement just ninety metres to the front. It was an impressive demonstration of accurate, timely and devastating fire power.

There was no let-up in the high pressure life of Cold War soldiering, but the next event was one of great pleasure as Her Majesty the Queen honoured the Royal Artillery in Germany by spending 22 and 23 May with the regiment. The events were organised by Major General Guy Watkins in his capacity as the Major General Royal Artillery at Headquarters 1st British Corps but hosted by General Sir Tim Morony — the Master Gunner — and also attended by the Director Royal Artillery, Major General Bill Cornock. Her first engagement was to attend a dinner for the more senior Gunner officers and their wives hosted by Lieutenant General Sir Martin Farndale where I was lucky enough to sit opposite Her Majesty and enjoy a fascinating conversation.

At the time there were fifteen Regiments of Royal Artillery in Germany and all were on parade next morning, less six batterys on exercise in other parts of the world. At 10.15 Her Majesty arrived on parade to take the salute and inspect this huge array of guns and missile launchers, over five hundred mostly tracked equipments on parade. Along with the other Commanders Royal Artillery and the Deputy Commander of the Artillery Division, I stood in front of the ninety-six guns of the 4th Divisional Artillery. The drive past was epic — a terrific roar of powerful engines and an unexpected deepening of the furrows caused by so many tracked vehicles in the grass sports fields that almost resulted in the last few guns bellying as they passed the Queen. Lunch with the Warrant Officers and Sergeants, which Ann and I also attended, came next, followed by a walk-about with equipment and other displays. Finally, we attended a Regimental Dinner for all the Gunner officers then stationed in Germany. It had been a memorable two days.

But the hectic life continued with the normal annual range of command post exercises, this year very much sharpened up as the huge Exercise Lionheart approached, with Exercise Javelin acting as a CPX rehearsal. At the same time my three regiments were training hard with five of their batterys deploying to BATUS in Canada.

Exercise Lionheart held in September 1984 in the operational area east of Hameln was the largest British Army exercise ever held since the Second

World War, with 131,000 British troops (plus thousands more NATO soldiers) exercising over 3,700 square miles. The deployment included thousands of regular units, Territorial Army units and army reservists from the United Kingdom. It was very much a political demonstration of the United Kingdom's resolve, as well as an exercise to demonstrate the nation's ability to reinforce the 1st British Corps rapidly and then fight a complex battle in depth. It was a clear warning to the Soviets that they would face a determined and active NATO should they attack the West.

The reinforcement phase, Exercise Full Flow, started on 3 September with its peak on 15 September as the Territorial Army units moved to Germany. Many reservists joined my regiments, in most cases having never seen them before or even trained for several years. The very efficient Territorial Army units quickly assumed the roles for which they had trained for many years, none more so that the Honourable Artillery Company stay-behind OPs and the Forward Observation Officer parties from 307 (South Notts Hussars Yeomanry) Battery RA (TA) who provided the third OP party for each of my batterys. Meanwhile we had been in the field since early September preparing our positions, checking plans, reconnoitring routes, digging defensive positions, laying the huge barrier minefields, preparing demolitions, outloading ammunition, fire planning and completing the confirmatory orders procedures. All these events were under strict radio silence.

The player formations were the 4th Armoured Division in the Main Defensive Position with the 3rd Armoured Division on the right flank, and the UK based 2nd Infantry Division (mostly a TA formation) in the rear area security role. Within the 3rd Armoured Division 6th Airportable Brigade with almost a hundred Milan anti-tank guided weapons was a fast helicopter deployable brigade while the 19th Infantry Brigade was a ground-holding brigade and their third brigade (4th Armoured Brigade) was identical to the three armoured brigades of the 4th Armoured Division. The umpire and control organization was provided by the 1st Armoured Division. The enemy, consisting of armoured divisions from German and Dutch forces reinforced by some Americans, was under tight control (whereas we had free play) and attacked at first light on 18 September to meet a Covering Force consisting of two armoured brigades, the 20th and 4th.

In the meantime there were scores of VIP visitors but none more amusing to my regiments than the United Kingdom and West German Ministers of Defence, Michael Heseltine and Manfred Wörner respectively, the latter having been a fighter pilot. They wanted to visit a fully dug-in

M109 155 mm howitzer battery of 27th Medium Regiment and I was told to be there to host them. Having sent the grid reference of a suitable landing site by the gun position, I waited and then spotted the ministers' German Air Force helicopter heading towards me. Suddenly it veered away (despite my waving) to the adjacent deception or dummy gun position, causing me to run the 400 yards to the landed helicopter. I explained to the ministers that they had landed in the wrong position, only to be told by minister Worner that as a former fighter pilot who had been in the co-pilot's seat he knew what he was doing and had landed by the gun battery. He soon realised that he had been cleverly deceived and moved to the real gun position, admiring the very clever layout and camouflage. As he left he told me that the Bundeswehr would adopt deception immediately.

The Covering Force battle proceeded as planned for some thirty-six hours before the enemy forces probed the Main Defensive Position with its huge minefields to slow them down allowing us to attack them with fire. After two days of heavy fighting the numerically superior enemy armoured divisions achieved some breakthroughs (just as planned) to allow the depth forces to have a battle.

This was the first exercise on which the new Tracked Rapier air defence missile system deployed with us. As they were designed to work well forward with the armoured battle groups, their battery commander spent most of his time with my headquarters to ensure that proper coordination was achieved. But the time had now come to demonstrate that the Counter Stroke manoeuvre would work and perform its task of massive destruction of the enemy breakthrough, and the 11th Armoured Brigade was the first to perform this difficult task. As I had suggested some months earlier, the devil was in the timing: not only did a Counter Stroke operation need to strike the flank of an armoured thrust, but we learned that even highly mobile armoured forces take time to launch such a complex operation. But all our technical artillery training over the previous two years paid off handsomely, as our regrouping procedures and fire planning proved well able to cope with the Counter Stroke.

As the exercise moved into its second week, other armoured brigades practised the Counter Stroke until the enemy forces were sufficiently weakened allowing a general advance to regain all the lost territory. This phase of the exercise involved a difficult crossing of the 'water sandwich' on to the Hohenegg Plain. Interestingly the regular stay-behind Observation Post parties from 32nd Regiment Royal Artillery, deployed high up on the huge chalk mounds in the area, provided vast amounts of accurate information on the enemy forces. As the exercise ended the more senior officers attended a series of 'wash up' conferences while the soldiers worked their way round the various positions occupied in recent days to fill in trenches and repair damage, and the Territorial Army and reservists soldiers hurried back to the United Kingdom to be in their various places of work on the coming Monday morning.

It had been a most satisfying exercise. My own headquarters and all parts of my 4th Armoured Divisional Artillery had performed magnificently and this was widely recognised. The demanding and imaginative training had paid dividends and raised individuals' self-confidence. At a higher level the inspired new operational tactics had worked well, as had the flow of reinforcements and the logistics. The message to the Warsaw Pact was a very clear one – you tangle with us at your peril. However, as an informed insider I knew that while we would defeat the Warsaw Pact First Echelon Forces of 3rd Shock Army, defeat of their Second and Third Echelon Forces, who would probably use chemical and possibly nuclear weapons, would be a very much harder task.

My Divisional Commander called me aside to tell me that I was required fairly urgently for a new post in the United Kingdom, a move that would reduce my tour by three months. As Exercise Lionheart had just ended successfully, I felt that I had in effect finished my tour on a high and a move earlier than planned was acceptable. So a few weeks and over a hundred confidential reports later I departed Herford. Fortunately, I was able to take Bombardier Brown with me to continue his duties as my driver.

CHAPTER 12

Commander Royal Artillery – the Second Time

H EADQUARTERS UNITED KINGDOM LAND FORCES (HQ UKLF) at Wilton had made a decision in the early 1980s that all their arms head-quarters such as Headquarters Royal Artillery would be moved from Wilton. Thus the Brigadier Royal Artillery (BRA) at Wilton was moved to Larkhill to become a Commander Royal Artillery (CRA), and retitled Commander Royal Artillery (South) to distinguish him from the CRA 2nd Infantry Division in York. With the return to the United Kingdom of the 2nd Infantry Division in 1982 to York, their CRA with his Air Defence deputy assumed responsibility for most UK based Air Defence and Territorial Army units that were designated 1st British Corps reinforce-ments. Subsequently another decision was made that the rusticated UKLF Arms Commanders would have a dual role. My new task as the Commander Royal Artillery (South) was to take over that role at Larkhill from Brigadier Trefor Jones and then move with my staff to Aldershot in December 1984 where I assumed the additional responsibility of Com-mander Aldershot Garrison from Brigadier Tony Clay with the existing Aldershot staff.

I spent no more than a week working at Larkhill as my new staff packed up the headquarters ready for the move. Major (later Lieutenant Colonel) Johnny Howard-Vyse, a member of my Battery in Detmold ten years earlier, took over as the Brigade Major Royal Artillery (BMRA) as we arrived in Aldershot. The United Kingdom Gunnery Training Team (UK GTT) under Lieutenant Colonel Tony Kingaby, another old friend from Gütersloh days, consisted of four instructors in gunnery and four assistant instructors in gunnery led by Warrant Officer 1 (Master Gunner) David Reid and was part of my new headquarters. Their role was gunnery instruction for all UK-based field artillery units including both the Territorial Army units and the University Officer Training Corps Artillery Troops.

I then went to Aldershot to take over as Commander Aldershot Garrison from Brigadier Clay, and in an instant the Ministry of Defence had saved one brigadier's pay as well as ensuring that he would be working all hours of the day and night! I combined the roles of Commander Royal Artillery (South) and Commander Aldershot Garrison with two entirely separate staffs from December 1984 until January 1988. As the Commander Royal Artillery I had three major roles. The first was as a staff branch of Headquarters United Kingdom Land Forces, responsible for the provision of special to arm artillery inputs to all command and staff matters. The second task was for the technical supervision of all training and artillery special to arm matters for the Royal Artillery Field Regiments stationed in the UK or training anywhere in the world, except for those based in West Germany as part of BAOR.

Following soon after the Falklands War, a tri-service planning head-quarters for Out of Area Operations (OOA) was established in Aldershot and called the Permanent Planning Group (PPG) of Joint Force Head-quarters (JFHQ). It reported to one of three potential Joint Operational Commanders (JOCs) under which the Major General Royal Marines (MGRM) commanded a division-sized force usually consisting of 1 Infantry Brigade, 3 Commando Brigade and 5 Airborne Brigade. The third role had the CRA and his staff as an integral part of this headquarters. As a result, with my staff I took part in the conceptual developments and planning, with training exercises in all parts of the world in this role, and ran specialised artillery live firing exercises.

As the CRA I reported to the Commander UK Field Army, Lieutenant General (later General) Sir John Akehurst based at Wilton. The regiments for which I had immediate responsibility, but not command, were 7th Parachute Regiment Royal Horse Artillery in Aldershot with the 105 mm Light Gun, 26th Field Regiment Royal Artillery on Thorney Island near Portsmouth with the 155 mm FH70 towed howitzer, 29th Commando Regiment Royal Artillery in Plymouth with the Light Gun, 45th Field Regiment at Colchester with the FH70, 94th Locating Regiment at Larkhill which included 5th (Gibraltar) Field Battery and 22nd Locating Battery, and the Gibraltar Regiment with the Light Gun. The Allied Mobile Force (Land) [AMF(L)] multi-national artillery component was commanded and run by 94th Locating Regiment and included 5th (Gibraltar) Field Battery as one of its eight gun batteries. This organization had several operational roles mostly on the flanks of NATO and exercised usually but not exclusively in Norway, Denmark, Greece and Turkey. Both 7th Parachute Regiment Royal Horse Artillery and 26th Field Regiment Royal Artillery included Blowpipe short range air defence guided missile units.

My task as Commander Aldershot Garrison was entirely different. There were over a hundred units in Aldershot of which more than forty were under my full command. Included in this disparate collection were the Headquarters and Training Centres of Airborne Forces, the Army Catering Corps, Royal Army Dental Corps, Queen Alexandra's Royal Army Nursing Corps and the Army Physical Training Corps; and a wide variety of units ranging from the Cambridge Military Hospital, Louise Margaret Maternity Hospital, a Women's Royal Army Corps Company, a Provost Company, a Workshop, Catering Centre and Ordnance Depot to a Royal Military Police Riding School, the Army's main sporting facilities and various TA units. More unusual units in my command were the Defence Land Agents organization run by Robert Sermon, the Royal Army Veterinary Corps headquarters run by Brigadier Andrew Parker-Bowles, the prestigious Prince Consort's Library, the Aldershot Military Museum, the Cadet Training Centre, the Army Physiological Research Establishment and many more. In addition many of the other seven brigadiers in Aldershot also had units under command, for example 5 Airborne Brigade and the RCT Training Group.

Within Aldershot Garrison and the surrounding training areas and ranges, I was responsible for all matters other than operations and training for operations (excepting Home Defence operations). This included maintenance of the buildings and estate, training areas, welfare, discipline, sports facilities and married quarters. During the period a major task was the demolition of substandard post-war married quarters and their replacement and the planning/rebuilding of all the major barracks. Home Defence responsibilities were planned and trained jointly with Hampshire Constabulary, with Commander Aldershot Garrison taking over the area post nuclear strike.

To achieve all this I had an excellent staff of mostly retired officers run by the Chief of Staff Lieutenant Colonel Richard Cross of the Royal Highland Fusiliers. I reported to the GOC South-East District, Lieutenant General (later General) Sir Geoffrey Howlett who was also one of the three potential Joint Operational Commanders for my operational role as CRA.

All this was a sizable and extremely demanding task, one that exercised me to the full at a formidable pace of work. Not least I had to initiate or write on more than six hundred officers' confidential reports each year, and this meant getting to know all these young men and women sufficiently well to judge their success or otherwise and identify their potential. But in Warrant Officer 1 Savage, an outstanding soldier who had spent most of his life in the Parachute Brigade in Aldershot, I had as my Garrison Sergeant Major a man who knew everything there was to know in the local area and who as a bonus had been the Regimental Sergeant Major of 40th Regiment just before my period in command.

In January 1985 the fabric of the military facilities in Aldershot was a disgrace: the remaining Victorian buildings were in an advanced stage of decay while the 1960s 'Poulson', mainly concrete, structures were not fit for habitation. There had been almost no maintenance money for many years. The problem had been recognised and my predecessor had initiated the plans to build new soldiers' married quarters, but nothing had started. I also found that the military community was divided into three parts with an amount of antipathy between them. The elite parachute units of the 5th Airborne Brigade were the top dogs while the many logistic units cut a low profile and the medical services adopted a superior 'above the fracas' attitude. I judged this to be unhelpful and set about bringing the various groups together. While the single soldiers' accommodation was appalling, the married quarters were even worse. I spent one morning every month visiting three or four married quarters, usually spending thirty or forty minutes in each. These wonderful stoical families put up with disgraceful housing. On one early visit I firmly touched a recently repainted interior wall and my finger went straight through to the outside.

But as urgent as this was, my mind had to jump across to artillery matters, not least as I was to be heavily involved in the annual winter deployment to Norway. The 3rd Commando Brigade and the Allied Mobile Force (Land) (AMF(L)) both had operational roles in Norway, the former to hold the narrow Bardufoss area in northern Norway facing the Finnish 'wedge', the shortest route for Warsaw Pact forces to gain a much needed foothold on the Atlantic. I went first to Andelsnes to watch 29th Commando Regiment under Lieutenant Colonel John Andrews conduct their winter warfare training, and then to Hjerkinn on the edge of the Dovrefjell Mountains where the AMF (L) artillery headquarters led by Lieutenant Colonel Ian Forward and 5th Field Battery were also completing their winter warfare training. There followed live firing on the snowy Hjerkinn artillery ranges covering much of the wild and inhospitable Dovrefjell plateau where at night I saw the incredible Northern Lights for the first time. After a short period back in Aldershot to attend to my other duties I returned to Norway to observe the multi-national Field Training Exercise (FTX) in the Bardufoss area to the north. The British soldiers, some of whom had spent twelve or more consecutive winters in north Norway, were most impressive: they were hardened professional soldiers equal to or even more at home in the mountains in winter than the Norwegian soldiers. It proved an interesting exercise allowing me to study the advantages to be gained if one battery of 29th Commando Regiment had a medium gun with its considerably greater range. At the same time I explored the advantages for the air defence of the entire brigade if their small short range Blowpipe Troop was supplemented by a Rapier medium range air defence battery. In the event both weapon systems took part in a similar exercise the following year.

On return the Director Royal Artillery, Major General Bill Cornock, called to ask me to take over as the chairman of Royal Artillery football. My protests that I had been essentially a hockey player were quickly overridden and so in the time-honoured way I was told to 'get on with it!' Almost immediately I was asked to join the Army Football Committee. Thereafter I enjoyed getting to know many dedicated and skilful footballers.

In Aldershot I raced around meeting the various units of the garrison as well as the other Royal Artillery regiments for whom I had responsibilities. Although the impressive 7th Parachute Regiment Royal Horse Artillery commanded by Lieutenant Colonel (later Major General) Nigel Richards were located only a few hundred yards from my office, I saw them most often on sports fields where they excelled. The medical units justifiably took much of my time. Both the Cambridge Military Hospital and Louise Margaret Maternity Hospital were staffed by military personnel but accepted a high percentage of civilian patients in order that their consultants were not restricted to dealing only with fit young men and women. I also faced the task of writing the annual confidential reports of all the brigadier and colonel consultants, and there were many, a matter on which I had to take advice from the Director General of the Army Medical Services. To achieve this I had 'white coat days' when I spent much of a day with the Hospital Commandants (both were colonels) touring the hospitals to meet the staff at work. I also had 22nd Field Hospital, then the Army's only instantly ready field hospital trained for major surgery anywhere in the world. The Royal Army Dental Corps Training Centre ran a wide range of courses as well as performing the most advanced dentistry in the armed forces. The Queen Alexandra's Royal Army Nursing Corps Training Centre ran a full range of courses from recruit training upwards.

I found myself much in demand taking the salute at pass out parades, mainly but not exclusively for recruits. They were always impressive occasions as young men and women with as little as ten weeks' service put on a show for me and their parents and families whom I always met afterwards. I developed a series of speeches both to try to capture the moment and suggest that as far as their careers were concerned 'the sky really was the limit'. I took the salute at recruit pass out parades of the Parachute Regiment in Aldershot, the Royal Artillery at Woolwich and the Queen Alexandra's Royal Army Nursing Corps at Aldershot, as well as presenting the 'Red Beret' to Parachute Regiment soldiers on qualifying to wear it and aircrew wings to the Royal Air Force Air Loadmasters at Odiham. I found these occasions exhilarating.

By this time – late March 1985 – the first major OOA Command Post Exercise (CPX) was approaching. Exercise Purple Wave was to be a seaborne passage by 3 Commando Brigade for an amphibious landing on Jamaica, and then reinforced by further brigades. Joint Force Headquarters (JFHQ) formed up at Plymouth under the Commander, Major General John Grey of the Royal Marines, before embarking in HMS *Invincible*. Unfortunately, while the CPX was set in Jamaica, we were actually sailing out into the Atlantic and then towards Norway before returning to the English Channel. This was to be my first experience of the Royal Navy and I enjoyed it hugely. All of the members of the Army and Royal Air Force were kitted out with 'Red Sea Rig', the most comfortable of all military evening wear. The CPX was imaginatively run by Colonel (later Brigadier) John Holman and his team from the PPG. We used the six-day passage to 'bed down' as a headquarters and prepare for the 'war' before going ashore. We were encouraged to tour the ship and I found a spare seat on Commander Flying's bridge where I spent many hours watching the Naval and Royal Air Force Harrier aircraft practising deck take-offs and landings. Headquarters 3rd Commando Brigade went ashore in Hampshire (pretending it was Jamaica) allowing JFHQ to mount a helicopter transfer to HMS *Fearless* located much nearer the shore where we conducted the exercise for another two days before moving the headquarters ashore to command the land battle for a further week. As the CRA, I was running, with my small staff, the artillery and air defence battles within the land battle. Although only a CPX and with no fighting troops on the ground, this was joint operations at its very best – interesting, stimulating, dynamic, and quite remarkable teamwork by all those involved. It was the first of a series of ever more complex exercises.

A few weeks later Exercise Purple Venture at South Cerney and Hullavington provided the opportunity for the JFHQ team to exercise in a scenario involving a fly-in followed by land operations.

Assisted by the Gunnery Training Team I had formed a view on the strengths and weaknesses of the UK-based Royal Artillery regiments. They were very well trained although slow and also lacking experience in artillery operations above regimental level. I amended and reissued in a different format some of the Artillery Notes that I had written two years earlier. I started to introduce the concept of exercises involving more than one regiment, and I reintroduced the use of my stopwatch to time artillery drills and procedures. For the gun detachments I set a maximum time of thirty seconds to complete the 'Image Lost' drill when live firing. Considerable competition grew up to be the fastest and for several weeks 7th Parachute Regiment held that honour with twenty-eight seconds, until the Gibraltar Regiment burst on the scene with an unbelievable twenty-one seconds. From then on whenever I visited a regiment all eyes were on my hands to see when they reached for the dreaded stopwatch, but the advantage was the introduction of an impetus to do everything more quickly.

As the CRA I had a duty to arrange for each of my regiments to complete a CRA's exercise every year, but as these regiments were not under my full command there had to be discussions with the relevant brigade commanders. In the event they all wanted their artillery regiments to do a CRA's exercise and in general these were arranged to suit the circumstances of a busy life, but they were less complex and demanding than those I had run in the 4th Armoured Division. Within 29th Commando Regiment, 148 (Meiktila) Commando Forward Observation Battery, based in Poole alongside the Special Boat Service (SBS), had a very specialised role within the Special Forces organization. Every man, including a few Royal Navy signallers had passed both the full parachute and commando selection tests, the only personnel in the Armed Forces for whom this was a mandatory requirement. All were trained as artillery and naval gunfire Forward Observation Officer parties and as Forward Air Controllers. These skilled and fearless men routinely parachuted in the Arctic Sea or exited submarines to make covert shore landings, normally in conjunction with the SBS. In June each year I travelled to north-west Scotland to watch them exercise with the NATO fleet conducting live firing on to the Cape Wrath ranges. Staying in the isolated Cape Wrath Hotel I walked each morning the three miles across the heather to the white sands of Balnakeil Bay and then up to the Faraid Head observation post. Sitting on the cliff edge there was no more stirring sight than the fleet approaching over the horizon to engage targets just below my position.

I had instituted a monthly Garrison Commanders' meeting in Aldershot to which every single unit sent its commander or a deputy. There had to be a 'carrot' and this was supplied by Colonel (later Brigadier) 'Tank' Nash whose Aldershot Catering Group invariably supplied the most delicious cakes or snacks to be taken with the coffee. These meetings became surprisingly popular to exchange information, air grievances, put forward new ideas and generally make the Aldershot military town a better place in which to live and work. Attendance rose to seventy or eighty officers each month and resulted in many improvements. On one occasion an officer commented on how dull the military estate looked in the spring with not a single daffodil. A few months later I saw great teams of men planting bulbs and learned that 40,000 daffodils had been planted. While I winced at the expenditure, the effect next spring was dramatic beyond belief causing the Mayor of Rushmoor to complain that his borough's considerable efforts had been massively surpassed.

I learned that the five local mayors whose areas include the Aldershot Military Town and training areas (Rushmoor, Guildford, Waverley, Surrey Heath and Hart) all took office in the spring. So each year I invited them with their five chief executives to my mess for a welcome-in lunch as soon as they assumed their office. It allowed them to get to know each other and provided a valuable platform for discussions on civil/military relations.

Life continued apace. No sooner had I spent a few days in the field with 26th Field Regiment commanded by Lieutenant Colonel Charles Nisbet than the Gibraltar Regiment commanded by Lieutenant Colonel Eddie Guerrero arrived in England for their annual firing camp at Sennybridge. They were well trained and as keen as mustard. Remarkably, on exercise, every word from any official artillery procedure was spoken in perfect English, while everything else was spoken in Spanish.

Exercise Purple Victory was a 5 Airborne Brigade FTX held at Otterburn in the autumn. The Royal Air Force took the lead in this exercise. As only one army brigade was involved, my staff formed a small artillery cell in Joint Force Headquarters but I was not involved, it being deemed, quite correctly, that there was no need for a Commander Royal Artillery to be present.

Instead I applied myself again to Aldershot where I arranged the sale of the old abandoned and rat-infested NAAFI building to a consortium who used the valuable site for a car wash and burger bar. We welcomed in the contractors who started a build of over three hundred excellent semi-detached two-, three- and four-bedroomed married soldiers' quarters in the adjacent southern part of the military estate, and I had the huge but totally tree-obscured statue of the Duke of Wellington opposite the Prince Consort's Library cleared and cleaned to mark the centenary of its arrival from Hyde Park Corner so that for the first time for many years it could be admired from the main road.

I took a very close interest in the Parachute Regiment Depot and Training Centre commanded by Major David Roberts, in particular in 'P' Company which ran the uncompromisingly tough parachute selection tests. I felt that this fine organization could always be vulnerable to accusations of bullying. I tried to see them every month and over the three years I took part in all the 'P' Company tests except the milling (no-rules fighting with boxing gloves) and the aerial agility tests. The speed march over Pen-y-Fan in the Brecon Beacons covered by two feet of new snow against a clear blue sky was a wonderful experience, while the gruelling stretcher race saw young men taken to and beyond their physical limits. The final timed run was magnificently controlled by the test staff who used every possible encouragement to get their men through. I was full of admiration for the selection system. It must be added that although I passed all the tests in the stipulated times, I was only able to do so because I carried nothing other than a water bottle! However, I was able to note that test times for the Parachute Regiment soldiers were marginally longer than those for soldiers from other regiments, a policy that had to be corrected.

Within Aldershot I adopted the habit of changing from uniform into a tracksuit for a run, but a run with a difference. At the time there were no security fences (despite the IRA threat) and so I was able to run inconspicuously through any part of the military town as my instinct took me. It provided the opportunity to stop to talk to anyone I saw – soldiers, families and civilians – and learn about their lives and problems. For 90 per cent, sub-standard accommodation was the main problem. I renewed pressure on those above me to bring forward modernisation. A junior minister from the Ministry of Defence appeared to see the soldiers' married quarters. The first dilapidated house I showed him he described as no worse than some of the council houses in his constituency, but backtracked a little when he learned that the occupant was a very highly qualified technician at the hospital laboratory. The second was a flat with huge damp problems that caused him to wince. But the *coup de grâce* was the third stop to see one of many quite appalling three-storey blocks with four flats on each floor. After a quick look round I took him to the master bedroom of a first floor flat where a carefully devised but covert playlet was put into operation. The wife told the minister that the walls were so thin that there was no privacy, at which stage the couple in the flat below staged a beautifully executed flaming row with every word clearly audible. As this subsided the couple in the bedroom above simulated some very passionate lovemaking with every groan and grunt clear for all to hear and imagine. The case was made and the decision taken to demolish this sordid estate within weeks, to be replaced with proper houses as our soldiers richly deserved.

One of my duties was chairman of the Aldershot Military Historical Trust. This organization maintained the military history of the area and ran the Aldershot Military Museum, one of eleven small military museums in Aldershot all of which were in a financially precarious state. I was tasked with amalgamating them onto one site, but sensing this would prove impossible owing to the many vested interests, I played it as long as I dared in the hope that my tour of duty would end before any firm plans emerged, and thankfully exactly this happened.

In November I travelled to Gibraltar to spend a week with the Gibraltar Regiment. The highlight was on the Saturday morning when most of the population turned out to watch a battery fire its 105 mm Light Guns. The targets were smugglers' confiscated speedboats moored in the bay to be destroyed by direct fire. Every hit was roundly cheered, to the chagrin of the owners who had been brought from the jail to watch. I found the inside of the rock fascinating. I was taken on the special military tour, seeing tunnels and stores not open to the public, including the hospital operating theatre where my wife's parents would have conducted surgery should the normal military hospital have been moved into the safety of the rock in the Second World War.

Back in Aldershot, as my first year ended so many of the leading figures changed. Lieutenant General Sir Michael Gray became my superior while Lieutenant Colonel Bill Bale took over as my Chief of Staff. In Plymouth Major General Nick Vaux as the incoming Major General Royal Marines became my main operational boss in his role as the Joint Force Land Commander, while Lieutenant Colonel (later Major General the Reverend) Ian Durie took over 29th Commando Regiment. In Tidworth, my old friend from Sandhurst and Colchester, Brigadier (later General Sir) John Wilsey, commanded the 1st Infantry Brigade that included 26th Field Regiment. Captain Gavin Kilgour joined my staff as the GSO 3 Artillery Operations from a busy tour as the adjutant of 7th Parachute Regiment RHA. My last act before the Christmas break was to tour the two hospitals to see the staff who would be on duty. Exceptionally, I could not resist talking to a patient wrapped in bandages with both arms and both legs suspended from the ceiling in traction. I asked, 'What on earth happened to you?' The patient replied, 'I was cycling to work, hit by a car, and ended up in the hedge.' So I asked why he had come to the Cambridge Military Hospital rather than a local civilian hospital. He replied that when the ambulance crew arrived he said, 'Please take me to the Cambridge,' to which the para-medic responded that 'in your state we would not take you anywhere else!' Such was the reputation of this fine hospital, only to be closed and lost for ever owing to the dogma of our politicians.

The year 1985 had flashed by, but it had been one of enormous interest for me. On the wider world stage Gorbachev had assumed power to discover that the corrupt Soviet Union was unravelling faster than his control, through financial mismanagement and the overcentralised Marxist command economy. The events of 1986 convinced the Soviet leadership that their policies had to change. The Soviet Union was broke and could never win the Cold War. But that nation staggered on for another six years, during which NATO had to maintain the pressure, turning the screw ever tighter.

Aldershot's single soldiers' accommodation now became the focus of my attention. The modernization of Lille Barracks was underway but the huge Montgomery Lines, home to three battalions, was beyond redemption. The huts of Mons Barracks dated from the 1940s while the site of Connaught Barracks was empty except for the listed, near-derelict, officers' mess. I went to the government buildings' architects to see their first designs for a new Mons Barracks and a new Connaught Barracks, the latter subsequently being named Normandy Barracks. Although impressed by the plans, I was able to suggest some improvements. Glancing at an adjacent desk I noticed that the buildings were all interlinked by covered walkways, so my final request was that all the barrack blocks in the new barracks should have similar covered walkways joining them with the dining hall, gymnasium and junior ranks club. 'Oh, that's difficult,' said the architect. 'The plans you saw on that desk are for a new prison, and government policy is that prisoners and prison warders must not be exposed to rain, but for soldiers that does not matter!' This simple statement just about summed up the policies of successive governments towards our nation's foremost asset, the people of the military.

Suddenly I found that I was off to Norway for the annual winter warfare training. I stayed in Hjerkinn where there were elements of no fewer than four Royal Artillery regiments in training. As ever 29th Commando Regiment and the AMF(L) components of 94th Locating Regiments were there in full. The newcomers were an FH70 155 mm towed howitzer battery from 45th Field Regiment and a towed Rapier medium-level air defence battery from the 16th Light Air Defence Regiment. Both batterys were in Norway to exercise for the first time with the 3rd Commando Brigade to determine whether it would be advantageous to add them to the brigade order of battle. The main problem was that they had large and relatively immobile equipment when compared with the light vehicles of the brigade. On the other hand they could make an enormous increase to the fighting strength of the brigade. I arranged for the regiments to fire together for one day in a small CRA's exercise that proved useful. As always my instructors in gunnery (who were also required to be both winter warfare trained and proficient skiers) exercised supervision of the live firing as well as reporting discreetly to me. The highlight of the week was watching the 29th Commando Regiment Battery Commanders and Forward Observation Officer parties conducting an advance over the mountains on skis, some towing pulks (military sledges for carrying equipment), while live firing. At last light they adopted a defensive position overlooking a large bowl into which they would be using illuminating ammunition for night firing. In the meantime Lieutenant Colonel Ian Durie and I went to his regimental headquarters for a meal before returning to the bowl in an over-snow vehicle to watch the night firing. We left his vehicle a mile or so short of the first OP position to make a tactical approach on skis using the fantastic white, blue, yellow and green streaks in the sky of the Northern Lights to allow us to find our way. After watching the live firing we decided to ski back to his vehicle, but the Northern Lights had finished, it became pitch black and we simply could not find the vehicle. We were lost. In conflict with every well-known regulation for winter warfare training, we were not carrying a shelter or sleeping bag, nor food or a radio. For more than two hours we skied in a pattern trying to find our (or indeed any other) vehicle. Eventually, we heard a noise, the engine of our vehicle that the driver had switched on to keep warm. It was a salutary lesson.

Knowing that the life of a commanding officer living within the confines of his regiment for three months in an Arctic winter does not permit much relaxation, I took myself off to the ski resort of Oppdal (just south of Trondheim) having summoned each of the four commanding officers to spend twenty-four hours with me in turn. For me at least it was a most enjoyable break. Each commanding officer was asked to arrive at 6 p.m. in time for a relaxed dinner prior to a day of downhill skiing including a leisurely lunch with a departure after tea. I enjoyed their company and I think they all enjoyed the change.

After two weeks in Aldershot I returned to Norway for the multi-national Field Training Exercise (FTX) in which 3rd Commando Brigade, (now commanded by Brigadier (later General Sir) Robin Ross with whom I had been at the Staff College, would practise their defensive role in the Bardufoss area, to the north of Narvik. For the first time 3rd Commando Brigade had medium-level air defence cover which vastly improved the confidence that the brigade had of its survival against concentrated air attacks in the narrow valleys in which so much of their combat support was confined. The deployment of the medium guns was of the greatest interest to all. With a range approaching twenty kilometres they could be positioned well back near the logistics base yet cover the whole area. For the Forward Observation Officer parties they provided a huge boost to the available fire power. But there was a downside: it needed a troop of Royal Engineers to clear the deep snow just to allow the medium guns and their ammunition to move and then deploy. The inclusion of Rapier and the FH 70 in the Order of Battle was considered a success. A Commando Rapier Battery was raised to become an integral part of 3rd Commando Brigade. The question of medium artillery was more complex. As Brigadier Ross said afterwards, 'We want and need a 155 mm battery but not with FH 70, which is too big and cumbersome.' A case was submitted for a lighter 155 mm gun and after some years it was produced, but by then the Cold War was over.

On return to Aldershot there was much to do, not least visiting every unit, however small, to see the people and what they were doing, and help to solve their problems. Relations with both the police and Rushmoor Borough Council were excellent. The Mayor and Council of Rushmoor very kindly invited the Royal Artillery to receive the Freedom and so, on 2 May 1986, the Freedom of Rushmoor was accepted by 7th Parachute Regiment Royal Horse Artillery (then stationed in Lille Barracks) in the presence of the Director Royal Artillery and myself on behalf of the Royal Artillery. Superintendent John Snook, an ex Gunner, ran the Aldershot Police with a firm hand and constantly assured me that almost none of his problems were caused by our soldiers.

A few weeks later saw my largest live firing exercise on Salisbury Plain with three regiments taking part (7th Parachute Regiment RHA, 26th

Field Regiment RA and 29th Commando Regiment RA), in total fifty-four guns plus a large number of helicopters. I selected a scenario of a division-sized force landing on an island, the island being designated by the outer boundary of the Salisbury Plain Training Area. Two of the 155 mm guns of 26th Field Regiment plus two command posts were extracted from the Training Area to use more distant gun positions so that they could simulate Naval Gunfire Support. It proved to be an outstanding exercise with all three regiments firing quickly and accurately, including three complex and successful divisional fire plans. No fewer than four generals came to observe, sharing my view that the three Royal Artillery regiments earmarked for possible Out of Area Operations were trained and ready.

Next came one of the largest UK Home Defence exercises. I shared responsibility for North Hampshire with Chief Superintendent (later Chief Constable of Cheshire) Mervyn Jones. In the event of war he controlled North Hampshire with the Armed Forces in support (with me as the Armed Forces Commander) until the first nuclear strike on the United Kingdom. Thereafter, I was to assume responsibility for North Hampshire with the police supporting the Armed Forces. It was an interesting and challenging exercise during which we learned a great deal, as well as realising the huge challenges should the UK ever be attacked with nuclear weapons.

As the exercise ended it was time to go to sea again for another exercise in the Purple Wave series, this time in HMS *Illustrious* as part of the Joint Force Headquarters. We followed the now familiar pattern of a Command Post Exercise set in some distant part of the world with our division-sized force being inserted into the area of conflict by sea and air. As in the previous year we cross-decked to HMS *Fearless* some two hundred miles from the exercise area to command the forces that had landed, and then went ashore ourselves for another most interesting exercise.

My sea time increased further as a result of the Armilla Patrol, a standing Royal Navy deployment in the Arabian Gulf. For a few years the threat of an Iranian Silkworm guided missile attack (or similar) had resulted in a Royal Marines Blowpipe air defence guided missile detachment being attached to every destroyer or frigate serving in the area. When asked if the Army would take over this role I agreed immediately, on condition that I could satisfy myself that the Royal Artillery Blowpipe detachments from 26th Field Regiment were fully integrated into the Ship's company. So it was arranged that I would spend twenty-four hours aboard each ship during

1. The Regular Commissions Board at Westbury in April 1957. The author is number 27. Robert Hall (2) and Bob Hastie (4) also passed. All three joined The Royal Military Academy Sandhurst in August 1957

2. The Inter-Seniors Obstacle Race at Sandhurst, November 1958. From l to r: in the air, Musa Bin Mohammed, the author, Peter Dwerryhouse and Mohammed Al Ali; and on the ground Simon Lowman and Jack Carter

3. Training in West Germany 1963 – a typically tense scene in the battery command post Saracen APC during a fire plan. The author, right, takes down the fire plan by radio while the Command Post Officer Lieutenant Richard Kidner, centre, prepares for the adjustment of targets. The TARA, Gunner Briggs, left, turns to see if a copy of the fire plan is available. From this position the author could hear the radio nets, observe the command post computational procedures, supervise the six guns and control ammunition distribution

4. The mutiny of the 11th Battalion Kenya Rifles in January 1964. The author with his 'platoon' drives through the barracks for the second phase of the operation with a smiling Sergeant Williams

5. End of mutiny; the author rounding up mutineers shortly after the attack

6. *The J (Sidi Rezegh) Battery RHA gun position and echelon at Thurmier in the Radfan April 1964. From l to r: WO 2 Smith, Major Tony Stagg and Captain Tim Thompson. Both officers were decorated for gallantry in the succeeding months*

7. A heavy machine-gun detachment of the 1st Battalion The Federal Regular Army deployed in the rocky and mostly barren hills of the Radfan where daytime temperatures reached 50°C (120°F), enabling an egg to be fried in about twenty minutes, some butter having been put on a suitable rock. The author dressed exactly as these soldiers when serving with them. The sangar provided essential protection from enemy fire

8. The 1st Battalion The Royal Scots command post at the head of the Wadi Misrah in the Radfan in May 1964 during a tense night when a platoon fighting patrol had been ambushed. From l to r: Gunner Ramsay, the author, Lieutenant Colonel Hugh Taylor and the intelligence officer, Lieutenant Robert Watson. The application of timely and accurate artillery fire allowed the platoon to withdraw without casualties.

9. A typical village on the Bakri Ridge with terraced fields. As every village had been built for protection, the area proved challenging for British soldiers. All movement was by night to avoid snipers, the terraces proving difficult to climb silently.

10. *E Battery RHA in West Germany in a non-tactical leaguer in 1973 with the six Abbot 105-mm howitzers to the right. The author's command vehicle is marked by the double aerial pennants*

11. *A typical scene in Hobart Barracks Detmold in 1975 with the soldiers of E Battery RHA taking a break during maintenance. Lance Bombardier Smith (second from left in standing group) had just been awarded a decoration for his actions in Belfast the previous year.*

12. *Visitors to the E Battery RHA base in Blairs Yard in the Short Strand area of East Belfast in April 1974; from l to r: General Sir William Jackson (then Quartermaster General), the author and Lieutenant Colonel John Learmont, Commanding Officer of 1st Regiment RHA*

13. *The guns of E Battery deployed in the wide-open prairie of the training area in Alberta in May 1975. As evening approaches the shadows cast by the camouflage nets indicate the presence of the widely spread guns*

14. *NATO conference, February 1978. From l to r: General Franz-Joseph Schulze (Commander in Chief Allied Forces Central Europe), General Alexander Haig (Supreme Allied Commander Europe) and the author*

15. *As MA to CINCENT the author (centre with the briefcases) was a frequent flyer around the NATO area. With back to camera in grey jacket is General Franz-Joseph Schulze while facing camera are Air Chief Marshal Sir Peter Le Cheminant (Deputy Commander in Chief Allied Forces Central Europe) and Lady Le Cheminant*

16. *Edinburgh, March 1980. During the 40th Field Regiment recruiting tour the Lord Provost accepted a statuette of a Gunner before taking the salute at a parade in the city. From l to r: the author, the Lord Provost, Regimental Sergeant-Major Tom McSherry, Captain Steve Sanderson and the Lord Provost's mace bearer*

17. Colchester 1981 – the author mounts an FH 70 howitzer for a final drive through 40th Field Regiment

18. Exercise LIONHEART in September 1984 was both the largest Field Training Exercise since the Second World War and a demonstration of political will to the Warsaw Pact. Here the author wearing the grey NBC suit of the time shows Michael Heseltine, Secretary of State for Defence, a battery gun position of 27th Medium Regiment. Behind, immediately below the window, is Manfred Worner, West German Minister of Defence

19. The Royal Artillery Barracks Woolwich 1985. The author is accompanied by Lieutenant Colonel David Evan during a Pass Out Parade of new recruits of the 17th Training Regiment Royal Artillery

its final work-up training at Portland. My first experience was not a happy one as, amongst other horrors, I discovered that there were no communications links between the detachments on the aft helicopter deck and the ship's operations room, and the soldiers had been allocated only a campbed each in a passageway, in my view unacceptable for a six months' tour of duty in the tropics. These problems were quickly rectified and never occurred again in other ships. The Royal Artillery Blowpipe detachments continued to serve with the Armilla Patrol for some years and all thoroughly enjoyed the experience.

To counter the threat from Guatemala, there was a continuous military presence in Belize, normally a battalion group split between the airport and the disputed frontier. A Light Gun Battery was an integral part of the battalion group. In August 1986 I spent ten days with the battery, some of which was spent live firing on the Baldy Beacon artillery range, a high plateau above the tree line and richly covered in wild orchids. There was time to explore the thickly jungled frontier area and travel south to the company camp at Punta Gorda that was almost on the beach.

Next came a large airborne exercise on Salisbury Plain where I spent a couple of days with 7th Parachute Regiment RHA who were exercising with the 5th Airborne Brigade, followed by time with 26th Field Regiment. My aim was to observe the live firing from the observation posts, sometimes setting fire plans. I preferred to visit the gun positions when they were not firing live ammunition as this gave me more time to talk to the soldiers without causing them to be distracted. My gunnery instructors were always present for live firing. I found that I saw them more often in the field at some distant location than in their offices alongside mine in Aldershot. The officer instructors in gunnery (IGs) were to be found at the observation posts while the warrant officer assistant instructors in gunnery (AIGs) were always at the gun positions. A few days later I attended the University Officers' Training Corps (UOTC) King George VI Trophy competition between their Gun Troops equipped with the 105 mm pack howitzer. Each troop had to cross a start line to deploy into a previously reconnoitred gun position, fire at various targets, and then move to a new position. They were highly skilled, well drilled, very keen – in fact highly impressive in every way.

The next Out of Area Command Post Exercise Purple Venture took place in June in Cyprus. It was followed in the autumn by Exercise Safe Seria using the Royal Air Force base at Masirah as an entry point for a Field Training Exercise in Oman that included a battalion parachute drop mounted from the United Kingdom. We had no doubts that the United Kingdom was demonstrating to the world that its armed forces could deploy rapidly and in strength to any corner of the globe. As both these exercises involved less than a brigade of soldiers, Major Johnny Howard-Vyse took Headquarters Royal Artillery while I remained in Aldershot.

As 1986 drew to an end I was very pleased to open the first of the high quality new married soldiers' quarters in the southern part of the Aldershot military town. They were superb and just what our soldiers deserved. But this was just a beginning, the first few feet of a mountain of reconstruction that was so urgently needed. I had become concerned that we were failing to make full and best use of the tens of thousands of acres of valuable training areas that surrounded Aldershot. So Lieutenant Colonel Barney Cockcroft joined my team to conduct a study into how better use could be made. He took me to places that were under my jurisdiction of which I had no knowledge, and I saw that the under-exploitation needed to be addressed. This valuable work produced all sorts of good ideas but there seemed to be a mental block amongst the principal major units. In effect they felt that they could conduct serious training only when away from Aldershot.

The start of 1987 saw more changes with Lieutenant Colonels John Lewin and Mike Smythe assuming command of the 7th Parachute Regiment RHA and the 94th Locating Regiment RA/AMF(L) artillery headquarters respectively. I felt like a curse on Mike as this was the fourth time he had served under my command. This was to be a particularly active winter in Norway. It started with an invitation from Brigadier Robin Ross to spend a few days with his 3rd Commando Brigade headquarters in Lillehammer, with strict instructions to bring my skis. Knowing that Lillehammer was the centre for Norwegian alpine skiing, I arrived with my downhill skis only to be told that it was the cross-country skis that were required. Fifty kilometres later . . . I was a very tired man.

I moved on to the familiar training areas at Hjerkinn, going out each day onto the artillery live firing area covered in deep snow to watch both 29th Commando Regiment and the AMF (L), in particular 5th (Gibraltar) Battery. I observed the live firing exercises, including setting a few of the more complex fire plans. After some very professional firing on the ranges in snow deeper than for many years and with temperatures well below zero there was time for a pause prior to the Field Training Exercise (FTX) further north. The FTX took place in the very far north in the area between Tromsø and the border, well inside the Arctic Circle. The Light

Gun Batterys of 29th Commando and 94th Locating Regiments were outstanding. Men and guns operated on skis throughout, with the Forward Observation Officer parties coping particularly well in the mountains and valleys while carrying huge loads. Later I went further north to observe the Allied Mobile Force (Land) winter live firing on the Setermoen artillery range.

I returned to Aldershot for a very brief period to catch up with Garrison matters before embarking in HMS *Ark Royal* with the Joint Force Headquarters led by Major General Nick Vaux for Exercise Purple Wave, a Command Post Exercise. As ever the Permanent Planning Group (PPG) had organised a testing exercise, with a scenario depicting a problem in a far-off land needing a seaborne approach with an amphibious landing, later reinforced by air once a runway had been secured. The reality was five days in the western approaches followed by a transfer ashore via HMS *Fearless* to one of the old Napoleonic forts in Plymouth Harbour where the land battle was conducted in a very cold April. My Headquarters Royal Artillery was very well integrated, working particularly closely with the air cell run by Group Captain (later Air Chief Marshal Sir) William Wratten. His staff and mine worked closely both on fire support to the ground forces and on air space control where we generally exercised control of the forward battle in the divisional and brigade areas while his staff controlled the rest of the airspace.

While planning my annual visit to Cape Wrath I had a phone call from the staff of the Commodore Amphibious Warfare (COMAW), Commodore Jeremy Larkin, asking if I could be at Stornoway Airport on the Isle of Lewis at 0900 hours on the third Tuesday in June. When I replied in the affirmative I was asked to be equipped to spend three days at sea followed by up to a week on land on exercise. I flew into Stornoway early to be met by the crew of a Wessex helicopter from HMS *Fearless* with an immersion suit for me to don. We flew hundreds of miles out into the North Atlantic where the exercising NATO fleet stretched across the horizon. There followed two very interesting days at sea with Brigadier Robin Ross and Headquarters 3rd Commando Brigade, including 29th Commando Regiment, prior to a night approach and first light amphibious landing east of the Cape Wrath range. I flew ashore to the Faraid Head observation post where Lieutenant Colonel Ian Durie planned the fire support of both the fleet's guns and his own batterys that had come ashore a few kilometres to the east, plus air support from fighter ground attack aircraft flying in from some distant airfield. It was another demanding but most interesting exercise demonstrating 'jointery', as tri-service operations had become known.

Lieutenant Colonel Mike Smythe, commander of the artillery elements of the Allied Mobile Force (Land) as well as commanding officer of the 94th Locating Regiment, received his AMF(L) orders from the Headquarters of the AMF(L) in Heidelberg in West Germany. This included welding together eight separate national batterys under his operational control with usually three live firing exercises each year, of which one had to be in Norway in winter. One of the 1987 exercises was held in eastern Turkey on the Sarikamis artillery range close to the Georgian part of the Soviet border. I flew into Erzurum and then joined the AMF(L) artillery near Sarikamis, a town of 23,000 soldiers and, it was said, only 230 females. It was certainly not a place to holiday. I watched the live firing with great interest. While the British gunners were by far the most professional (as I would have expected) it was quite clear that they 'lifted' the standards of the other nations who sought to emulate them. And of course it was not lost on the Soviet Union that six nations had flown artillery batterys into their border region to train together.

I returned to England briefly before setting off for the Falkland Islands. There was no longer a battery permanently based there but the batterys for which I was responsible went there on a regular basis, partly to become acquainted with conditions on the island but mainly to train with the resident infantry battalion. I had left England in mid-August to arrive in mid-winter, and to discover that the Falklands tend to experience all four seasons roughly once each hour. Having spent two very interesting days watching the artillery live firing, I had chance to visit the permanent residents, in particular the Rapier air defence positions all of which seemed to be sited on the most exposed and coldest points of the southern hemisphere. But I also had to do some detective work in the knowledge that my Light Gun regiments were very short of gun sighting systems, particularly anti-tank telescopes. My suspicion was that all the spares had been sent south during the Falklands War and had never been returned. So I strong-armed my way into the Ordnance Depot (all previous requests from my visiting batterys having been refused) where I found haphazardly stored a large number of the missing items which, having at some stage lost their labelling, were just sitting on shelves. Their rescue more than paid for my trip.

My work in Aldershot continued apace with my efforts to foster improved cooperation within the garrison gathering effectiveness. Almost every military member of the garrison took part in the half-marathon run while my mess developed into an extremely lively community, marking much improved cohesion between the various units. Relationships with the local community thrived.

Exercise Purple Warrior in November 1987 was the largest Field Training Exercise in the UK for many years. Involving three brigades, several ships and a large number of aircraft, the exercise was the largest and most complex since the Falklands campaign five years earlier. As the CRA, my role with my headquarters as an integral part of Joint Force Headquarters (JFHQ) under Major General Nick Vaux was to command and control artillery and air defence support to the land operations. The airfield at West Freugh in Dumfries and Galloway was secured in a novel operational assault to allow further operations to commence after a swift build-up of forces. A live enemy had established themselves in Dumfries, Galloway and South Ayrshire, rugged hill country. JFHQ was flown in at an early stage to set up in a disused hangar at the West Freugh airfield from which we ran the 'war'. It was a demanding yet fascinating exercise that both confirmed the realism of the many CPXs that had preceded it, and showed that the UK could mount a tri-service operation quickly and efficiently. I was very proud to be a part of this team.

As the entire exercise had been conducted on private land as a goodwill gesture by Scottish landowners, my Aldershot Garrison Headquarters had been tasked with the organization of a Regimental Dinner on completion of the exercise to thank the landowners. Lieutenant Colonel Bill Bale took on this task with skill and imagination. The beautiful Culzean Castle on the South Ayrshire coast was hired, where the military hierarchy, all in full mess kit, entertained the landowners in the candlelit hall to a sumptuous dinner accompanied by the Army's most skilled pipers. As dinner ended, Moira Anderson, one of Scotland's finest singers, came to the end of the table to sing traditional Scottish ballads. The encores were such that a half-hour engagement extended well beyond an hour. I looked at our guests and very few had not shed tears, such was the place and the occasion. I stayed in the Adam Suite in the top of the castle keep, next morning to look out over Ailsa Crag and the Island of Arran – it had been a wonderful finale to five years as a Commander Royal Artillery.

Back in Aldershot I embarked on a long round of farewells, but not before I had a very curious visitor. My personal assistant had booked in a gentleman from British Rail but with no idea of the subjects to be discussed. A very pleasant young man duly appeared to explain that as the

British Army was British Rail's largest customer, he had come to see me on the direction of the MOD to learn what I thought of the service they provided. As I had hardly travelled on a train in years and had no knowledge of the service they provided to the military, I was completely stumped. After thirty minutes of verbal sparring, my visitor said that he had to return to his boss with something, so please could I just ask for anything. I blurted out without thinking that I would like to drive a high-speed train from London to Bristol and back. 'Impossible!' my visitor said, as I showed him to the door, to which I replied, 'Well, just try!' Some eight months later, by which time I was working in the MOD in London, my phone rang and this same young man asked if I could make platform nine at Paddington at 2.15 p.m. the next Thursday. I duly arrived on time where I was met with a large smile and introduced to the most senior of all high-speed train instructors. I sat in the right hand seat of the HS125 train all the way to Bristol Temple Meads with the train consistently travelling at 125 mph. The return by night was even more impressive. I learned a lot and never ever criticized our rail system again, having seen how close the margins are, and how dependent the train drivers are on the signalmen. The final high-speed night approach into London with a mass of lights ahead verged on the scary.

I had enjoyed the depth and variety of my work in Aldershot for three years as both a Commander Royal Artillery and Garrison Commander, but early in this period it became clear that the Commander Royal Artillery and his staff should never have been removed from Wilton, and so I had worked hard to have that decision reversed. I was also mindful that every brigade commander in the Army combined his brigade command with command of the local garrison, except for the Aldershot-based Commander 5th Airborne Brigade. In January 1988 I handed over my duties as Commander Royal Artillery to Brigadier (later Major General) Mike Tennant who with the HQRA team returned to Headquarters United Kingdom Land Forces at Wilton. Command of Aldershot Garrison was passed to the Commander 5th Airborne Brigade, Brigadier David Chaundler, who entrusted day-to-day Garrison matters to his deputy commander, a colonel, who worked closely with the Chief of Staff of Headquarters Aldershot Garrison. I was very sorry to say farewell, after seven years as my driver, to Bombardier Brown and his family but pleased that he joined my successor.

CHAPTER 13

Starting Training Simulation

G ENERAL SIR JOHN CHAPPLE was the Chief of the General Staff (CGS) in 1987 when he received a briefing on advances in technology with the potential to revolutionise Army training. Although the Directorate of Army Training (DAT) held the responsibility for the development of new training methods, General Chapple wanted a team to examine these technologies independently and in depth and produce a plan for their introduction. This was to be my next job, working in the Ministry of Defence in London, with a small team: Lieutenant Colonel Tony Clark of the Parachute Regiment, Lieutenant Colonel Chris Nind of the Royal Signals and my personal assistant, Sergeant Jan Corryer from the Women's Royal Army Corps.

The task split into two sections. Tactical Engagement Simulation (TES) allowed two-sided war fighting practice in which every soldier and weapon carried an eye-safe embedded laser firer and laser receivers linked to computers that allowed a totally realistic and authentic hit/kill or hit/disable chance, with the 'killed/disabled' soldier, tank, helicopter, etc. unable to continue in the battle. An infantryman could 'kill' another infantryman with his rifle but not a tank, although he could 'kill' an exposed crew member. A tank could 'kill' almost every target on the battlefield. Lieutenant Colonel Tony Clark was the project officer for TES.

Command and Staff Trainers (CAST) was the second task, with Lieutenant Colonel Chris Nind as the project officer. For many years the Army had two Battle Group Trainers that had later been enlarged to undertake the training of Brigade Headquarters (BBGT). They were located in old military buildings, one at Bovington in Dorset and the other in Sennelager in West Germany. A Brigade or Battle Group Headquarters would deploy close to the BBGT in which were located all the Lower Controls (LOWCONS) and a Higher Control (HICON) necessary to run a Command Post Exercise (CPX). But there was very little computer assistance and much reference to probability tables with a strong dose of military experience thrown in. The task was to introduce computer systems to allow more demanding, realistic and refined CPX training for head-quarters ranging from battle group up to corps.

We assembled in February and received an outline of the work completed so far by Colonel Brian Hamilton-Russell. Whereas the two Brigade and Battle Group Trainers (BBGT) were up and running, almost no work had been started on their upgrading and enlargement. A UK company, Centronics, had produced a simple laser system for TES by the name of ISAWES (Infantry Small Arms Weapons Effects Simulator) that was being used haphazardly mainly in recruit training centres, and with very little benefit to the army at large. Additionally the Royal Armoured Corps used, but had little faith in, a small number of SIMFIRE and SIMFICS systems.

Our first task was to learn what other armies were doing and to update ourselves on the existing and emerging technologies. Centronics had sold some of their TES systems to the military in Jordan and Singapore, and so I spent a few days with the Jordanian Army watching an Armoured Brigade battle in which impressive use was made of the TES systems. The US Army had used their MILES (Multiple Integrated Laser Engagement System) for several years. The most interesting development was an embryonic Swedish system from Saab, originally designed as an anti-tank missile training simulator but adapted to use a two-way laser that allowed an interrogation between attacker and target to provide total fidelity. This was quickly identified as the way forward for TES, a recommendation only accepted after long and sometimes fierce argument.

The time had come for the TES/CAST Team to make some serious visits, the first to the United States. In April 1988 we started at Headquarters TRADOC (Training and Doctrine Command) in a fine old citadel, Fort Monroe near Norfolk, Virginia for briefings, before going on to the US Army National Training Centre at Fort Irwin in the Nevada Desert, an area the size of a typical English county. We watched an armoured brigade in battle against a simulated Soviet-style force known as the OPFOR (Opposing Force) whose tanks and armoured personnel carriers were modified with plywood to provide a passable imitation of the existing Soviet vehicles. Every person, vehicle and most helicopters were equipped with a MILES system, each hit being marked by an automatic coloured smoke discharge. There was much filming and record taking of the various actions to allow highly organised and sometimes controversial After Action Reviews (AAR) to ensure that training lessons were well learned. It was a most impressive facility although we identified three major flaws: a lack of fidelity as a result of the one way MILES system; the lack of an area weapons effects simulator to enable artillery and mortar fire, minefields and aerial bombing to be included in the battle; and a tendency to stifle initiative owing to the AAR system forcing leaders to conform to doctrine.

We moved on to the Joint Readiness Training Centre (JRTC) at Fort Chaffee in Arkansas which, although similarly equipped, was organised for light-force training. We spent two days following a National Guard battalion through the snake-infested swamps and then watched it suffer badly during a poorly executed attack. But it was excellent training, thanks to their MILES systems and to the AAR process that really did mean that lessons were learned and then passed on.

In Florida we visited the University of Central Florida to see its specialist simulation faculty and the adjacent US Army Office for Simulated Training Development and Purchasing, and then moved on to MOD Canada for similar discussions. These visits proved of the very greatest value, and it has to be admitted that the opportunities provided to use spare time to experience the Gettysburg battlefield, Niagara Falls, Las Vegas and Disneyworld were accepted and enjoyed.

Our visits had alerted the MILES sales team that a MOD UK purchase was planned and so we found ourselves under considerable pressure to adopt their one-way laser system. But all our instincts pointed us towards the embryonic high fidelity two-way laser system that, although more expensive, would provide far superior training.

Our next visit was to the US European Command Training Centre at Hohenfels in Bavaria where a small but nevertheless valuable facility had been set up for the two US Corps based in southern Germany. They too had the MILES system and were making very good use of it, despite its limitations. This visit proved extremely valuable as, by chance, we were shown a new prototype training system called Simulated Networking (SIMNET) that networked hundreds of affordable simulators in real time to practise joint collective war-fighting skills. It consisted of a large number of wooden mock-ups of tanks, armoured personnel carriers and helicopters with their vision and weapon sights replaced by interactive monitors, all of which were linked in one battle with the ability to fire weapons in the normal fashion but with a computerised engagement outcome facility. Suddenly our concept for the future of training became clear: by linking this new SIMNET system to a new BBGT and to a TES facility it would be possible for a corps to be exercised with one division engaged in a TES exercise, a second division in a CAST training facility while a third division used SIMNET. Thus a corps headquarters could be exercised with all its divisions engaged in different kinds of simulated battles, but on the same piece of ground against a common enemy. This was exciting stuff.

Back in England the time had come to start talking to senior officers about the general direction of our thinking. The Commander UK Field Army, Lieutenant General (later General Lord) Sir David Ramsbottom, took a keen interest supporting our ideas. From time to time I would receive some thirty minutes' notice that General Chapple would drop in for an informal chat. He would sit on my desk and ask for a ten-minute verbal brief on what we had done and what our thinking was for the next stage of work. He always nodded agreement and gave encouragement.

So far CAST had taken a back seat compared with the TES study, but a breakthrough occurred when the US Army presented us with the complete software package for their equivalent developing system. Not only would this save a large amount of hard work, but it would allow interoperability on a grand scale. However, I had reckoned without the obtuse interference of the main MOD committee on information technology systems who, it seemed, were deeply affected by the 'not invented here syndrome'.

Sergeant Corryer was promoted and in her place I was asked to take Corporal (later WO 1) Jinder Parkes as my personal assistant. She came to the office to meet me and I could hardly ask her to join the team quickly enough for she was one of the most beautiful women I had ever seen, and charming with it. I could see that my two colonels were willing me to accept her. She was an outstanding personal assistant.

By the end of 1988 we felt that we had a fairly clear idea of the way ahead, although some firm evidence was required to support the emerging plan. Lieutenant General Sir David Ramsbottom agreed that all the existing ISAWES should be pooled for a Field Training Exercise on Salisbury Plain in which the 1st Battalion The Argyll & Sutherland Highlanders and an enemy force would engage in all phases of war. A large number of important visitors assembled for the final phase, a formal attack to capture Imber Village, after which the visitors were invited to question the participants. Both observation of the attack and discussions with the participants provided overwhelming evidence of the value of the TES system.

I therefore asked General Chapple to spend two days with the US Army at their National Training Centre in the Nevada Desert to which he readily agreed. Before departure we updated him on our thinking, giving our views on the strengths and weaknesses of the US system. Once again we saw an amazing training exercise, after which General Chapple confirmed that he broadly agreed with our plans.

We had been wrestling with the problem of a lack of an area weapons effects simulator to enable artillery and mortar fire, minefields and aerial bombing to be simulated in the battle. A number of technologies were examined, the most promising being a triangulation system of directional radio waves that could inflict either a hit/kill or a hit/disable on men/vehicles in a specific area. A technology requirement for an Area Weapons Effects Simulator (AWES) was put out for development.

The rest of the year was spent writing the Army Simulation Strategy Paper, circulating it for comment, rewriting and then recirculating it, and then the same again in the time-honoured MOD fashion until it was agreed by all who mattered. In essence the plan was for two purpose-built CAST facilities both based on computerised war gaming technologies suitable to exercise operational headquarters from battle group up to corps, one to be located in Germany and the other on Salisbury Plain. Interestingly the concurrent US Army project paper consisted of three Vufoils that their general signed off after just an hour's discussion!

The TES plan was more complex. We recommended that training at BATUS in Canada for BAOR-based battle groups should be split between live firing and TES training with a permanent OPFOR based mainly in obsolescent Scorpion tracked vehicles modified to appear to be a Soviet tank. In the UK we recommended a similar TES organization based on Westdown Camp making use of the whole of Salisbury Plain with the Infantry Demonstration Battalion providing the OPFOR, but noting that, owing to the requirements of many other range users and the risk of serious environmental damage, there would have to be a strictly limited number of exercises each year. A further recommendation was that smaller TES facilities should be provided in the UK at Stanford, Aldershot and Catterick, and in BAOR at Sennelager and Soltau for four reasons: to provide company level TES training as an introduction to higher level training, to reduce the risk of environmental damage by overuse of major training areas, to allow dismounted infantry to train in areas that offered natural cover and to allow more battle groups each year to benefit from higher level TES training. As far as TES technology was concerned we stated very strongly that a two-way laser system and the introduction of an Area Weapons Effects System were very necessary.

As my task did not include the use of SIMNET-type interactive technologies to enhance simulated training, I noted in my final report that further study should be made into this exciting new technology.

By the late autumn of 1989 my work was completed, although it must be said that a huge amount of staff work remained to be done before any of the systems could reach the invitations-to-tender stage for the equipment and the work services that would be required. Lieutenant Colonels Tony Clark and Chris Nind moved with their projects into the Directorate of Army Training where they made progress towards realisation. Of all the recommendations in the plan only the lower level of TES training failed to be funded. I was sad to leave but I had to move on. But, as I did so, the citizens of Berlin tore down the Berlin wall on 9 November 1989 to mark the beginning of the end of the Cold War.

CHAPTER 14

Tackling Combat Clothing and Personal Equipment

A T THE 1988 DIRECTOR ROYAL ARTILLERY annual conference at Woolwich I bumped into my old friend Brigadier (later Major General) Brian Pennicott, now the Deputy Military Secretary responsible for brigadiers' postings. He led me into a corner, reminded me that I had only about four years left to serve, and suggested it was time I called in to see him. So a few months later I went to his tiny 8th floor London office in MOD Main Building on a Monday morning to have my palm read. His first question was to ask if I saw myself being promoted to major general, and my honest reply that I very much doubted the possibility was met with a nod of the head, so at least that was crystal clear. Brian handed me several sheets of A4 paper which had listed every brigadier's post in the army, with annotations by his staff against those I might expect to have a chance of getting, suggesting that I take it home and discuss options with Ann.

I should explain here that, at the time, we had three children at boarding school, and that new regulations required the receivers of boarding school allowance to reside within fifty miles of their place of work, or move into quarters at their place of work. In addition, I knew that I was on a list to become either the Commandant of the Royal School of Artillery at Larkhill or the Garrison Commander at Woolwich, both far more than fifty miles from our home even to the straightest flying bird. And it would have been crazy to move out of our own home, where we had lived very happily for the past five years, for my last job before retirement.

So I took the piece of paper from Brian and without delay marked a figure '1' against Director of Clothing and Textiles (DCT) at Andover; '2' against Chief of Staff South East District at Aldershot; and '3' against Director of Army Recruiting in London. Brian took the paper and put in directly into his briefcase, saying, 'Thanks. You'll receive a posting order on Friday.'

I replied, 'Many thanks, but you didn't look to see the appointments I marked.'

'No need,' he replied with a smile. We chatted on about other matters but I was still perplexed by his promise of a posting order on Friday. Like the Cheshire cat he smiled but said no more. Astonishingly, Friday's post included the familiar buff-coloured envelope, and inside was a posting order to become Director of Clothing and Textiles in November 1989 for four years. Long enough to see me through to retirement. Hurrah! And many, many thanks, Brian.

Having been an operational soldier for almost all of my thirty-two years' service at that point, I knew very well that the British soldier had been very poorly provided for with combat clothing and individual personal equipment. The Falklands War had proved just how bad it was. There was a big job to be done and I relished the challenge.

So in November 1989, I set off for my first day at Andover to meet the existing incumbent for a day of briefings, after which I would be in the chair. The talk was of saving money here, using cheaper materials, maintaining the lowest possible stock levels (there was only a 34 per cent availability of stock of the basic clothing scale when I took over), delaying in-to-service dates, the importance of spending a day a week in MOD Main Building to keep up with the gossip and almost nothing about improving the lot of the soldier. Some of his staff were infected with the same spirit. It was a miserable day and so at 4 p.m. I pushed him out of the door and called my management group into the conference room. A new broom had arrived.

This was the first and only time in my military career when my takeover of a new appointment left me feeling angry at my inheritance. I looked at the members of the management group and told them that I was disappointed with all that I had been told during the day, citing the general attitude of short changing the soldier by selecting the lowest standards, lowest costs, accepting low stock levels and lowest use of the budget available. I asked them if, now that I was the Director, they themselves sought a change of direction or policy in their general corporate responsibility towards providing the best soldiers in the world with the proper combat clothing and personal equipment to do the job. I looked round the table in a clockwise direction at each person present and asked them one by one if they shared my views or, on the other hand, were they entirely satisfied with the way the Directorate had been doing its job. I received eight or nine negative reactions. I dismissed the meeting, telling them all to do some hard thinking overnight and be prepared to provide some more thoughtful comments at 8.30 a.m. the following morning.

I returned home deep in thought, almost colliding with a deer crossing a narrow lane near Bradley on my forty-two mile drive back to Haslemere. There was a great deal of thinking to do before the morning meeting. In fact my mind buzzed away all night as I thought through the way ahead.

At precisely 8.30 a.m. the meeting commenced, the attitude quiet but unmenacing, but certainly not yet on my side. Again I went round the table in a clockwise direction inviting views. There were none, none at all. I did not have a script, and nor did I make contemporary notes but I vividly remember making a speech approximately thus:

I arrived here yesterday knowing that the current standard and provision of combat clothing for the British soldier were a long way below the quality and availability required. During the day, I learned of the deliberate policy of selecting the cheaper options, of the policy of underspending the allocated budget, of the policy of accepting that some of the clothing range would be out of stock at any one time and delaying by various means the introduction of new items into service. I also learned that there is no overall corporate policy for the development of new items, and that there is no well-defined and clear research programme. I now understand why, as example one, eight years after the Falklands War the combat boot is still not right, and example two, the majority of soldiers cannot fire their rifle fitted with a night sight when wearing the helmet, or indeed wear the helmet properly when wearing a respirator.

We will start two new programmes from today. The first will be a development programme which will five years from now introduce a totally new combat clothing and personal equipment system using existing textile technologies. It will be an integrated system treating the soldier as a complete system based upon the layer principle. It will be known as Combat Soldier 1995 (CS 95) and will enter service in April 1995. (It was most rewarding when, a little over ten years later, Prime Minister Tony Blair unveiled the Millennium Dome Spiral of Innovation for which the Design Council had selected Combat Soldier 1995 as one of two hundred examples of creativity and innovation to improve our lives at the beginning of the new millennium.) The second will be a research programme which will provide a minimum of ten years' military textile research in order to introduce a replacement for the temporary CS 95 system, using newly developed smart materials, again in a fully integrated system. It will be known as Combat Soldier 2005 and will enter service in that year. In parallel, we will work up a counter-surveillance research and development plan with the aim of introducing a multi-spectral camouflage system.

This is the way this Directorate will move forward. Additionally, we will never again accept the cheapest materials, never underspend the budget (but we will not overspend it either), we will ensure that stocks allow every soldier to have available his entitlement and, in short, we will make things work properly. Are there any questions or comments?

I went round the table again. There were no comments until I came to my budget manager and senior civil servant Mike Warne. He ventured, 'You'll never do it. The financiers will pick bits out of your system knowing full well that once they succeed in extracting one new item as a savings measure, the whole concept will collapse, and then they will take all the money.' I challenged back, 'No – my job is to ring-fence the whole system and ensure it remains ring-fenced.' There were no more comments and the meeting broke up. I guessed this had been a larger change of substance as well as style than they had bargained for, but I was already enjoying the challenges, and they came thick and fast.

The next day I was asked if it would be convenient for a small group of the staff to brief me on an important matter. They filed in led by my deputy, Colonel Mike Mounde, a highly experienced MOD officer, sat down round my office conference table and, after a moment of very obvious discomfort, let the bombshell explode. 'We have a problem,' one of them said. 'A very serious problem,' another announced. For many years almost all of the army's (poor quality) combat boots had been manufactured by a large boot and shoe manufacturing company in South East England. Such was the confidence in this sole supplier that the quality assurance staff had stopped visiting earlier in the year. The consequential catastrophic quality failure led to the rejection of over 70,000 pairs of combat boots, the majority of which were not fit to issue. This rejection meant that there were now no combat boots in stock, and that it would not be possible to purchase any more combat boots for more than six months, by which time the deficit, it was calculated, would be in excess of 230,000 pairs. This had explosive tabloid newspaper banner headline potential: 'Barefoot British Squaddies' or probably worse. We spent several hours struggling with the problem. I organised people to examine the ramifications, and the news was not good. Even before the problem, second- (and even sixth-) hand boots were being issued in the TA. Now only soldiers on operations and recruits would get a pair of new boots. The boots of soldiers leaving would be reissued, and some soldiers would have to wear cooks' boots in lieu of combat boots. It became an acute problem that was not eased until well over a year later. But more of that later.

As I entered my office on day three, I felt fairly confident that it would turn out to be easier than days one and two. Wrong. I started, as planned, by doing a walkabout through my staffs' offices to try to get to know them, to see how much work appeared to be facing each of them, and to learn what (apart from me) their main problems were. But I was soon asked to return to my office. It was my General's chief of staff asking if he could speak to me and the gist of his conversation was that £14 million from my procurement budget of £82 million for the current year had to be cut. To make matters worse I was required to present my proposals to achieve this next morning in the Ministry of Defence to the Vice Quartermaster General. So an hour later a worried Mike Warne came to my office clutching reams of computer printouts, but the start point was the need to explain to me how the procurement budget worked, for which a day had been programmed the following week. We poured over lines and lines of stock figures, planned expenditure figures and cross-referenced these with contracts currently in the manufacturing stage. Not only had I been given an impossible task, but the people who had given this order should have known better. It was extremely unprofessional of staff officers in the budgetary chain of command to demand such a cut when, with less than four months of the financial year remaining, it would have been poor planning by my staff not to have had all this money either at contract (and for the contracts to have been completed and delivered by the following February), or alternatively the money handed back.

Nevertheless, the following morning I entered the Ministry of Defence prepared to hand back a couple of million pounds for items (mainly combat boots!) which we thought would not be delivered in the next three months. I explained the situation to the major general who, having been in the RAOC all his life, should have understood immediately that once a contract is awarded, it is a very expensive matter to alter it. But no, he only wanted to find another £12 million worth of immediate savings. For three hours he crawled over all the figures. 'Why are you buying a hundred and twenty 9 feet × 9 feet shelter tents?'

'Because a hundred and twenty were issued last year to replace those lost or damaged, and these are to go into stock to replace next year's losses.'

'So why can't you stop this contract now to save £2,400?'

'Because ninety of these tents have already been delivered and the remaining thirty are actually in production now.' This conversation was repeated again and again: berets, rucksacks, bearskins, shirts, sleeping bags and a thousand other items were all dissected in budgetary terms, and we never did find a way of saving the £12 million. But it was a sobering experience to witness at first hand the sheer amateurism of the thought process. I was to learn during the following months and years that much of this could be laid at the doors of the budgetary civil servants (and ultimately at those in the Treasury) who exercised power without responsibility.

After these first three days, life did become more reasonably paced. The most important task was to visit those parts of my responsibility not located in Andover. But first I had a most agreeable interview with my immediate superior Major General Jerry Hulme, the Director General of Ordnance Services, whose message was – do not bother me unless something is going wrong. What more could I ask for?

My first visit was to the then named Stores and Clothing Research and Development Establishment (SCRDE) at Colchester and known to the whole Army as Screedy. While responsible for doing work for all three services, this was very much an army organisation, and skilfully commanded by Dr Steve Cole, an eminent MOD scientist. I found there a lively and charming collection of scientists and textile engineers with a diverse range of skills. The total strength was a little over a hundred and fifty, but worryingly there were only about forty-five scientists and development engineers, and an awful lot of what I was told were essential hangers-on. They were designing new combat clothing and personal equipment for the jungle, desert, arctic and temperate climates, and with camouflage nets, tents and shelters to match. At the same time new in-barracks clothing was being developed, and body armour and shoes of every description and a thousand and one other items. Although there was an annual scientific evaluation of their work, it was immediately crystal clear that an unfocused corporate research and development policy had led not only to a lack of clear direction in their work, but in some cases valuable resources were being wasted. The worst case was of a very senior member of staff who informed me when questioned that he had spent the last seven years working on a means to defeat Warsaw Pact image intensification surveillance and weapon sights. As the Warsaw Pact did not have any such sights, but did have a plethora of battlefield surveillance radars, I was somewhat concerned, the more so when he explained that he had done this work because he found it interesting, and had never enjoyed working with radars. It was changed, although not without difficulty, for the scientist concerned considered it important to complete his somewhat unnecessary and self-imposed task. But SCRDE gave me a thoroughly good feel and I had a stimulating first day with them.

My next visit a few days later was to the Stores and Clothing Quality Assurance Division (QAD [S & C]) at Didcot where, including four outposts at Glasgow, Manchester, Leeds and Plymouth, some hundred and sixty inspectors conducted quality-assurance tests on the myriad of items coming from industry. The range was enormous – cooking utensils to helmets, regimental colours to camouflage nets, and rucksacks to combat boots (although sadly not satisfactorily of late with the latter). The organisation was headed by a sometime textile engineer who was, over the next three years, to become increasingly a thorn in my side. In my opinion, he seemed to delegate much of his work to a senior member of his staff to allow him time to develop a new computer software programme exclusively for QAD (S & C). When I insisted that this project had to be fully interoperable with the other computer systems within the Directorate I was told (eventually) that not only was it impossible, but that it never could become possible.

My third visit in that first December was to another disaster area, the stores and clothing Contracts Branch in Glasgow. It is worth telling the story, for the inheritance I received from both the MOD and the European Commission combined to produce a set-up of mind-boggling inefficiency. For many years the stores and clothing Contracts Branch had been an integral part of the DCT organization, ideally located in Leeds, the centre of the textile industry. A MOD official decided that a small isolated Contracts Branch in the right place and chain of command and with a small band of highly experienced and dedicated contracts officers could not possibly be efficient. However, the real truth was that 'they' wanted to assemble in Glasgow sufficient contracts staff to justify a grade 5 civil servant as the chief. Sadly no other consideration mattered. And to make matters worse this senior contracts officer was not even in the Quartermaster General's command chain. So in mid 1989, after all but one of the Leeds-based DCT Contracts Branch staff had declined to move to Glasgow, an entirely new team had to be recruited and trained under a new chief, Liz McDonald, who tended to follow the letter of the regulations.

At this first visit, I spent the day getting to know the new staff, discussing their training and the contracts that they were currently arranging, and trying to get them to understand the military. It appeared that not one had ever served, even in the TA. It was immediately clear that very few contracts had been let since the move from Leeds the previous summer, and that few contracts would be let in the next few months as the new staff struggled with an unfamiliar system. I tried to visit the Glasgow Contracts Office every month during the next three years. I always took my uniform, changing on arrival and before departure. Had I not done so, the young and highly intelligent Glaswegians who had joined the office would neither have seen a soldier, nor probably known that I was a serving officer.

A few days later, Liz McDonald let the European Commission genie out of the bottle. Brussels had passed a law stating that henceforth all government contract invitations to tender had to be advertised in the European Commission Contracts Journal after which no tender could be accepted for six months in order to allow other nations a chance to bid. As all the MOD maintenance stock reordering was based on annuality linked to the in-year budget, the no-notice imposition of a six months' delay would clearly play havoc both with the budget and, worse, with the stock levels which in many cases were non-existent. There was a let-out clause. Military operational items were exempt. 'No problems then!' I said. 'For body armour, load carriage equipment, combat boots, sleeping bags and combat clothing are all operational items.' But unbelievably the only item they accepted from the whole inventory was the combat helmet, and so once again the soldier suffered.

My next visit was to the clothing equipment management branch of the Directorate of Supply Management (DSM), an organization of around forty people (a few were serving RAOC officers and non-commissioned officers) who received every demand for clothing from the army and then authorised the issues in the right priority. Furthermore, it was they who informed my Directorate where we were short of stock (at the time almost everywhere), and what we should be purchasing to return the stock to a working level. In other words they were at the centre of many of our crisis areas. At the time a male recruit's basic kit issue was of forty-eight different items. Yet nineteen of these, including some of the most important, were not available. Although their work was an integral part of the functioning of my Directorate, they were very questionably outside it. Later I tried very hard to persuade their director that this group should be transferred to my line management but he would have none of it. However, as soon as he himself was appointed as my successor he instigated the transfer and it proved a great improvement.

I also visited the School of Infantry to meet the small but very valuable section in the Infantry Trials and Development Unit, headed by Major Peter Andrews of the Duke of Wellington's Regiment, which was responsible for all the field trials of the infantry soldiers' combat clothing and individual equipment. They were worth their weight in gold and the closer we worked with them the better the result.

During these first few weeks I determined my priorities in more detail and also made the biggest mistake of my tour. I was to learn that the larger the delegation that came to see me, the more suspicious I should be of the briefing I was to receive, and this was never more true than with the replacement sleeping bag, or the 'Sleeping Assembly GS'. The main part of this was a new sleeping bag to replace both the small down-filled bags which soldiers had used for the previous twenty-five years and the far larger special arctic bag used only by 3 Commando Brigade and a few others. The new bag was heavy and vast. There was no way it could be carried by an infantry soldier, and I should have turned it down on the spot. But the delegation had come armed to the teeth with trial reports, acceptance reports and every piece of paper that could possibly justify a bag with a performance down to −35° Celsius when 98 per cent of the land forces rarely operated in temperatures below −5°. But then the senior financier waded in. 'As we have removed the money from the budget line for the second bag, you have no choice but to confirm this plan which your predecessor agreed over two years ago.' Foolishly I relented, and the result has been that countless infantry soldiers have either carried an overweight bag with a performance they did not need, or they have left it elsewhere and missed the opportunity to grab much needed sleep. A bad mistake.

There were many more visits which needed to be made. Early in January 1990, Dr Trevor Tees, my Research and Development Advisor, took me on a three-day trip to the cotton spinning and weaving mills in Lancashire and Yorkshire to teach me the raw principles of textile technology. It was an amazing experience. The first mill visited in Oldham was spinning cotton on eight floors under a British manager. However, the workers on the eight floors were from eight different Indian castes that apparently could not be mixed.

Aware that soldiers were spending enormous sums of their own money on combat clothing and individual equipment, I determined to visit infantry battalions on a regular basis. I quickly found a formula that worked well: thirty minutes with the commanding officer followed by an hour with the quartermaster. But the meat of these most interesting visits was a lengthy session with the recce platoon, with a few rifle platoon commanders plus the regimental sergeant major also present. I used to ask the recce platoon commander to arrange for all his men to bring in to the meeting place (normally the gym) every item of combat clothing or individual equipment they had purchased because the issued equivalent was below standard or not available. My visit to the 1st Battalion The Green Howards, commanded by Lieutenant Colonel (later General Sir) Richard Dannatt, was amongst the most stimulating. There must have been

£80,000 to £100,000 worth of privately purchased kit all neatly laid out. I took each item by turn, having a long and totally open discussion on the reasons it was better than the official issue. Taking as just one example, sleeping bags, I examined all the different bags, compared them with each other and their differing characteristics, discussed the pros and cons of all the factors, and then informed the soldiers what I was doing about it and why. These were highly valuable and interesting discussions with people who had thought deeply about their requirements and priorities, and knew what they were talking about. I could also advise them, for example, that it was extremely unlikely that a privately purchased combat suit or rain suit would have infrared reflective dyes in the camouflage pattern, and the wearer would be wearing the equivalent of a Day-Glo suit to an enemy with an infrared weapon or surveillance sight.

I made similar visits in the first few months of 1990 to many units, mostly infantry, in the UK, Germany and Northern Ireland, and benefited from them all. In Northern Ireland, I found to my horror that every soldier was being ordered to buy chest webbing at £45 per set before his tour began, because it is much easier to wear in urban operations and when using vehicles. So I went to Headquarters Northern Ireland and asked them if they had authorised this or demanded to have chest webbing issued. They had done neither. I was cross and then discovered that the staff officer responsible for combat clothing and individual equipment had totally ignored this responsibility, as had his predecessors. So I sorted that problem and several others.

During all these visits and discussions, it became very clear that my initial concepts of Combat Soldier 1995 and Combat Soldier 2005 were bang on target, so I next turned my attention to their further development. I decided to make a wide-ranging visit to a number of institutions in the United States, beginning in April 1990. I started at the US Army Infantry School at Fort Benning where the British liaison officer, Lieutenant Colonel David Shepherd of the Queen's Regiment, hosted me. I had asked to see the TEXCOM (Testing and Evaluation Command) team at Fort Benning. On arrival I started by briefing them on my ideas for the future. Amazingly, they were working in precisely the same areas and so they threw away the prepared programme and gave me a very full briefing on their new Soldier Integrated Protective Ensemble (SIPE) concept. David Shepherd was very surprised, for none of this had reached him. Knowing that my next port of call was to Headquarters TRADOC (Training and Doctrine Command) at Fort Monroe in Southern Virginia, they called ahead so that my programme there could be adjusted to include the SIPE concept. It was, and it was most interesting to compare concepts and ideas. They were without any doubt far ahead of the UK (for we had done nothing) in the field of improving command and control and the weapon effectiveness of the dismounted infantry soldier, but I sensed we were level in terms of integrated combat clothing systems. My final visit was for two days at the US Army Natick Research, Development and Engineering Laboratories some thirty miles west of Boston, and the equivalent of our own SCRDE at Colchester. The TEXCOM team had once again phoned ahead of me and so a fascinating two hours was inserted into an already crowded programme, so that the SIPE programme manager, Carol Fitzgerald, could show me all the work she had done. It was absolutely clear to me that the US and the UK were at one on the advantages of developing the efficiency of the individual infantry soldier, but I had not reckoned on the diehard attitude of one or two at Warminster, but more of that later.

The main purpose of my visit to Natick had been to discuss every aspect of the common ground between their organization and mine in the provision of combat clothing, individual equipment, camouflage, tentage, testing, trials and a host of related matters. I made many friends in doing so, the majority of whom I still counted on seeing regularly ten years and more later. Charlie Williams, Bob Lewis and Larry Symington were prominent amongst them but there were many more, too many to be named here. I determined that as many as possible of my staff should visit Natick, and from this initial visit a series of further staff visits took place, including the exchange of scientists for one year.

After visiting Natick, I travelled south again to Delaware to meet research and development staffs at the DuPont headquarters in Wilmington and the W.L. Gore headquarters in Elkton. These meetings, while enjoyable and interesting in themselves, proved of the greatest value to my work over the next few years. I also went to Germany to units of the 1st British Corps where all I had learned in my earlier visits was confirmed. As ever I particularly enjoyed visiting the infantry battalions. A highlight was a day with the 1st Battalion The Argyll & Sutherland Highlanders, commanded by the flamboyant Malcolm McVittie, who amongst other things paraded a complete company, every man of whom was in a different form of so-called official regimental dress. At the Quartermaster's Department I surprised the QM by demanding to see the hitherto secret Argyll kilt mountain. After much unlocking of doors I was shown the results of careful accumulation over many years. I took the opportunity of calling in to see my old friend Lieutenant General Sir (later General the Lord) Charles Guthrie, now the Corps Commander, to whom I explained my priorities both for improving availability of current combat clothing and for the introduction of Combat Soldier 1995. He gave me unqualified and very positive support both then and on a number of subsequent occasions.

By now it was clear that my interests and almost total motivation as the new Director of Clothing and Textiles was the improvement both short and long term of the combat clothing and individual equipment range. I paid very little interest to the barrack and ceremonial clothing responsibilities, leaving those responsible to run them almost without supervision. But I was enjoying the appointment enormously, despite the frustrations, and this drove me on to try to win every battle.

However, people still tried to pull the wool over my eyes. In fact they must have thought me both naive and stupid. Very early in 1990, having worn a self-purchased Norwegian Army shirt myself in cold weather for several years, I called a meeting of my staff in order to plan its introduction into service. At the time a very high percentage of soldiers were buying these excellent shirts, and many were being ripped off by unscrupulous dealers selling them cheap imitations. My staff tried to tell me that the Shirt GS, a cotton shirt with a conventional collar, epaulettes and chest patch pockets, had a better TOG (measurement of warmth) rating than the Norwegian Army shirt. They told me that they had already run comparative TOG tests, but, when I demanded to see the results, they were never forthcoming. So we then ran some tests, issued a specification, found some money in the budget and started procurement action, aiming to start issues to the soldiers serving in Norway in winter. My budget manager Mike Warne came to my office a few weeks later to inform me that the Assistant Under Secretary Quartermaster General (AUS[Q]) – a two-star civil servant – had halted the procurement because it broke Treasury regulations. Apparently there could not be an increase in the soldiers' clothing scale without a compensating reduction. I was livid. So I made contact with the School of Infantry Sergeants' Course at Brecon – by far the toughest military course in the world – and arranged to take the AUS(Q) there for a day in the middle of winter, and one during which it rained continuously. We arrived at the rendezvous about two hundred metres above a steep valley at the bottom of which the course were receiving confirmatory orders prior to a twelve kilometre uphill live firing attack. As we descended, AUS(Q) slipped and completed the two hundred metres downhill on his back, sliding on the long wet grass. We then met a number of the soldiers, all of whom were soaked and very tired, and by chance were all wearing self-purchased Norwegian Army shirts, not to mention Gore-Tex® rain suits. Fortunately, the Start Line for the attack was the far side of a waist-deep swollen and swift-flowing river, so our intrepid civil servant soon experienced how it is to be soaked. We had a long hard day following the attack uphill and watching at close quarters the most extraordinary physical feats of these young men, who unlike us, were all carrying a full battle load. At the end we spoke to many soldiers about the suitability of their combat clothing and individual equipment. Despite their fatigue, they were honest and clear thinking about the requirements of the infantry soldier. We then adjourned with the senior instructors to a public house for lunch in front of a roaring fire, and again some very sensible ideas were put forward.

After a shower, AUS(Q) and I drove in a staff car to Cardiff railway station. After discussing what we had seen, and in what seemed to be a more positive attitude to providing the soldier with his needs, I produced from my briefcase the necessary authority for the introduction of the Norwegian Army shirt for AUS(Q) to sign. He read it most carefully, and after much hesitation pulled out a pen and got as far as the first letter of his name before pausing. 'On reflection,' he said, 'I would like to sleep on this over the weekend!' I was staggered that another weekend would be needed for such an obvious and simple decision. Two weeks later, after further badgering, I received the signed paper and we proceeded to introduce the Norwegian Army shirt. This was a long overdue move and it was all too easy to see the disbelief on the faces of soldiers when they heard of and saw such needless prevarication.

Throughout my service I had been concerned that my beret fitted properly. The issue beret had an outrageously large crown that pulled down well below the ear, so every soldier had to boil his new beret to shrink the crown down to a sensible size. Inevitably this also ruined the leather rim that soon deteriorated beyond use. As a result, soldiers (and officers) had to buy their berets from the local garrison tailor who miraculously could provide an identical beret with a small crown. So I decided to visit a beret factory in Witney to see the army berets being made. At the end of my tour I complained to the manager that the crowns of the berets were too big. 'Well,' he said, 'that row of discs on the wall to the right are for the MOD contracts – they are what your office tells us to make. But those discs to the left are what we use for the non-MOD contracts, because that is what the soldiers want.' I could not believe that for thirty-five years I had spent hours and pounds shrinking berets simply because some official was too idle to amend the specification. But that was the simple truth. So I ordered him to destroy the MOD discs immediately, but being a wise old bird he declined until he had received a written contract amendment from my contracts office. To cut a long and at times very tense story short, it took me another three weeks to get this matter corrected, and then only when the person responsible had become clear that dismissal beckoned very close. This was a sad and crassly stupid story, but is just one example of what I came across time and time again – bureaucratic indifference to the needs of the soldier and total ignorance of the principle of providing the best value from the taxpayers' money.

On 11 May 1990 I received the honour of being appointed to be an aide-de-camp to Her Majesty the Queen, a position I held until retirement from the army in November 1993. This is an honorary appointment that in my case did not involve any actions at all. I was very pleased to receive this prestigious appointment that meant that I wore the words 'ADC' on my rank badges plus the heaviest and thickest of the gold aiguillettes on my right shoulder. Of course everyone also knew that this award meant that I would certainly not gain further promotion.

By mid 1990 I felt that my senior staff had, in the majority of cases but by no means all, taken on the vast majority of my ideas with enthusiasm and vigour. In particular they were sold on the principles of a planned and scientifically conducted upgrade of the soldiers' combat clothing and individual equipment items, and on the imperative of getting rid of the appalling shortage of basic clothing items. I had appointed Major Richard Simonds to design and introduce a new system to control budget expenditure in the right year and on the right items in such a way that we spent all our money in the correct time frame. Richard worked for hours and hours on this, but his work did allow us to regain total control. The result was that at the year end we came out exactly as per the budget, and within two years every shortage had been eradicated and stocks were very high. But we had to take measured risks to manage the budget accurately. In the textile industry there is a measurable percentage of late delivery. In the past DCT had generally planned to overspend by 2 per cent, but clearly this had not worked. So I adjusted this figure up to 8 per cent which caused my budget manager Mike Warne to become concerned, but it worked.

Another success story was Lieutenant Colonel Alan Forestier-Walker of the 7th Gurkha Rifles who had joined the same day as me, and I daresay learned his new trade at about the same speed as me. His views and ideas matched mine exactly so he was an excellent person to move my concepts forward. Alan took the lead in the staffing of Combat Soldier 1995 and, as a result, the army owes much to his efforts.

As Combat Soldier 1995 developed I decided I should seek a meeting with the Director of Infantry. So in June 1990 I called on the major general in his Warminster office to explain the concept of my Combat Soldier 1995 and 2005 projects as a means of improving the combat efficiency of the dismounted soldier. I also explained to him that, while these two projects were entirely in my gift as the Director of Clothing and Textiles, the emerging US Soldier Modernisation Plan (of which SIPE was but a part) also included new man-portable concepts for fire control, command and control and battlefield information which, when taken all together, would very substantially improve the fighting power of the infantry soldier. He told me that the infantry was already highly efficient and did not require any of the improvements I was suggesting. I left his office surprised. However, his successors backed the Soldier Modernisation Plan concept, introducing the Future Infantry Soldier Technology (FIST) development project.

I referred earlier in this chapter to the combat boot crisis that had struck on my very first day. By mid-June 1990 this was coming under control, for David Smith, managing director of G. B. Britton, which was the premier division of the UK Safety Group, had taken on 90 per cent of our production requirements. Careful juggling of the forty-seven different sizes allowed us to plan production with David to ensure that we just kept ahead of a really major crisis. Slowly, more and more combat boots were released to those who really needed them and the war maintenance reserve stocks even had a few pairs allocated to them.

The standard combat boot which was issued too quickly in the mid-1980s was named the Boot Combat High. It was a failure owing to a Treasury insistence for down-engineering to reduce the price. The result was a harrowing number of foot injuries. I had been all but crippled by the Boot Combat High. Urgent modifications were introduced to prevent tendonitis and the new boot was somewhat unimaginatively named the Boot Combat High (Improved). At the time we were working so closely with G. B. Britton to overcome the combat boot shortage that David Smith offered an entirely new private venture combat boot which he assured me would be a winner. After trials it was very readily accepted into service. My staff came to me to inform me they had decided to name this new boot the Boot Combat High (Improved) Mark 2. I stopped this immediately for the Boot Combat High carried such a bad reputation that I did not want the new very superior combat boot tainted by the name. So I called it the Combat Assault Boot, or CAB, and since that day well over a million pairs have been made, and worn almost without a single complaint.

I continued my regular visits to both Regular and TA units. One which sticks in mind was the 1st Battalion The Devonshire & Dorset Regiment commanded by Lieutenant Colonel Chris Biles, a man with an outstanding sense of humour. I was invited to arrive for a lunch that all officers attended. Every captain and subaltern came in to the mess wearing boots so old that I could see their socks between the uppers and the soles. It was an excellent leg pull, but it soon emerged that they had no idea how serious the real position on the supply of combat boots remained.

At this time I became embroiled for the first time in the Gore-Tex® problem, which was to last another eighteen months. The standard issue combat rain suit was made of neoprene, an impermeable material that made the wearer sweat heavily: indeed the wearer was usually wetter on the inside than on the outside. Reflecting their arduous duties, soldiers in Northern Ireland had been issued with the vastly superior breathable Gore-Tex® combat rain suits, a policy that had been extended to the parachute brigade. In consequence, a thriving market had developed in the private purchase of apparently identical Gore-Tex® combat rain suits at extortionate prices, but without the magic infrared reflective printing inks in the camouflage. So I decided that the only solution was to replace neoprene with Gore-Tex® for all the soldiers of the Field Army. We could never afford to re-equip the whole army, and frankly nor did we need to. So I started technical studies to gain precise knowledge on what Gore-Tex® and similar materials could do and could not do in terms of breathability and waterproofness.

By August 1990, we were making significant progress on all fronts, although the availability of the basic combat clothing scale had only just reached beyond 50 per cent – a very serious matter. Then came another thunderbolt from the blue – the Gulf War. On 2 August 1990 Saddam Hussain's Iraqi Army invaded Kuwait and it soon became very clear that the major nations of the world would be involved in one way or another. As UK policy several years earlier had clearly stated that British Forces would no longer be committed east of Suez, all stocks of desert-coloured combat clothing, camouflage nets and similar had long since been sold. Indeed the remaining stocks of three-colour desert camouflage clothing had been sold to the Iraqis in friendlier times. It was immediately apparent that my team had much work to do.

The combat clothing and camouflage designers at Colchester set to work with great haste. Within two days they had designed and checked a new camouflage colour system, and amended all the manufacturing drawings so that we could go out to contract. Shadow contracts were drawn up and even small quantities of garments were ordered within the same week. SCRDE did an excellent job in a very short time. In the meantime, the UK presence in the Gulf began to appear to be an RAF-only operation, so keen were they to redress the Falklands War when they took very little part in offensive operations.

However, by mid-August all the indications were that the UK would send an Armoured Brigade, and this was announced in mid-September by the Secretary of State for Defence, Tom King. The most urgent requirement, for it was still very hot in the desert in early autumn, was for desert sand combat kit – jacket, trousers and hat. For 7,000 soldiers it was decided that 20,000 sets were needed as soon as possible. However, the wretched civil servants delayed over several weeks the allocation of funding to the contracts for the combat suits and hats, presumably in the hope that the Iraqis would withdraw in line with the UN resolutions. They ignored the fact that it takes a minimum of ten weeks from the signing of a contract until garments start to leave the production line, for cotton has to be sourced and then spun and woven, dyed and printed before cutting and sewing can start. The effect of this needless delay was that the Americans were able to get into the market ahead of us and buy up the world supply of readily available cotton and most of the production sites. A decision was soon taken to send a full armoured division to the Gulf, 37,000 men in total. Our requirement for desert combat suits now rose to 185,000. By October, television pictures were being beamed back to the UK every night. Our soldiers were still all dressed in green camouflage (and every single item of the British light weight jungle uniforms stock had already been issued). It became very clear that neither Margaret Thatcher nor Tom King enjoyed seeing British soldiers in green and so great pressure was applied to try to speed up the introduction of the desert uniforms. I visited factories to talk to the work force to get them to work weekends and nights, brought in new factories, and moved production into Morocco, where my people were stoned. But the problem was always time.

One day I was summoned to the office of Tom King to inform him personally why there were such delays and what I was doing about it.

Coffee was not offered! It was interesting that none of the chain of command offered to accompany me, but I took the precaution of taking with me some very clear flow charts showing exactly how the ten weeks was needed. Tom King had, in earlier days, managed his family textile manufacturing business and so recognised instantly that there were no short cuts to be had. I warned him that the other major problem was capacity, the Americans having beaten us to so many factories. There was nothing indecisive about Tom King. He immediately picked up the phone and rang Lord Rayner, Chairman of Marks & Spencer, to ask for one factory to be turned over to the manufacture of desert combat suits with immediate effect. I was given a telephone number to ring two hours later, and the following Monday arrived at William Baird's Oswestry factory with a small team to set the operation into action. This went well and certainly helped to relieve the pressure. Baird's manufactured 30,000 suits in all and in very quick time. At the end of the contract their managing director told me that he thought manufacturing for Marks & Spencer was bad enough, but having had six weeks of MOD bureaucracy, he would never manufacture ever again for the MOD. But the sting was in the tail, for some months later a National Audit Office team started to make my life difficult on the subject of the much higher price paid for combat suits from this one company. I directed them to the Secretary of State, and heard no more.

During the period of the war in the Gulf, we had to process over a hundred and sixty Urgent Operational Requirements to provide clothing and equipment that was either not in the inventory or in very short supply. The total cost was over £62m. and the largest single item was for desert camouflage nets that in total cost more than £12m. The second largest item was the introduction of Combat Body Armour for all soldiers, a development project completed three years earlier but consistently denied funding by the Treasury. These brief statistics hide a vast amount of work completed in very quick time by my staff. They all played a leading part, none more so than Katrina Hutchison of the Contracts Branch, who worked with amazing dexterity to get contracts let in record times. Others heavily involved included those who not without difficulty arranged for all the garments manufactured in Morocco to be delivered to Gibraltar from where the RAF picked them up to get them to the Gulf. At the end of the war, there was not a single criticism of any item we provided, only of the wait to receive them.

There was an amusing story over desert combat boots. One day the

American Gulf War commander, General Norman Schwarzkopf, strode into the operations room wearing the first of the new US desert combat boots. A pair was soon offered and provided to the British Commander, General Peter de la Billiere, who in turn requested that all British soldiers in the Gulf should also have desert combat boots. This was quickly achieved thanks to David Smith and Paul Cockburn at G. B. Britton Ltd and a pair presented to the US commander. The two generals thereafter wore the opposite nation's desert combat boots.

Earlier in 1990 I had conceived the concept of a 'Briefing to Industry' seminar. This took place in the new Whitworth Conference Centre at Shrivenham over two days during which we gave a series of presentations on our requirements, contract and quality control procedures and ideas for the future. Every delegate paid £200 that entitled him or her to attend a full military guest night as well as all the other hospitality. This also allowed me to gather all my senior staff for an earlier day of rehearsals and meetings. This was not only the early days of the mobile telephone, but also a time when Gulf War contracts were being let by the hour. So during every break in the presentation programme, the industrial delegates retired to various corners of the car park to do their contract bidding. The Briefing to Industry seminars continued for several years and proved highly successful.

In 1991 I had a real stroke of luck, for Maurice Campbell, a gentle but clear-thinking Highlander, was appointed to be my head of contracts. He immediately overturned his predecessor's arcane policies and, from that day on, our contracts were more sensibly and successfully managed. Maurice's team of Katrina Hutchison, Gerry Harvey and Paul Lund did a wonderful job and became much admired throughout the industry.

By now it was more than a year since the end of the Cold War and a peace dividend was required. The government introduced the Options for Change programme, in effect dismantling the army in which I had served for over thirty years and which had won the Cold War. These were painful times. Major General David Botting, a most supportive and enjoyable man, was now my boss and faced the inevitable amalgamation of his much-loved Royal Army Ordnance Corps with the Royal Corps of Transport, the Army Catering Corps and others. As a member of his Management Board I sat through all the deliberations on Corps policy towards these considerable changes, and I like to think I contributed a little. For example, I asked the question: if the future RAOC consisted of only around 3,000 men, did this represent mass enough to sustain their heritage?

The Gulf War duly ended and this allowed me to continue with my work modernizing the Army's combat clothing and personal equipment. By this time General Sir John Learmont (my commanding officer twenty years earlier) had become the Quartermaster General and gave me unstinting support. New projects came up thick and fast. One which proved enormously successful was the development of a complete new range of non-operational uniforms for females. This was the brainwave of Major Jackie Smith who devised a most enterprising design competition using all the major UK schools of art and design plus the staff of SCRDE. It culminated in a top-class fashion show in London, with catwalk, professional models, gilt chairs, etc. and led to a forty-minute television programme followed by newspaper double spreads. Thousands of service-women are indebted to Jackie Smith, who sadly died suddenly without seeing her work completed. Thankfully, Major Lorna McGregor saw the project through.

I spent a week on winter warfare training in Norway and a week at the Jungle Warfare School in Brunei to take a long hard look at the special clothing items we produced for these regions. I decided to add hot climate, temperate climate and special forces committees to the very forceful arctic warfare clothing committee in order to improve soldier effectiveness. These meetings not only allowed the experts from these specialist groups to influence our developments but, equally importantly, it allowed my experts to spend time in the jungle and similar inhospitable places.

In the meantime the Warsaw Pact was under increasing strain and by the summer of 1991 the Soviet Union had begun to unravel, with Yeltsin challenging Gorbachev, leading to the replacement of the Red Flag by the national tricolour of Russia in Moscow on 31 December.

During all these years I had continued to be a member of the Executive Committee of the Army Football Association. In 1991, I was suddenly asked to become the vice-chairman of Army Football, effectively the chief executive. Major Terry Knight was more persuasive than I would have liked (mainly because he knew that there were no other brigadiers who would take it on) and so I agreed for one year only. A week later, Terry sidled up to me with a smile and said, 'Did I mention that by rotation it will also be the Army's turn to run the Combined Services, and you will become their chairman?' I exploded, but Terry merely smiled and said quietly, 'Of course it will mean that you will lead the Combined Services' two-week tour of Saudi Arabia and the Oman.' I duly did so and had a wonderful time. This was one of the ways these two nations thanked the British for their contribution to the Gulf War, and their hospitality was boundless. The seventeen players were the pick of the Armed Forces in every way, and they were a joy to be with. They played fine football and wherever we stayed they ran youth coaching days, proving to be fine ambassadors of our country.

In the meantime, General Sir John Learmont, the Quartermaster General, asked me to use an hour of his allocated time at the Chief of the General Staff's annual conference to describe the evolving Combat Soldier 1995 (CS 95) clothing system. This offered the ideal opportunity to have one or two tricky changes approved (such as where badges of rank are best positioned) and for widespread approval in principle to be gained. I enlisted two of the best corporals in the army to do much of the talking: one was from the Infantry Trials and Development Unit, and the other from the Armoured Trials and Development Unit. Both had been heavily involved in the CS 95 trials. General Sir (later Field Marshal The Rt. Hon. Lord) Peter Inge had assembled every three-star and more senior serving general in the army. I introduced the presentation and then handed over to my two corporals who quite brilliantly combined expert knowledge, user experience and soldier humour. General Inge and General Guthrie, both highly experienced infantrymen, led the discussion giving strong support. But then a potential show-stopper, the Second Permanent Under-Secretary in the MOD (responsible for all expenditure), took to the floor first to ask Dr Steve Cole if this was a scientifically sensible project, and to ask me how I would fund the project. My reply that I would fund the project from my existing budget as long as I received no more cuts was enthusiastically supported by everyone present.

As we entered the first few months of 1992, I received an unwelcome shock. My four-year final tour of duty as DCT was to be shortened to three years, with a departure at the year's end. So I would be left with a rump nine months to serve until my retirement in November 1993. What would I do? The answer came from my good friend General Sir John Stibbon, Master General of the Ordnance but also the President of the Army Football Association. He took me aside after a match at Aldershot and said, 'Look, Richard, I know about all the things you have done as DCT. You would be very wise to become a consultant in this field when you leave the army.' And thus the idea was born.

CHAPTER 15

Into Industry

MY OLD FRIEND Brigadier LLoyd Body made contact with me at about the same time. Having been the Director of Clothing and Textiles some ten years before me, he had worked since retirement for one or two days per week as a consultant for the European part of DuPont. His main tasks had been to help with the introduction into Western Europe of Kevlar® for lightweight ballistic protection, and Nomex® for fire and heat protective clothing. LLoyd's proposition was simple. He now wished to stand down, and would I like to take over his role? I had met his colleagues in the DuPont team and so knew a reasonable amount of their work and future priorities. Most importantly I liked them all. This was a fantastic opportunity.

I was invited to the DuPont headquarters in Geneva by Reiner Nassauer to discuss the proposal. It appeared very interesting. Reiner recognised my need to work a five-day week by introducing me to other business units within DuPont with an existing or potential military/police interest. Within a few weeks I had enlarged my work portfolio from only Kevlar® and Nomex® to include Cordura® (material for rucksacks, load carriage systems and military combat boots), Nylon (parachutes and shelter sheets), Coolmax® (sweat wicking/quick drying underwear and socks), Dacron® Insulation Systems (sleeping bag and cold climate clothing insulations), and the Tyvek® range of materials to provide protective clothing against chemical and biological warfare agents. Simultaneously, I had been discussing work with the G. B. Britton division of the UK Safety Group in Bristol, almost the sole UK manufacturer of the full range of combat boots. Within days David Smith and Paul Cockburn invited me to join their team for a half-day of work per week, a plan readily agreed by DuPont.

I formed a private limited company called Individual Fighting Systems Limited (IFS) that would employ me as a consultant and marketing advisor with a series of annual contracts with DuPont and the UK Safety Group. My future seemed assured: I retired from the Army on my 55th birthday on 15 November 1993, and started my new career the following day without realising that fourteen vibrant, exhilarating and stimulating years would follow.

There were during the mid to late 1990s two events that enhanced my ability to grow my influence and my company. The concept of the Soldier Modernisation Plan (SMP) had been conceived during the final years of the Cold War but accelerated by the Gulf War and the concurrent development of the digitized land/air battle. It was becoming increasingly clear that the dismounted soldier needed to become an inclusive part of the whole battle with the same standards of information and information technology as soldiers manning complex equipments. The second was the growing importance of advanced low-burden protective clothing against chemical and biological warfare agents brought about by the chemical weapon demilitarization requirements of the Chemical Warfare Convention (CWC), the realization that advanced armies may have to fight in hot climates in full NBC protection, and more sinisterly the increasing threat of the use of chemical and biological warfare agents by terrorists. These influences stimulated the realization that the soldiers' (or police officers') combat clothing and personal equipment (or equivalent) had to be a thoughtful and scientific combination of every single item worn/carried from the skin outwards into one single total system. Uniquely, my Company's 'hand' of materials included every single requirement other than the rubber or latex for the respirator.

My military career had, during operations and training, spanned every type and aspect of doctrine and training in all parts of the world. I was both an 'armoured' soldier and a 'light' soldier; I had served in support of the police and spent several weeks at sea with the navy; I had even trained and flown as a back seat passenger in a Harrier fighter aircraft. Now these skills proved of the greatest value as I developed a method of explaining integrated protective combat clothing systems (and the police equivalent) to both my clients, DuPont and the UK Safety Group, and to Ministries of Defence, Infantry Schools and Police Schools. I became deeply involved in specialist aviation clothing, in particular for fast jet aircrew, including survivability aspects. Furthermore, it had become well known that I had originated Combat Soldier 1995 in the UK, a concept that was to be followed by every European army, and so I was able to pass on the benefits of my experiences.

As the years passed 100 per cent of my work was for DuPont, while my activities for the UK Safety Group tailed off by 2001. It was a remarkable experience to work for a large international company that had a presence in all the world's major nations. Typical was an informal dinner just outside Paris in 1997 at which fifteen DuPont team members enjoyed an evening together, and they came from fifteen different countries, ranging from China to Columbia and South Africa to Russia, all speaking in English. My life became very international. I was just as likely to be working with South African colleagues in South Africa, French colleagues in France, Russian colleagues in Russia or Turkish colleagues in Turkey. I worked in every country in Europe except Spain, Serbia and some of the smaller CIS nations such as Moldova, in several Middle Eastern nations and in South Africa. I also spent time in the United States and Canada.

DuPont was very similar to the military. Personnel seemed to do three-year tours and then get a posting to a new department. Most, but not all, of those with whom I worked had a Ph.D. in chemistry or chemical engineering, but only a very few had any military experience and that was mostly as a one-year conscript. Promotion was generally upwards until the maximum capability/performance platform was reached, and thereafter all postings were sideways. There were the fighting elements (research, sales and marketing), the supply parts (manufacture and distribution) and the administration (travel, legal, etc). There were five very large business groups, each divided into six or eight sectors, with each sector sub-divided into business units. In general the DuPont business was based on extremely clever and very well developed processes for mixing advanced polymers with a range of chemicals to produce materials with properties far in advance of any seen before. These materials were used in road building, car manufacturing, house building, medical equipment, agriculture, safety equipment, electronics and many more. It was after all a $US27 billion business with 60,000 employees spread all over the world in seventy different countries.

A fascinating aspect of my work was bringing together the various business units of DuPont, who, while sharing an interest in protecting the man, were not only located in different European countries, but did not even know each other. So I became an increasingly indispensable link, able to assemble the right people in any country for a conference, seminar or exhibition, or simply to introduce colleagues. As the years passed I became the corporate memory. Often my colleagues would ask, 'Richard, we are thinking of doing so and so – what do you think?' I was able to say, 'We tried that or similar five years ago but the problem was . . . and so we did not pursue that direction further.'

Kevlar® is a para-aramid fibre of greater strength than steel on a weight for weight basis, and was invented by Stephanie Kwolek in 1965 in the US, with the first production plant outside the US being opened near

Londonderry in Northern Ireland in 1988. Initia.
the manufacture of ballistic protective helmets,
followed by body armour, and subsequently for the
faced plates to stop high velocity bullets, and later for ar.
and aircraft. Nomex® is a meta-aramid fibre designed
remarkable protection against fire – it simply does not burn   be
manufactured into garments far more comfortable than cotto.   r into
lightweight structures for aircraft. My work in this area started with fire-
and heat-protective operational clothing systems for aircrew, ships' crews,
armoured vehicle crews and police officers on riot duty and later moved
into complete high-performance combat clothing systems for all soldiers.
Much of my time with DuPont was spent assisting the sales and marketing
teams introduce and then expand sales of Kevlar® and Nomex®, initially in
the western European nations, then the eastern European nations and South
Africa, and a little later in the Middle East and North African nations.

As I joined the DuPont organisation, I was also asked to become the
Honorary Regimental Colonel of 40th Regiment Royal Artillery. This
was a welcome and most enjoyable appointment that allowed me to
spend up to two weeks with the regiment each year, normally three or
four days at a time. I found that there were around a hundred soldiers
who had served with me more than thirteen years earlier, most of whom
welcomed me as an old friend. As a bonus my visits allowed me to keep
up to date with equipments related to my new career. I was to continue
in this role for seven years, handing over to Brigadier David Creswell in
2000.

For my first seven years the Kevlar® sales and marketing team members
combined their responsibilities with the Nomex® product range. My first
colleague was Michael Koerber, a German citizen, who covered the United
Kingdom, Scandinavia and Germany. Michael and I quickly discovered
that a frank, open and honest confidence-building seminar with many
technical diagrams and pictures displayed on a screen was the best approach.
It allowed for a logical exposition of the product range, followed by
discussion and questions. Military and police audiences needed to see
garments and items of personal equipment. Quite rightly they needed to
feel the material, look for shine, ensure there was no rustle when the wearer
moved, and consider every item as part of a complete fighting ensemble
usable in all climates. These seminars soon developed into very sophisticated presentations. Sometimes we started with an audience of five or six
people that quickly grew to twenty or more as urgent phone calls were

...de to summon additional people. On occasions they lasted well beyond the planned timetable, extending as long as seven or eight hours.

The new Soldier Modernisation Plan (SMP) concept for integrated and more efficient clothing systems allowed me to develop an initial presentation to demonstrate how all these new DuPont technologies could be combined to meet SMP objectives. From these early days we were able to build a position of considerable value to Ministries of Defence and similar, and many demanded an annual seminar which they treated as a study period for all members of their staffs.

As Michael Koerber moved to a new appointment, my work with Kevlar® and Nomex® extended. Michael was replaced in the UK and Scandinavia by Heather McAndrews, who was American, and so I started work with Ctirad Panek, Czech born, but a naturalized German, in all the German-speaking nations plus eastern European former Warsaw Pact member nations. This proved fascinating. We faced a massive gulf in thinking between the older pro-communist Russian-speaking majors and colonels, and the younger pro-NATO English-speaking officers who wanted to be aligned with the west. I worked with William Maldonado, who was Columbian, and later Beatrice Moureaux, a French citizen, in the French-speaking nations. In Italy and Greece I enjoyed working with Matina Skalkou, who was Greek. As the South African apartheid years ended, with sanctions lifted, DuPont needed to regain this market, and so I worked closely with Rob Price, a South African, in DuPont Southern Africa with both the military and police, and achieved much success, as well as making many new friends in that beautiful country. Our work was supported by a very powerful technical team in Geneva. Kevlar® was extraordinarily well supported by Nicolas van Zijl, from Luxembourg, Jianrong Ren, a Chinese citizen although university educated in England, and Nicolas Pont, a Frenchman, all of whom became the very closest friends, as were the Nomex® technical team of Tony Stocks, from the UK and Yves Bader and Andre Capt, both French.

Since the very first days I also worked for the DuPont Tyvek® team who were mostly based in Luxembourg at the Tyvek® manufacturing plant. The invitation was from Jens Engelhart, a German citizen, who offered a simple proposition. 'We have a new product called Tyvek 'F' which we think will stop all chemical and biological warfare agents. I will pay you one US dollar for every coverall you sell anywhere in the world!' Had I accepted I would have become a millionaire several times over, but I explained that I would be very pleased to join his team as the military and police specialist as well as organizing the testing and certification of the entire Tyvek® (later renamed Tychem®) range of materials. I worked with Helmut Eichinger, an Austrian based in Geneva, mainly on policy, and Aloyse Wilmes, of Luxembourg, who was the DuPont senior chemist at the huge manufacturing plant in Luxembourg on testing and certification. This project required a vast amount of work with both the MOD UK Laboratories at Porton Down and the TNO Laboratories in the Netherlands, followed by watertight documentation. I became heavily involved with officers and scientists in R & D centres in many nations ranging from Norway (Bjorn-Arne Johnson) and Finland (Matti Puutio) in the north to Philip Coleman in South Africa, as well as many others as far apart as the United States and Turkey. In the UK I worked very closely with Jim Battensby and Paul Young as well as many others at Porton Down. I persuaded Vic Raines and John Martin of the UK company Remploy that they should take on the design and manufacture of a range of military and police protective garments. They achieved considerable success selling these all over the world and establishing the Tychem® range (Tychem® 'C', 'F' and 'TK') as the garment of choice for all those facing the threat of attack from either military or terrorist use of chemical and biological warfare agents.

The next string to my bow in this new life was based on DuPont's unique high tenacity Nylon, type 6.6. One type that had been texturised and named Cordura® was the material of choice for all military load carriage equipment from rucksacks to belts (and also combat boots). The texturising process removed any shine and produced a natural non-reflective surface to an extremely tough material. The same material in a lighter version was used as the outer layer of all the military and police Gore-Tex® waterproof jackets and trousers. The non-texturised Nylon, also extremely strong at very light weights, was used for a massive range of military requirements, from parachutes to sleeping-bag covers and waterproof bags to small tents/shelters. For the first nine years I worked with Sig Hardarsen, who was from Iceland but based in Geneva. Together we moved from a situation where Cordura® in particular was used only by a very few nations to a position where it was the natural material of choice for almost all, not just western and eastern Europe, but also in South Africa and the Middle East. As the use of body armour increased, so Cordura® was selected for the outer covers to allow the carriage of radios, ammunition, etc. on the body armour cover, and so the business grew and grew. The focal point of the DuPont Nylon business was switched to

Gloucester and I found myself working in succession with three very different but talented government business managers, all British and with impressive doctorates in chemistry: first Tim Anson, a man with an encyclopedic knowledge of how the business worked, then the diminutive but superbly organized Julie Gretton, and finally the more cautious John McEvoy. It was a pleasure to work in this team with similar aims but a quite different system to tackle the various markets.

The final aspect of my work fell into two quite different material uses but controlled by one DuPont management team. These were Coolmax® for use as a knitted, fast sweat-wicking and quick drying, very comfortable material to be worn next to the skin in all climates as underwear, socks or gloves; and the Quallofil® and Thermolite® ranges of lightweight insulations for sleeping bags and cold climate clothing. When I started with this team, only the older Quallofil® insulation was used by the military in a few countries. My work started with Giancarlo Pomati, from Italy, switched to Bob Dyke, from the UK, and then Jean-Christophe Rouyer, a Frenchman, followed by Jordi Lopez, from Spain. We used every opportunity to explain the advantages afforded by these new much lighter and more efficient materials and over the years gradually persuaded the various military users to change to these DuPont materials. Military operations in the hot climates of Iraq and Afghanistan accelerated their adoption, as did the wearing of body armour for which Coolmax® under-layers did much to alleviate problems of achieving efficient body heat management. Soldiers became hugely enthusiastic about the advantages of socks made from Coolmax®. Sales reached tens of millions of pairs.

With the UK Safety Group I joined the development team faced with two tasks: the design and production of the 'ultimate combat boot'; and increasing their military export market. Paul Cockburn and I had previously realized that any combat boot design originating from a government or academic environment was not likely to be manufacturable on a commercial scale at a realistic price. So we decided to design the best possible combat boot that the UK Safety Group factory could make, and then submit it for test. The 'PRO-BOOT' was born. The first sixteen pairs were given to the SAS in Hereford to test. They were so good that the testers, all very experienced SAS senior ranks, refused to return them after the three months' trial period. The word was out, that at long last the army had a really good new combat boot, and the impetus of this success led to a ten-year long development and manufacturing partnership with MOD UK, covering boots for all purposes. Even the Royal Air Force adopted the

'PRO-BOOT' as a result of aircrew pressure, despite the obvious risk of FOD (foreign object damage) from the land forces tread pattern.

Overseas sales were less successful. The United States Marine Corps tested the 'PRO-BOOT' and declared it the best boot that they had ever seen, but then stated that they would never buy it because it was not American! The Quartermaster General of the Norwegian Army, Brigadier Reidar Melheim, would have liked to adopt the UK combat boot but explained that to do so would end all Norwegian combat boot production, effectively killing off the livelihoods of the populations of two remote valleys near Trondheim. Nevertheless, overseas sales did increase but never reached the levels anticipated mainly because of traditional national supply systems.

Turning back to DuPont's Kevlar® and Nomex® products that remained the backbone of my work, the requirements for advanced ballistic and fire/heat protection for both military and police personnel increased significantly from the late 1990s onwards. Rob Price moved from South Africa to Geneva to head the technical team and look after the UK markets. Elzbieta Wojciechowska-Zalewska, from Poland, assumed responsibility for Scandinavian nations and for the development of new business in all the non-Soviet former Warsaw Pact nations. I made many visits to the military and police authorities in Poland, Hungary, the Czech Republic, the Slovak Republic, Romania, Bulgaria, Croatia and Slovenia at the exciting period of their developments from conservative thinking communist nations into increasingly wealthy EU and NATO members, making many friends in the process.

Further east in Russia and the Ukraine my work for DuPont was with Sergey Zavadsky from the Ukraine. We ran several seminars in both countries for the military, police and Ministry of the Interior organizations. These occasions were very open, frank and of the greatest interest to me. Sergey was assisted by Colonel (Retired) Nikolai Stelmakh, also a Ukrainian citizen, who had spent his entire career in the elite Soviet Rocket Forces SS 20 force, which was a devastating missile system that we in the West had spent much time trying to locate during the Cold War. We had many interesting conversations comparing our experiences during the Cold War. I told him that I would like to see a real SS 20, having previously only seen very grainy photos. Within the hour he had taken me to the Kiev military museum where the actual SS 20 TEL launcher system he had commanded at the start of his career held pride of place. As the chief Soviet negotiator at the disarmament talks, Nikolai has saved his very first rocket launcher for the museum in his home city, Kiev.

It was also most interesting to attend meetings in Russia concerning the removal and destruction of the vast stock of old chemical weapons, as required by the terms of the CWC.

Personnel changes in the DuPont team in western Europe in the years after 2000 were matched by substantial organizational modifications. At the strategic level, DuPont decided to move away from being a chemical production company of staple products to become a science-based innovative company producing specialist materials where profit margins would be higher. The Cordura®/Nylon business was renamed Invista® and sold to Koch Inc., a privately owned US company. The European part of the Coolmax® and insulations business was renamed AdvanSA® and sold to the Turkish company Sabinci. Nevertheless, the synergies resulting from the need to equip the man with a complete integrated system allowed me to continue working for all my clients as before.

Realignment within DuPont altered the separate Kevlar®, Nomex® and Tyvek® businesses to become Life Protection (Kevlar) and Personal Protection (Nomex and Tyvek). Jeroen Jacobs, of the Netherlands, became the head of the new Life Protection Kevlar business at a time of massive increases in demand resulting from the wars in Iraq and Afghanistan, and brought a fresh dynamism in thinking with a new team and so in the UK and French/Spanish-speaking countries I found myself working with Rodolphe Besnard, from France, in the German-speaking countries with Kai Hutmacher, who was German, in Eastern Europe with Martin Jirousek, a Czech citizen, in the eastern Mediterranean with Tufan Tiryakioglu from Turkey, and in the Arabic-speaking nations with Mahir Emil, an Egyptian. At the same time the Personal Protection Nomex® and Tyvek® businesses placed a renewed emphasis on the provision of protection for personnel facing dangers both in war and in the event of terrorist attack. Andreas Fries, who was German, headed the marketing team and much of my work in the UK and Scandinavia was with Stewart Richardson from the UK, in the German-speaking countries with Helmut Scheckenbach, also German, in the French-speaking countries with Monika Rigoulot, who was a Hungarian citizen, in Eastern Europe with Ljubica Cesnik, a Slovenian, and in the Eastern Mediterranean with Arinc Aktan, who was Turkish. It was a privilege to work with these outstanding people, and many others, from so many nations. Not only did I travel extensively but, more importantly, I enjoyed meeting and working with thousands of military, police and industrialists in many nations, all of whom proved to have points of interest for me over and above the information I could give them. Looking back, our combined efforts succeeded in altering the materials used for military and police combat and equivalent clothing across one quarter of the world, and most were from DuPont with by far the largest percentage manufactured in Europe.

By 2005, I began to feel that both I and DuPont needed a change. So I selected 30 March 2007 as my retirement date, promising my clients that I would find a successor. In mid 2006 Brigadier (Retired) William Cook emerged as the perfect successor, our three months' handover period commencing on 1 January 2007. As promised many months earlier, I switched my computer and communications systems off at 1200 hours precisely on Friday 30 March 2007 and, after a stimulating and enjoyable working life of almost exactly fifty years, started a busy retirement.

Epilogue

THE AIM OF THIS BOOK WAS always to provide a record of military life during the Cold War years, a period that combined an arms race with more than forty years in which two huge military power blocks faced each other, sometimes coming close to a war that would have destroyed the world. Having never kept a diary I am grateful to many friends and colleagues for their help and advice as I struggled to remember the details and dates of events in my military service.

While choosing to write my account in an autobiographical framework I have mentioned very little of my family, just a few key moments. But, like every other serviceman, I am very grateful for the love and support freely given to me by my wife Ann and our children Victoria, Elizabeth and Alexander. All three were born in military hospitals in West Germany and like so many other service children found that every two to three years the family moved and so new friends had to be made and different schools mastered.

Always in the back of my mind was the awful thought that, if a conflict had become imminent or started, then Ann and our children would, alongside many thousands of other families, have to make a dash for the channel in the most difficult of circumstances.

I am most grateful for the considerable support and help provided to me in the writing of this book by the very supportive Lynn Davidson of the Memoir Club, and by her colleagues Eileen Finlayson, who has been a most helpful and accurate editor, and Rosie Readman, the production manager with an astute eye for detail.

Haslemere, Surrey
January 2009

Abbreviations

AAR	After Action Review – US Army procedure
ADC	Aide de Camp
AFCENT	Allied Forces Central Europe – commanded by a four-star general
AFV	Armoured Fighting Vehicle – tank, armoured personnel carrier, etc.
AIG	Assistant Instructor in Gunnery – sergeant-major gunnery instructor
AMF(L)	Allied Mobile Force (Land)
AP	Advanced Post (in a Sound Ranging Troop) or Ammunition Point
ASOC	Air Support Operations Centre – a NATO air control headquarters
ATAF	Allied Tactical Air Force – commanded by a three-star general/air marshal
AUS(Q)	Assistant Under Secretary (Quartermaster) – civil servant finance controller
BAFV	British Armed Forces Voucher
BAOR	British Army of the Rhine
BATUS	British Army Training Unit Suffield – a live firing battle school
BBGT	Brigade and Battle Group Trainer – controls for a CPX
BMRA	Brigade Major Royal Artillery – chief of staff at an HQRA
BRA	Brigadier Royal Artillery – artillery commander at a HQ above division
CAB	Combat Assault Boot – British Army combat boot from 1992
CAST	Command and Staff Trainer – controls for a CPX
CENTAG	Central Army Group – headquarters for four to six army corps
CINCENT	Commander in Chief Central Europe – commander of all land and air forces Hamburg to Swiss border

COMLANDJUT	Commander Land Forces Jutland and Schleswig-Holstein
COMAW	Commodore Amphibious Warfare – the UK amphibious fleet
CPO	Command Post Officer
CPX	Command Post Exercise – no troops involved except HQ and radio units
CRA	Commander Royal Artillery – commander of three to six artillery regiments in a division
CS95	Combat Soldier 1995 – UK clothing system
CS05	Combat Soldier 2005 – UK clothing R & D plan
CWC	Chemical Warfare Convention – to reduce chemical weapons
DAT	Director of Army Training – in MOD UK
DCINCENT	Deputy Commander in Chief Central Europe
DCT	Director of Clothing and Textiles – responsible for UK clothing and most personal equipment
DC	District Commissioner – in a UK colony
DSACEUR	Deputy Supreme Allied Commander Europe
DS	Directing Staff – at the UK Staff College and similar
DSM	Director of Supply Management – part of MOD UK
FCE 7	Fire Control Equipment number 7 – air defence radar with predictor
FOD	Foreign Object Damage – mud, stones, etc. in an aircraft system
FOO	Forward Observation Officer – for directing artillery fire
FRA	Federal Regular Army – army of South Arabia until 1967
FTX	Field Training Exercise – field exercise with all troops involved, but no live firing
GPO	Gun Position Officer – of an artillery battery
GOC	General Officer Commanding – of a division or similar
GS	General Staff or General Service
GSO (Ops)	General Staff Officer (Operations) – normally the key staff branch of a HQ
GTT	Gunnery Training Team – group of UK gunnery instructors
HAC	Honourable Artillery Company – London based TA unit providing special OPs

HICON	Higher Control – for a CPX
HMS	Her Majesty's Ship – of the Royal Navy
HQRA	Headquarters Royal Artillery
IG	Instructor in Gunnery – officer gunnery instructor
IRA	Irish Republican Army – terrorist organization
ISAWES	Infantry Small Arms Weapons Effects Simulator – laser designator fixed on rifle or machine gun
JFHQ	Joint Force Headquarters – with navy, army and air force representation
JOC	Joint Operational Commander – three-star or higher commander of a combined navy, army and air force deployment
JRTC	Joint Readiness Training Centre – US Army training centre
KBE	Knight of the Order of the British Empire – British honour
LI	The Light Infantry – British Infantry Regiment of five/six battalions
LP	Listening Post – for mortar locating radars
LOWCON	Lower Control – for a CPX
MA	Military Assistant – personal staff officer for a three-star officer or higher
MC	Military Cross – British honour for gallantry
MDP	Ministry of Defence Police
MGRA	Major General Royal Artillery
MGRM	Major General Royal Marines
MILES	Multiple Integrated Laser Engagement System – for TES training
mm	millimetre
MOD	Ministry of Defence – UK armed forces HQ
NAAFI	Navy Army and Air Force Institute – UK armed forces canteens and shops
NATO	North Atlantic Treaty Organization
NBC	Nuclear, Biological and Chemical warfare
NORTHAG	Northern Army Group – headquarters for four to six army corps
OBE	Officer of the Order of the British Empire – British honour
OOA	Out of Area – UK term meaning beyond NATO area

OP	Observation Post – for artillery observers
OPFOR	Opposing Force – enemy when TES training
ORBAT	Order of Battle – organization of a fighting force
'P' Company	Parachute selection company
Para	Parachutist or The Parachute Regiment
PPG	Permanent Planning Group – for Out of Area operations
PX	Post Exchange – US Army shop
QAD (SC)	Quality Assurance Directorate (Stores and Clothing)
QM	Quartermaster – supplier of material
RA	Royal Artillery
RAF	Royal Air Force
RAOC	Royal Army Ordnance Corps
RASC	Royal Army Service Corps
RCT	Royal Corps of Transport
R & D	Research and Development
REME	Royal Electrical and Mechanical Engineers
RHA	Royal Horse Artillery
RHQ	Regimental Headquarters
RMP	Royal Military Police
RSDG	Royal Scots Dragoon Guards
RSM	Regimental Sergeant Major
RTR	Royal Tank Regiment
Rt. Hon.	The Right Honourable (a member of the Privy Council)
RUC	Royal Ulster Constabulary
RV	rendezvous
SACEUR	Supreme Allied Commander Europe – commander of all land and air forces North Norway to Eastern Turkey
SAS	Special Air Service
SCRDE	Stores and Clothing Research and Development Establishment
SIMMO	Simulated Ammunition
SIMNET	Simulated Networking – computer based training system
SIPE	Soldier Integrated Protective Ensemble – US Army development
SLTA	Soltau Luneberg Training Area – in West Germany

SMP	Soldier Modernisation Plan – development to improve total capability of dismounted soldier
TA	Territorial Army
TARA	Technical Assistant Royal Artillery – soldier responsible for calculations to align gun to target
TES	Tactical Engagement Simulation – laser simulation of weapons on exercise
TEWT	Tactical Exercise Without Troops – talking through tactical situations
TEXCOM	Test and Experimentation Command – US Army
TOG	a metric unit to describe the insulation properties of cloth (1 TOG = 0.645 clo)
TRADOC	Training and Doctrine Command – US Army
WRAC	Women's Royal Army Corps
UDA	Ulster Defence Association – terrorist organization
UK	United Kingdom
UKLF	United Kingdom Land Forces – UK HQ
UKMF	United Kingdom Mobile Force – division-sized force to reinforce NATO
UOTC	University Officers Training Corps
US	United States
UVF	Ulster Volunteer Force – terrorist organization

Index

Military ranks shown in the index are the highest achieved by the named person, rather than the rank held in the particular year referenced when that person may have held a more junior rank.